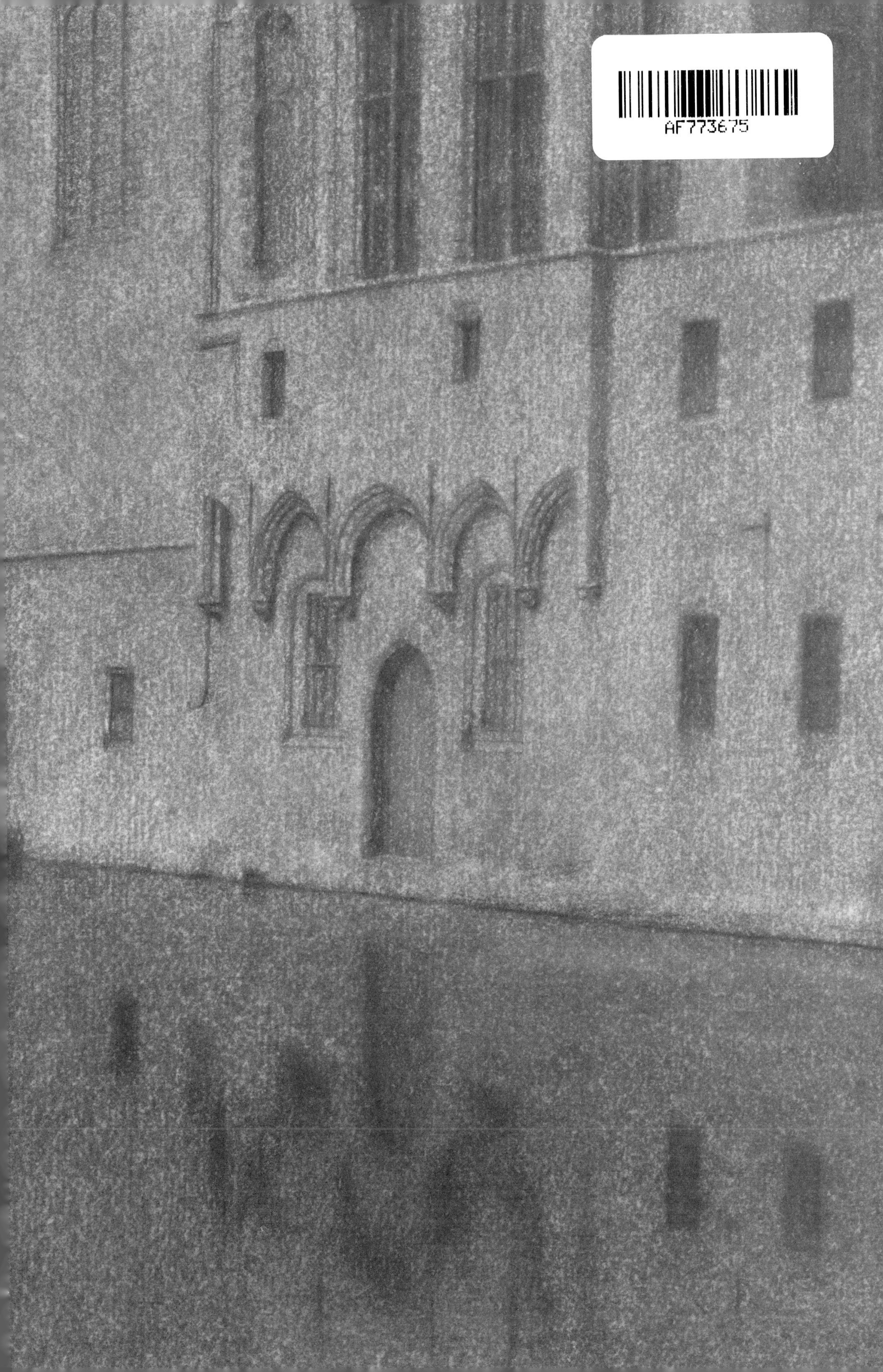

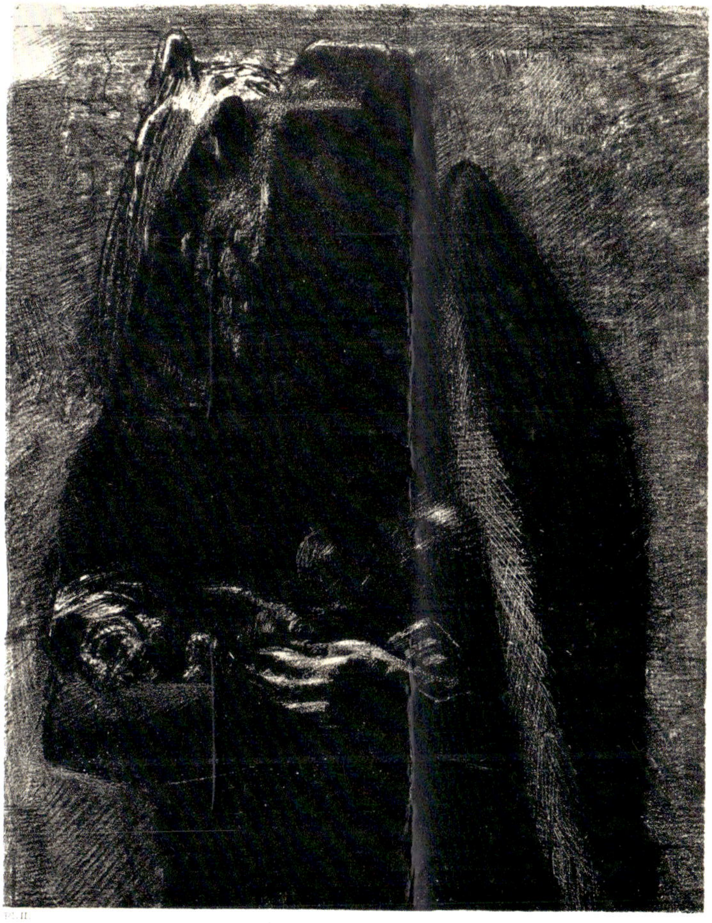

Pl. II.

C'est le diable, portant sous ses deux ailes les sept péchés capitaux.....

THE DARKER SIDE OF LIGHT

THE DARKER SIDE OF LIGHT

ARTS OF PRIVACY, 1850–1900

Peter Parshall

with S. Hollis Clayson, Christiane Hertel, and Nicholas Penny

NATIONAL GALLERY OF ART, WASHINGTON

in association with Lund Humphries

The exhibition is organized by the National Gallery of Art, Washington

EXHIBITION DATES

Hammer Museum, Los Angeles
April 5–June 28, 2009

National Gallery of Art, Washington
October 1, 2009–January 18, 2010

Smart Museum of Art, University of Chicago
February 11–June 10, 2010

Produced by the Publishing Office
National Gallery of Art, Washington
www.nga.gov

Judy Metro, Editor in Chief

Chris Vogel, Deputy Publisher

Ulrike Mills, Senior Editor

Brad Ireland, Designer

Sara Sanders-Buell, Photography Rights Coordinator

Wendy Schleicher, Design Manager

Edited by Laura Jones Dooley

This book was typeset in Bembo by BW&A Inc., Durham, NC, and printed on GardaMatt by EBS Group, Italy

ENDPAPERS

front: Fernand Khnopff, *Memory of Flanders: A Canal* (detail, fig. 21, p. 38)

back: James Ensor, *The Cathedral* (detail, fig. 9, p. 18)

DISPLAY ILLUSTRATIONS

page II: Odilon Redon, *This Is the Devil* (detail, fig. 2, p. 9)

page X: Eugène Carrière, *Sleep*, 1897, National Gallery of Art, Washington, Rosenwald Collection

page XII: James McNeill Whistler, *Nocturne* (detail, fig. 7, p. 16)

page 40: Edgar Degas, *Woman by a Fireplace* (detail, fig. 18, p. 74)

page 80: Käthe Kollwitz, *Scene from "Germinal"* (detail, fig. 16, p. 114)

page 126: Louis-Oscar Roty, *France Mourning the President of the Republic* (detail, fig. 13, p. 151)

LIBRARY OF CONGRESS CATALOGING-IN-PUBLICATION DATA

Parshall, Peter W.
The darker side of light: arts of privacy, 1850–1900 / Peter Parshall with S. Hollis Clayton, Christiane Hertel, and Nicholas Penny.
p. cm.
Issued in connection with an exhibition held April 5–June 28, 2009, Armand Hammer Museum, Los Angeles, October 1, 2009–January 18, 2010, National Gallery of Art, Washington, and February 11–June 10, 2010, Smart Museum of Art, University of Chicago. Includes bibliographical references.
1 Prints—19th century—Exhibitions. 2. Art and society—History—19th century—Exhibitions. I. Clayson, Hollis, 1946– II. Hertel, Christiane, 1958– III. Penny, Nicholas, 1949– IV. Armand Hammer Museum of Art and Cultural Center. V. National Gallery of Art (U.S.) VI. David and Alfred Smart Museum of Art. VII. Title.

NE485.P37 2009

769.9'03407473—DC22

2008044664

ISBN: 978-1-84822-021-8 (alk. paper, museum edition)

The paper used in this publication meets the minimum requirements of the American National Standard for Information Sciences—Permanence of Paper for Printed Library Materials, ansiz39.48.1992.

Published in association with Lund Humphries.

Lund Humphries, Wey Court East
Union Road, Farnham, Surrey,
GU9 7PT, UK, and
Suite 420,
101 Cherry Street
Burlington, VT
05401-4405, USA
www.lundhumphries.com

Lund Humphries is a part of Ashgate Publishing

10 9 8 7 6 5 4 3 2 1

NOTE TO THE READER

Dimensions are given in centimeters. Height precedes width.

CONTENTS

DIRECTOR'S FOREWORD VI
ACKNOWLEDGMENTS VIII
LENDERS TO THE EXHIBITION XI

LOOKING WITHIN THE CELL OF PRIVACY
S. Hollis Clayson 42

SCULPTURE AND PRIVACY
Nicholas Penny 128

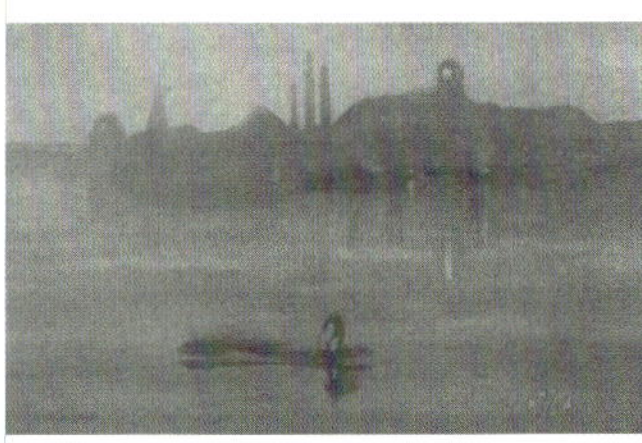
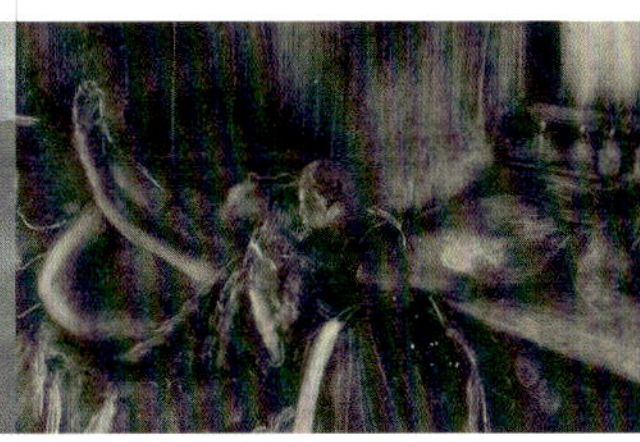
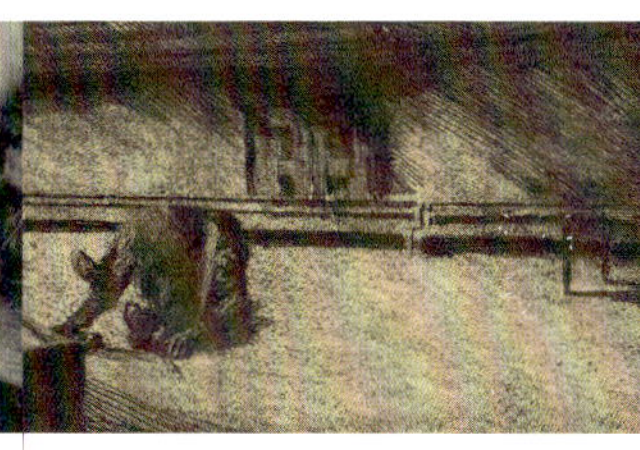
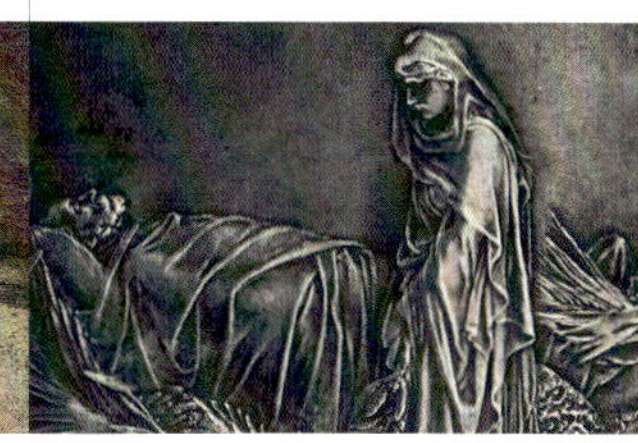

A DARKER SIDE OF LIGHT:
PRINTS, PRIVACY, AND POSSESSION
Peter Parshall 2

THE WORLD INSIDE:
PRIVACY ACCORDING TO KLINGER,
LIEBERMANN, AND KOLLWITZ
Christiane Hertel 82

NOTES 152
CHECKLIST 171
INDEX 178
PHOTOGRAPHY CREDITS 180

The practice of art collecting as we often think of it really started in the Renaissance. Not only popes and princes but also prosperous merchants and scholars were accumulating private collections of art and antiquities, for example drawings and prints, small sculptures, ancient coins and cameos. Once objects such as these were acquired in significant number they were typically stored away in cabinets and albums to be taken out on special occasions for solitary enjoyment or sharing with a friend. To some extent this practice has remained unbroken to the present day. Most old master prints that are now housed in museums were originally brought together in this manner until they found their way into public collections such as the National Gallery of Art.

This exhibition is a celebration of that particular kind of collecting: acquiring works of art for occasional delight rather than the everyday pleasure that we take in seeing a painting that hangs on our wall. Here we are acknowledging what is most compelling about works of art on paper: their inherent fragility and their particular brand of quiet intimacy. Stored collections have something in common with books in a library: we choose the moment to enjoy them rather than have it come upon us in the normal course of our activities. This exhibition is about that act of deliberate private viewing.

The National Gallery's collection of prints, drawings, and rare books numbers around 80,000, and only a small portion can be on view at a given time. Otherwise they are safely stored away in archival boxes, cabinets, and drawers adjacent to our study rooms where they are made available to the public by appointment. In this regard the modern practice of viewing prints and drawings in museum study rooms is part of a long tradition. When visitors come to the Gallery to request a box of etchings by Rembrandt, they are able to relive something of what a nineteenth-century collector must have felt on a quiet afternoon in the study.

The late nineteenth century was an era when print collecting in particular was especially widespread. Etching societies were formed with the idea of publishing prints in order to cultivate and improve the tastes of the urban bourgeoisie. Subscribers with comfortable but modest means might receive half a dozen or so prints three to four times a year, often beginning with a specially commissioned title page to adorn the annual portfolio. In addition to such organized efforts there were many independent dealers and book shops in Paris, London, Berlin, and elsewhere that sold prints, drawings, and small sculptures by artists of various schools. These were the places where private collections were gradually formed.

The Darker Side of Light is drawn primarily from the National Gallery's own substantial collection of nineteenth-century European and American art. Our own history as a museum explains the exhibition's primary emphasis on French art, an area where we have benefited not only from the extraordinary gift of Lessing J. Rosenwald, but also those of R. Horace Gallatin, and more recently Mr. and Mrs. Daniel Bell and Ruth and Jacob Kainen. Our exceptional collections of work by the German artist Max Klinger and the Norwegian Edvard Munch reflect the continued generosity of the Epstein family. We express our deep gratitude to Sarah Epstein, Mr. and Mrs. Charles Hack, Virginia and Ira Jackson, Mrs. Paul Mellon, Dr. Richard Simms, the Baltimore Museum of Art, and the Princeton University Art Museum for additional and critically important loans to the exhibition.

I thank the directors of the two institutions that will host the exhibition, Ann Philbin, director of the Hammer Museum at the University of California in Los Angeles, and Anthony G. Hirschel, director of the Smart Museum of Art at the University of Chicago. Last, sincere thanks are due to curator Peter Parshall, who conceived the idea for this exhibition and carried it through to completion.

Earl A. Powell III NATIONAL GALLERY OF ART

The subject of this catalogue and the accompanying exhibition represents a significant departure from my accustomed area of research, the Renaissance. To be sure the problem I have chosen to address in the nineteenth century has its roots in that much earlier time. Nonetheless, the surroundings were at first relatively unfamiliar to me, and the requirement for remedial learning has been unremitting. The boldness to undertake such a project required a host of better-versed colleagues willing to offer their advice and expertise, first among them my co-authors. S. Hollis Clayson chose to write her catalogue essay on the problem of psychological interiority in its relation to women and the domestic interior, primarily but not exclusively in France. Christiane Hertel examines the question of privacy in the context of politics and art theory as it affected German printmaking. Finally, Nicholas Penny explores "in the round" certain of the more elusive intimacies in the experience of late nineteenth-century sculpture. Each of these essays takes its departure from the guiding theme of private aesthetic experience. Each makes a distinctive contribution to the subject, and all extend beyond the particular works that are included in the exhibition.

In addition to my co-authors, a great many friends and colleagues have provided invaluable assistance in the research and writing of the catalogue. For their expertise in relevant areas of the art of the period I am particularly grateful to Jay A. Clarke, Samuel Danon, Jay McKean Fisher, Laura Giles, Eik Kahng, Linda Parshall, Elizabeth Prelinger, Pierre-Lin Renié, Kimberly Schenck, Martha Tedeschi, Pamela Warner, Jeffrey Weiss, and Helena Wright.

For their assistance in realizing the exhibition I express my gratitude to Earl A. Powell III, director of the National Gallery of Art; Alan Shestack, former deputy director and chief curator, and his successor, Franklin Kelly; D. Dodge Thompson, head of exhibitions; Andrew Robison, senior curator of prints and drawings; and Gregory Jecmen, associate curator of old master prints. For the publication of the catalogue we are indebted above all to the editor in chief, Judy Metro, and her staff, including especially the designer Brad Ireland, our editors Ulrike Mills and Laura Jones Dooley, and deputy publisher Chris Vogel.

To present the arts of privacy in the form of a public exhibition in itself requires an exercise of the imagination, not to say a feat of ingenuity. A conscious adjustment is expected of the visitors who must linger and reflect patiently in order to cultivate a frame of mind complementary to the art surrounding them. Accordingly, the institutions installing such a project must consider the ways in which a compelling degree of intimacy can be created for the display of these works of art. For this we extend our appreciation to the staff. At the National Gallery of Art, I thank Mark Leithauser, Jamé Anderson, and John Olson of the design department; Michelle Facini and Marian Dirda in the department of paper conservation; as well as my curatorial intern Elizabeth Rudy and our Andrew W. Mellon Curatorial Fellow, Naoko Takahatake.

For their vigorous support in orchestrating the two additional venues for the exhibition and all that this entails, we are deeply grateful to Cynthia Burlingham and her colleagues at the Hammer Museum in Los Angeles, and to Anne Leonard and her colleagues at the Smart Museum of Art at the University of Chicago. I am especially pleased to have the opportunity of working with two museums closely associated with universities, the second of them my alma mater. Increased collaboration between museums and the academy is the single most promising development in art-historical scholarship over the past generation, and a maturing relationship that has contributed substantially to our mutual vitality and the enrichment of the discipline. Thus, it seems appropriate that we should celebrate it here.

Peter Parshall CURATOR AND HEAD OF DEPARTMENT OF OLD MASTER PRINTS
NATIONAL GALLERY OF ART

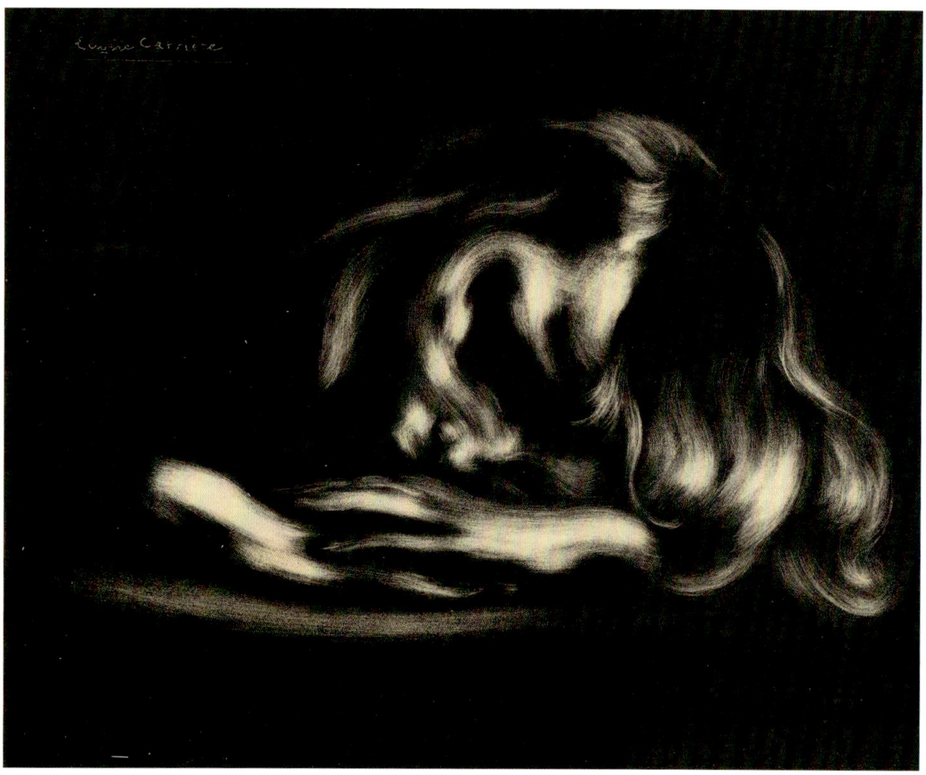

LENDERS TO THE EXHIBITION

Baltimore Museum of Art

Epstein Family Foundation

Hearn Family Trust

Virginia and Ira Jackson Collection

Mrs. Paul Mellon

National Gallery of Art, Washington

Princeton University Art Museum

Dr. Richard A. Simms

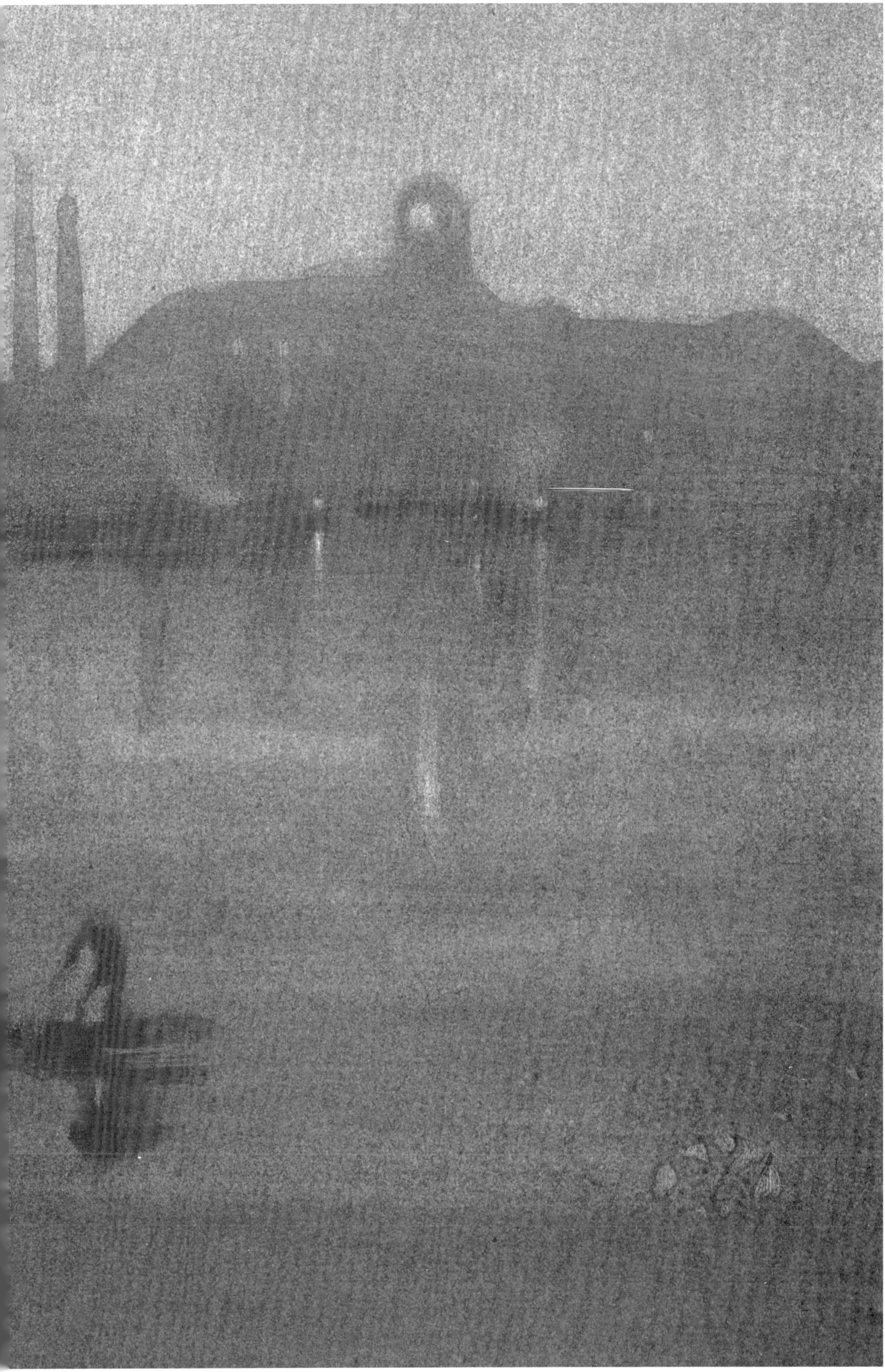

A DARKER SIDE OF LIGHT: PRINTS, PRIVACY, AND POSSESSION

Peter Parshall

A PRINT—

THE SPONTANEOUS, IMMEDIATE EMANATION OF AN ARTIST'S GENIUS—MUST BE WELCOMED, SAVORED A LITTLE AS ONE WOULD A CONFIDENCE, IN THE INTIMACY OF STILLNESS AND WITH THE DEVOTION OF SILENCE.

—*Roger Marx*

The collector J.-J. Claussin (1766–1844) is reported to have tucked his portfolio of Rembrandt etchings under his pillow at night so that when a particular print wandered into his dreams, he might wake up and reflect on it directly.[1] This is an unusual means of engaging a work of art—encouraging a subconscious haunting through a kind of sympathetic magic and then measuring it against the reality of the object seen before one's wakened eyes. Mostly we think of an aesthetic encounter in the opposite way, where the direct contemplation of a work of art becomes a means of transporting us out of ourselves. Nevertheless, what remains common to both experiences is the condition of privacy.

Privacy can be achieved in silence or incantation, in the solitude of a monastic cell or in the throng of a crowded museum. Here we are concerned with retreat and the intimacy that comes from holding a work of art in the hand. This is an experience particular but not peculiar to prints, and it has a history of its own. As a manner of relating to an object, the private and premeditated encounter was greatly significant for artists, collectors, and critics in the nineteenth century. Small sculptures ask to be lifted and handled. A print or a drawing must be singled out from its portfolio and tilted to the light, much as a book is pulled from the library shelf. Furthermore, as the art critic Charles Blanc observed at the time, it is better to store a collection of drawings and prints rather than put them under glass and hang them on the wall, because such familiarity would detract from the subtleties they have to offer. "There are, among the treasures of art and curiosities, riches that one must always have visible to keep the sacred fire going in one's soul.... But there are things that it is important not to see at every moment, from morning till evening, because one will finish by becoming indifferent to the pleasures they give."[2] Sequestering an object establishes the conditions for experiencing it. Cycles of paintings were often commissioned for discrete spaces such as the Renaissance *studiolo*. Medals and rare coins were put away in cabinets just as collections of prints and drawings were kept in albums and, later, in portfolios. And for the sake of propriety, collections of erotica have always been concealed.

Under these conditions, encountering a work of art was a determined activity, not a random occurrence such as pausing before a painted landscape in the drawing room. The conditions of privacy were therefore both physical and psychological and, in the latter case, historically unrecoverable. We will never know what went on in Claussin's mind when he woke up and rummaged under his pillow for the Rembrandt album. And yet, there is much to say about the longing for private aesthetic experience and the kind of art made to satisfy it. The habit of intimate collecting was pronounced among the nineteenth-century European bourgeoisie, which cultivated an appreciation for this shadowed world and the quiet of a time and a place set aside for it. There was a fascination with the interior, not only in the architecture of the private house but in the obscurity of human consciousness. One material, the other subjective, these are the spaces of silent contemplation.

The element of darkness was a proclaimed aesthetic property, both formal and iconographic, naturally conveyed in the clouded atmospheres and tonal contrasts of black and white that are inherent in the printed media. In the preface to the first portfolio of prints issued by Alfred Cadart for the newly founded Société des Aquafortistes (Society of Etchers) in 1863, the critic Théophile Gautier delivered an intoxicated description of Rembrandt's etching style, offering it as an example of what the medium could accomplish: "His resources, seemingly so bounded, furnished Rembrandt with the trembling light, the mysterious shadows and deep blacks which he required for his renderings of *philosophes* and alchemists in search of the microcosm; for the synagogues of solomonic architecture; his Christ resuscitating the dead; his landscapes crossed with shadows and rays of light; and all the phantasmagorias of his dreaming imagination, powerful and bizarre."[3] This rapturous account is very much of its moment, a romantic response to the defining genius of a medium. Rembrandt's importance for habits of collecting, for perceptions of the artistic imagination, and for the very concept of a work of art in the nineteenth century cannot be underestimated. For Gautier and most other critics in his time, Rembrandt was not only the paragon of etchers but also the grand magician of darkness and light. Darkness became a visual language understood as encouraging the exploration of shadowed kinds of subjects and indeterminate states of mind.

"The darker side of light" is meant as a paradoxical play on different levels. It is a reference to Paris, the City of Light and the capital of nineteenth-century avant-gardism. This well-known sobriquet recalls the fact that Paris was also a center of the Enlightenment. Furthermore, it was among the first cities to make broad use of gaslight and, by the 1880s, electric street lighting. Paris was also the birthplace of impressionism, the painting of light in celebration of the countryside and popular entertainments. But the artists and writers who captured that contented public image also knew something of what lay behind it. The somber reality reflected in Émile Zola's novels, the etched fantasies of Charles Meryon, the poetry of Stéphane Mallarmé, and the dark tales of Edgar Allan Poe told another story. This was the post-romantic world as reconceived by Charles Darwin, Karl Marx, Jean-Martin Charcot, and later Sigmund Freud, in which the human condition came to be defined in material terms, and the prospect of change was no longer spiritual but psychological, social, and political.[4] Sensuality was expressed openly, often indecently, and society was seen to be an agent of isolation as much as community. Illness was understood as a mental as well as physical condition. Above all, death was vivid and ever present, and resurrection an unlikely outcome. Whether consciously aestheticized or not, whether artificial or genuinely felt, the pictorial vocabulary of this period betrays an uncertain and often distressed worldview. Our intent is not to illustrate that culture but to re-create something of its circumstances and sensations through the introspective nature of its imagery.

ETCHING: AN AUTHORIZED ART

Of the many objects collected in the late nineteenth century, prints were among the most common and most often written about. They were, moreover, the defining art of privacy. Much was said about the aesthetics of the print, and its promotion across the major cities of Europe was a public affair conducted at a high level by critics of various stripes largely in the pages of periodicals and newspapers.[5] The so-called etching revival in England, France, Germany, Belgium, and Austria in the 1860s through the 1880s and, later on, in the United States, was the result of a movement by artists, critics, and, most important, print publishers to encourage the acquisition of original works of art, to support amateur drawing and printmaking, and along the way to elevate public taste.

Such ambitions lay at the center of a critical discourse over what was then and is often still termed the "original print"—that is, a print of original composition executed by the artist responsible for its design. This primarily meant etching but sometimes included lithography, both in effect techniques of drawing. Such prints were touted as genuine works of art in contrast to the labor-intensive and costly engravings that reproduced masterpieces of painting and sculpture, the type of print that dominated the market and claimed the attention of critics in reviews of the annual salons. It was a battle for position in a hierarchy of prestige, and the skirmish over the issue of originality soon established a second front to defend against the successes of photography. This eloquent campaign enlisted some of the most articulate and highly regarded writers of the period, and it may be that in the long term the writing generated by the revival proved more influential than the art itself.[6]

The initial declaration of the rebirth of etching as an artistic medium was delivered by Charles Baudelaire in his landmark essay "Peintres et aquafortistes," published in 1862, the year of the founding of Cadart's Société des Aquafortistes.[7] Though he praised etching as the ideal medium for the expression of deep artistic sensibility, Baudelaire nevertheless feared that the relative ease and accessibility of the technique would foster a deluge of amateur work, as he saw happening in England. Indeed, he pointedly resisted the taint of popularity fostered by the revival. As he put it: "A little unpopularity is a sort of consecration."[8] In contrast to the aspirations of print publishers, Baudelaire was an unapologetic elitist.

The debate surrounding the "original print" in the second half of the nineteenth century is thus curiously hyperbolic, which surely betrays a certain defensiveness about the print's secondary status in the hierarchy of media. In retrospect, the revival of the original print is a notable instance of co-option in which publishers sponsored a rhetoric in support of their ambition. The writers who proclaimed the virtues of the original print in newspapers and periodicals were the same critics who wrote the prefaces to the annual portfolios of the etchers' society.[9] The commercial value of prints had long been a concern, and in the face of increasingly sophisticated techniques of reproduction, the various contrived means of inflating the worth of an impression were much discussed. Again Charles Blanc makes the crucial point: "An etching, as we understand it, is purely a drawing... but it is also a design with a number of copies, and—especially bizarre—in the world of the *curious,* where all value is augmented by rarity, a plate from which one can pull a fairly large number of impressions is often more esteemed than a unique drawing. It is certain that the most beautiful wash drawing by Rembrandt has never fetched as high a price as an impression of the *Hundred Guilder Print* or the *Burgermeister Six.*"[10] But Rembrandt was a different case. The British art critic Philip Gilbert Hamerton, close enough to the situation to be right about it, could not understand how his contemporaries made any money from their prints, even given the facility of the technique and the newly developed advantage of steel-facing.[11] In fact, within five years Cadart's operation faltered and went under for a time. Perhaps the best of these artists did indeed etch mainly for love.

The view still persists that the official or institutional etching revival contributed little of lasting significance to the more creative dimensions of late nineteenth-century art. Yet, most critics writing in support of the revival were drawn by seemingly incompatible ideas: a program in favor of bourgeois enlightenment and an investment in the more arcane, self-revelatory capacities of the medium. Baudelaire not only declared that etching glorifies the artist, but also asserted that the technique itself makes it "difficult for an artist not to describe his most intimate personality on the copper."[12] Here in the urgent defense of the technique is the curious implication that an etching is in some essential way more revealing of its author than a pen or watercolor sketch. It is as if incising the etching ground and committing the plate to acid somehow entailed a sense of finality that required an uncommon degree of artistic integrity.

An etching was thus perceived to be at its most compelling as a mode of confession (precisely the sense of the epigraph to this essay). A print is something to be "savored a little as one would a confidence." In a self-congratulatory claim, Baudelaire closed the circle of initiates even more tightly. Etching, he wrote, "is really too *personal,* and consequently too *aristocratic,* a genre to enchant people other than those who are naturally artists."[13] The inherently private character attributed to etching was an attempt to separate that medium from the mechanical aspect of printmaking and associate it with a basic romantic idea: the experience of an object as a means of direct communication with the artist. That this might best be achieved in a replicated medium is an odd shift in the inherited sense of the power of the original, or what has come to be referred to as the "aura" of a work of art.[14] Whether consciously heretical or a straightforward declaration of faith, in retrospect Baudelaire's extraordinary claims for the etching medium seem remarkably postmodern.

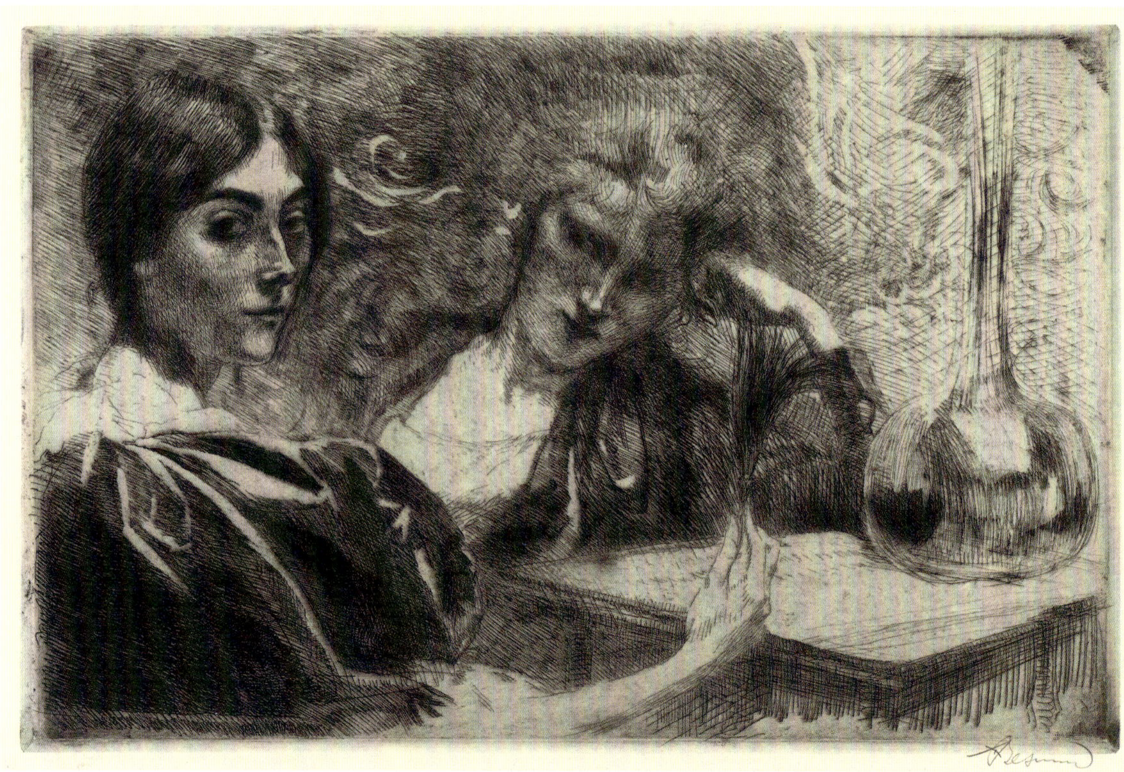

1 Albert Besnard, *Morphine Addicts,* 1887, etching, 23.7 × 37, National Gallery of Art, Washington, Rosenwald Collection

2 Odilon Redon, *This Is the Devil,* 1888, lithograph, 25.1 × 20, National Gallery of Art, Washington, Ailsa Mellon Bruce Fund

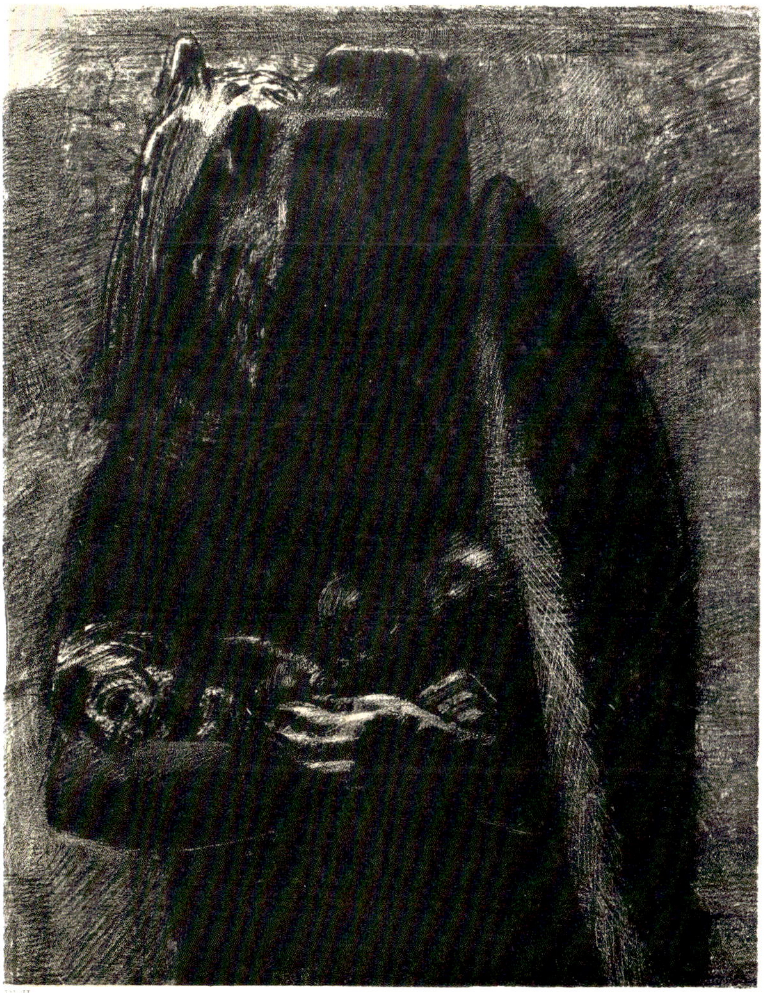

Pl. II

C'est le diable, portant sous ses deux ailes les sept péchés capitaux.....

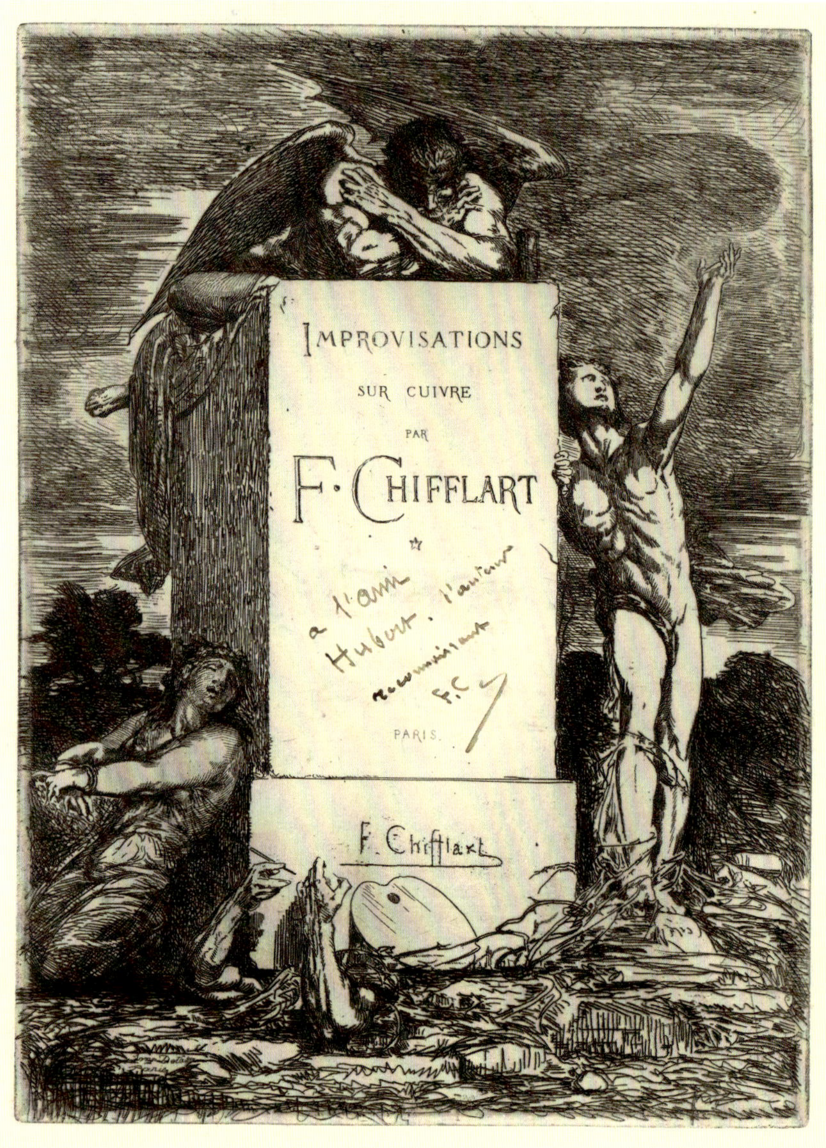
IMPROVISATIONS
SUR CUIVRE
PAR
F. CHIFFLART
PARIS.
F. Chifflart

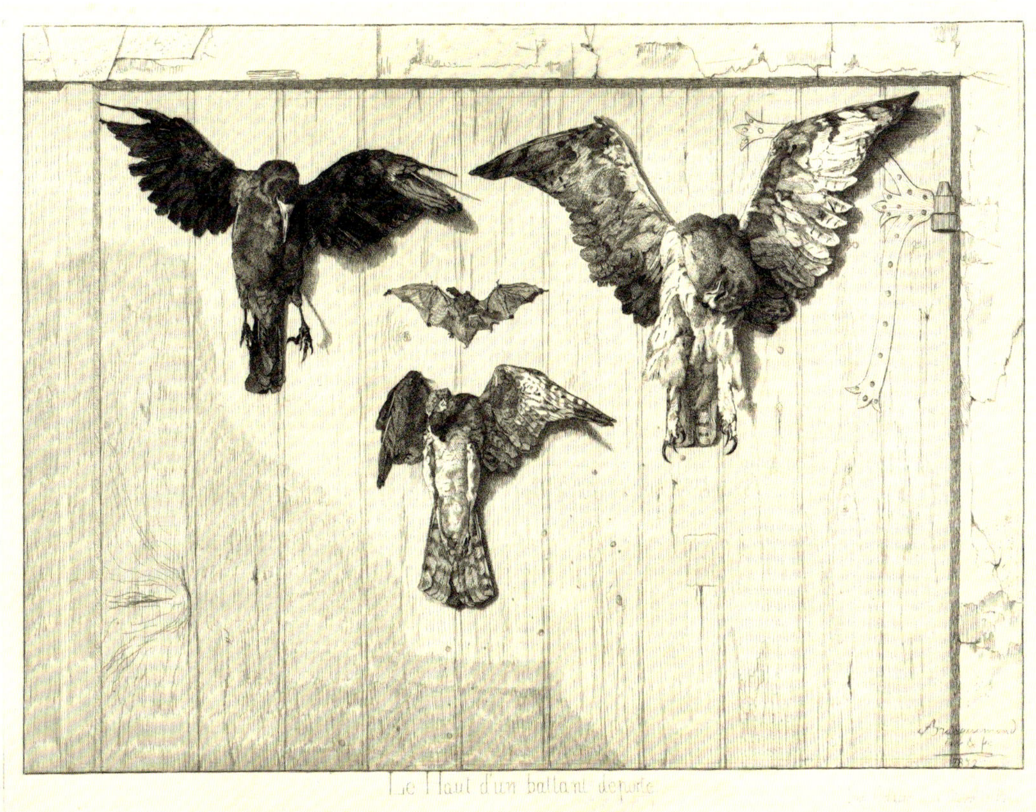

3 François Nicolas Chifflart, title page for *Improvisations on Copper,* 1865, etching, 32 × 24, National Gallery of Art, Washington, Ailsa Mellon Bruce Fund 2002.136.1

4 Félix Bracquemond, *Top of a Barn Door,* 1852, etching, 28 × 38.3, National Gallery of Art, Washington, Rosenwald Collection

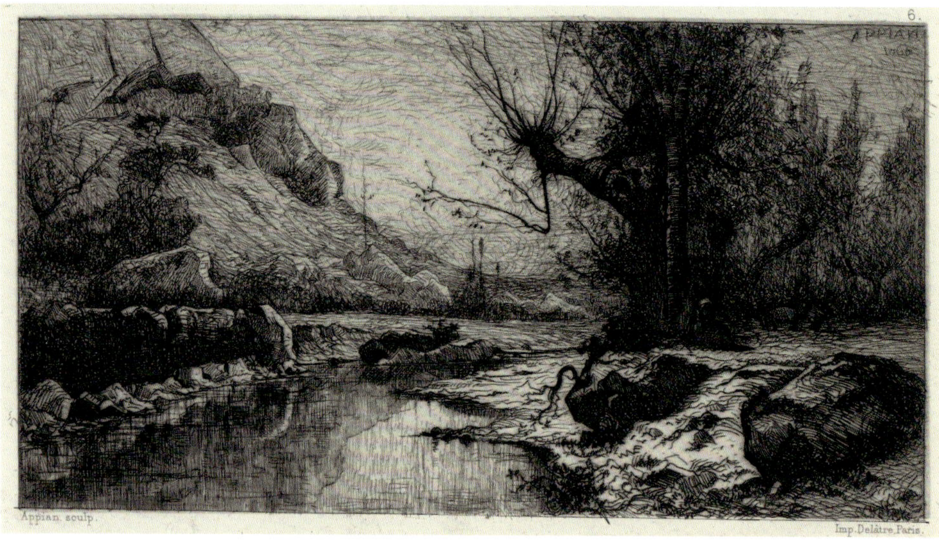
6.
Appian. sculp.
Imp. Delâtre, Paris.

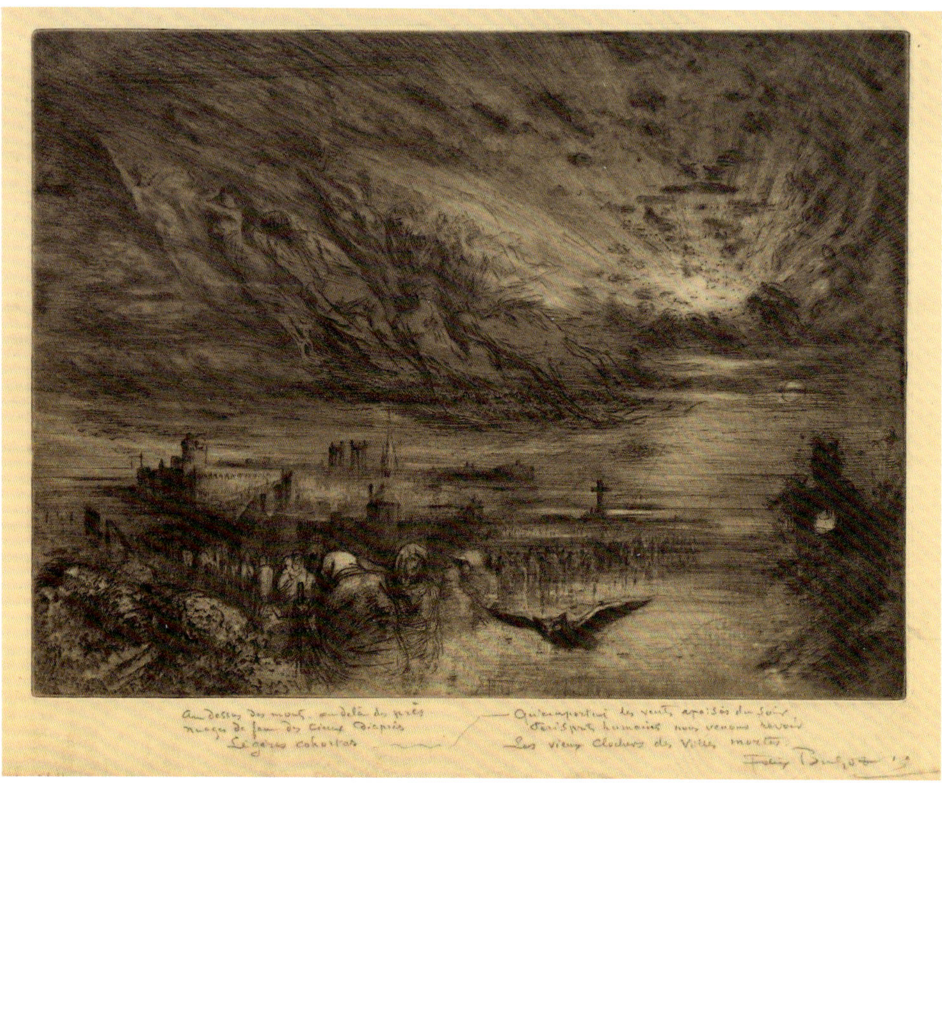

THE DARKER THEME

The culture of printmaking has always been ecumenical. Because it is an art form of the open market, it is less subject to the strictures of convention, and therefore artists, and by extension collectors, are freer to invade unfamiliar territory in their choice of style and subject. Throughout its history there have been times and local circumstances wherein various forms of official and unofficial censorship have restricted the publication of images. But given its prospective mobility and scale of production, printing is inherently difficult to control. Accordingly, printed images, like printed texts, have always had a high potential for transgression, and throughout the nineteenth century they carried on a background conversation shadowing the more public discourse of competing academic movements and aesthetic ideologies. This had been true before. In the Renaissance, in seventeenth-century Holland, and in Bourbon Spain, for example, prints regularly breached expected standards of decorum in religion, politics, and everyday life. The same was true from the 1860s onward, when lithography, wood engraving, photography, and especially etching became newly vital territories of invention, entrepreneurship, and the exchange of ideas.

A good example is the now little known academic painter Albert Besnard (1849–1934), a student of Alexandre Cabanel and a recipient of the Prix de Rome, who gained recognition as a society portraitist and painter of murals for civic and commercial buildings from the 1880s on.[15] Whereas his paintings are for the most part regarded as sophisticated banalities, inflecting a saccharine academicism with elements of impressionist style and an occasional whisper of symbolist allegory, in his off-hours Besnard made etchings of often remarkable and disturbing subjects, such as two fashionably attired morphine addicts in a state of delirium (fig. 1). For him the discreet nature of the medium lifted the constraints of etiquette that governed his paintings and especially his commissioned work. Etching not only exercised Besnard's skill as a draftsman, but it also drew him into the domain of dark and light in both senses. His successful career as a painter has largely been written out of the history of modern art,[16] yet his early etchings done in the 1880s explore marginal subjects in often unsettling ways that both evoke the brooding novels of Zola and presage the art of expressionism.[17]

When Rembrandt began making his radical sketch plates in the 1630s, he initiated the print as a brilliant medium for informal improvisation. This potential was given new implication by the vigorous promotion of etching and lithography as distinctly autograph techniques with a license to experiment. Prints might operate as a form of poetry and be allotted all the tolerances of obscurity, nonconformity, and loucheness that poetry allowed.

5 Adolphe Appian, *At Valromey*, 1868, etching with drypoint, 10 × 19.1, National Gallery of Art, Washington, Gift of Gaillard F. Ravenel and Frances P. Smyth-Ravenel

6 Félix Hilaire Buhot, *The Spirits of Dead Cities*, 1885, etching, roulette, drypoint, lift ground, aquatint, scraping, and burnishing, 28.8 × 39, National Gallery of Art, Washington, Rosenwald Collection

It became a medium suited to playing out an idea in a suite of images, an old format invested with new possibility. The lavishly designed portfolio containing a group of prints became a regular scheme for publication during the second half of the nineteenth century. Often these suites were improvisations in the proper sense: loosely connected if not random groups of images intended for sampling rather than reading in sequence. Odilon Redon's two series of lithographs based on Gustave Flaubert's unfinished episodic dialogue *Temptation of Saint Anthony* (fig. 2) is a cycle that cannot hope to capture more than a few fleeting and unrecollectable passages of the text. Max Klinger's several compilations of etchings—each given the indeterminate title "Opus"—sometimes form a tightly coherent sequence and sometimes do not. They are at times consistent in scale and orientation, and at times not. François Nicolas Chifflart's suite entitled *Improvisations on Copper* (fig. 3) is likewise a mélange of compositions embracing a variety of themes, moods, and settings—in short, an invitation to respond as if leafing through a volume of Mallarmé, pausing here and there to read a stanza or savor a line.

For the most part, prints of this kind remained offstage in the exhibitions and salons, being a less public repertoire issued for a discrete clientele with literary inclinations.[18] Thus, in print shops, printing studios, and artists' ateliers one could discover, at a modest price and with no commitment to a public expression of taste, the art of realists, academics, impressionists, and symbolists, many of them invading one another's territory. Baudelaire classified Edouard Manet as a realist. Academic painters like Besnard and Chifflart etched subjects of a more disturbing nature than their paintings. Félix Bracquemond, among the most celebrated masters of etching in the period, was an animal specialist whose images range from the conventional to the unnerving (fig. 4). "Rembrandtists" such as Seymour Haden, Barbizon artists such as Jean-Baptiste-Camille Corot and Adolphe Appian (fig. 5), and impressionists such as Félix Buhot (fig. 6), Max Liebermann (Hertel, fig. 2), and James McNeill Whistler (fig. 7) were prolific etchers. Gustave Doré, the great storyteller and most imaginative of illustrators, generated absorbing images in the late romantic mode (fig. 8). In many respects the most print-centered of all were the symbolists, including Klinger, Redon, and James Ensor (fig. 9).[19] And there are the many who through their choice of direction elude conventional labeling: the realist-fantast Charles Meryon, probably the most widely collected printmaker of the period; the academic impressionist James Tissot (Clayson, fig. 19); the social realist–expressionist Käthe Kollwitz (Hertel, fig. 9); and the naturalist-symbolist Félicien Rops.

Of the original prints made in this period the vast majority were destined not for framing on the wall but for portfolios. Among those images best savored in chosen moments of leisure were many obscure subjects, allegories either learned or whimsical, mild and not so mild erotica, political and social satire, and innumerable explorations of strained states of mind and social circumstance that would have disrupted the decorum of the proper bourgeois interior. In the same category were bound volumes of etchings, lithographs, and wood engravings, and the suites of etchings issued between fashionably designed covers, often series of landscapes or city views but also explorations of lofty philosophical and literary topics. Print collecting had a broad compass, including subjects ranging from erudition to impropriety. The practice of collecting came along with the promotion of the print as fine art, and inevitably the one had to be joined to the other. From this followed the necessary decision to make a place for keeping prints, and thereby a place for the private and occasional diversion of consulting them.

THE GENDERING OF PRIVACY

What were the parameters of privacy in private collecting? Collecting works of art had by this time become a bourgeois more than a princely activity and therefore something to be advised, written about, and occasionally mocked. It is a standard assertion that the modern concept of domesticity in Western culture evolved in the nineteenth century, and that its essential symptom was the woman's assumption of responsibility for the household. This applied not only to the daily running of the house but also to determining its interior appointments—that is, the arena for the expression of taste. In its particular manifestations this shift cannot have been uniform across cultures and class boundaries, and certainly it varied by wealth and social custom. It also varied according to available housing. For example, middle-class urban families in London aspired to live in individual, vertically arranged houses with gardens, whereas in Paris and other European capitals they customarily lived in apartments. Nonetheless, the self-proclaimed tastemakers were in broad agreement about the need for a well-supervised domestic environment, not just as an expression of social and moral well-being but as a requirement for maintaining it. They also agreed on how such a household should look.[20]

In 1871, Jacob von Falke published a widely read study on the history of the house from antiquity to the present. The concluding chapters offer instructions for designing an interior, and the last, entitled "Women's Aesthetic Mission," considers the special qualifications of these newly assigned guardians of domesticity. Falke's conception of the woman's role and his definition of taste are very much of the period. The understanding of higher beauty—art—is exclusively the prerogative of men, yet below this, "there is still a wide-spread domain which is governed by beauty, and in which the

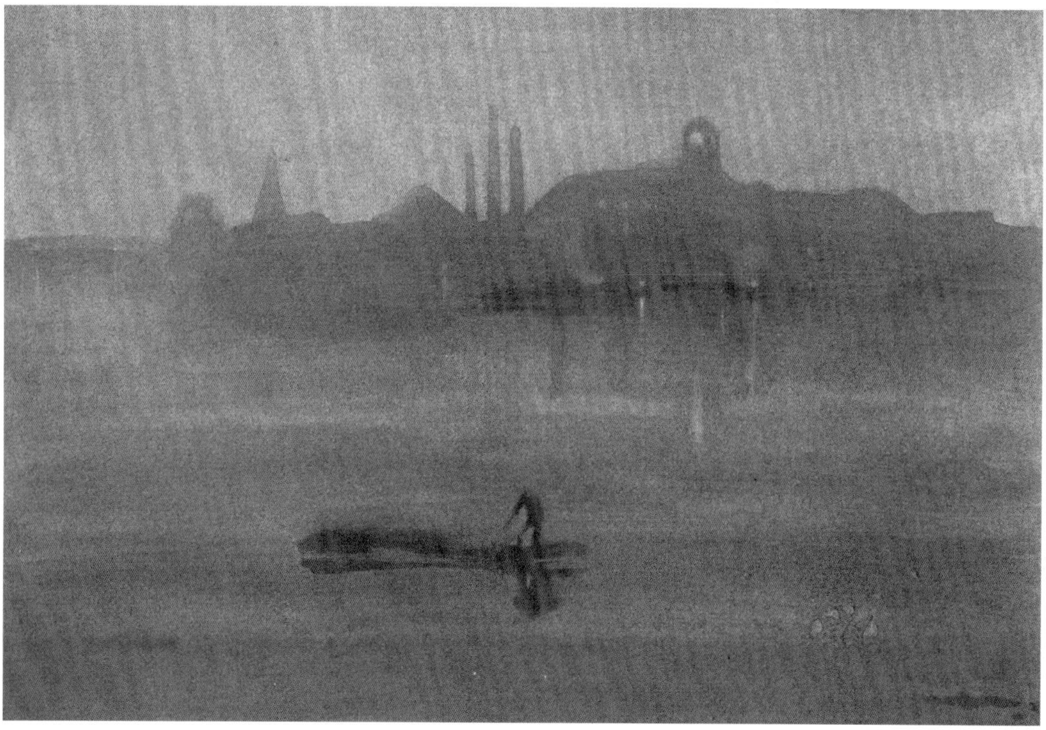

7 James McNeill Whistler, *Nocturne,* 1878, lithotint with scraping, 17.1 × 25.7, National Gallery of Art, Washington, Rosenwald Collection

8 Gustave Doré, "Houndsditch," 1872, wood engraving, from Blanchard Jerrold, *London: A Pilgrimage* (London, 1872), National Gallery of Art, Washington, William B. O'Neal Fund

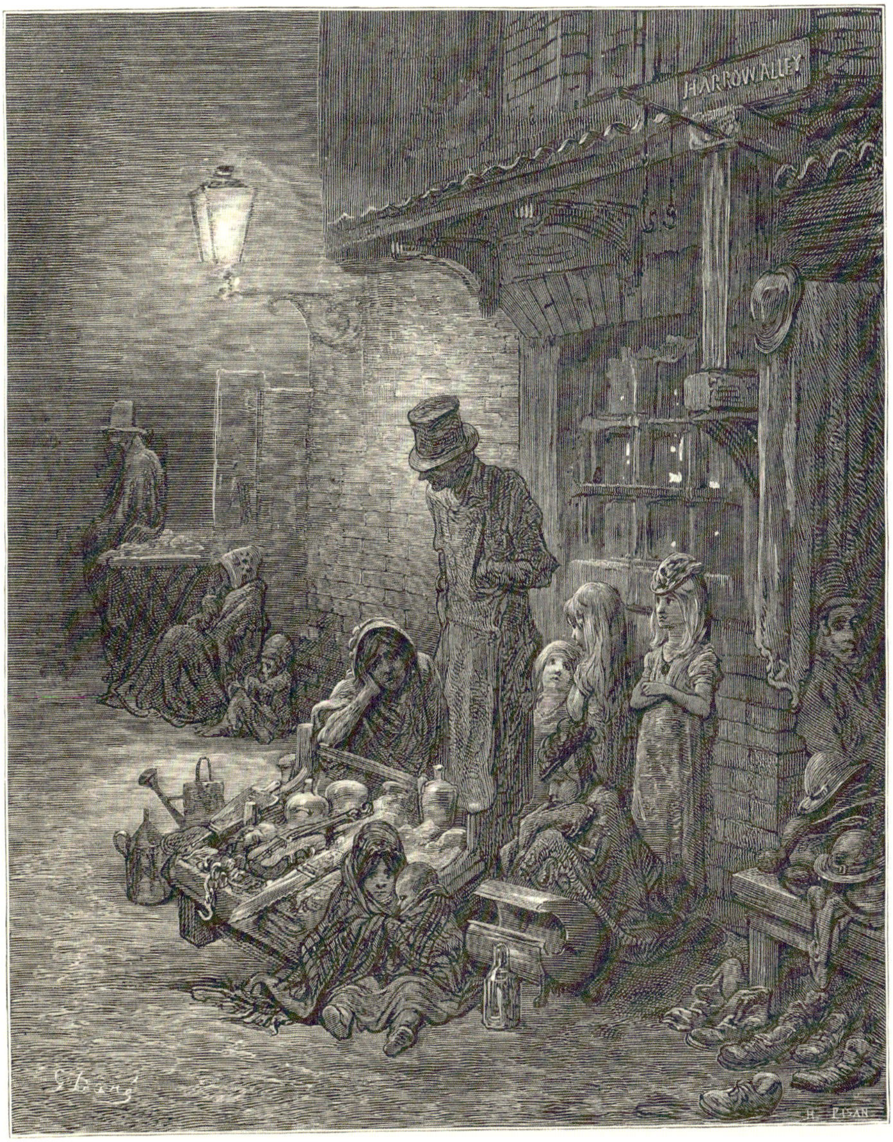
HARROW ALLEY

beautiful and the useful are united." This he terms "the realm of taste," the true province of a woman and "natural to her sex."[21] The home is her proper place, and her particular synthetic intuition (implicitly not her intellect) qualifies her by nature to create and preside over those precincts that both reflect the family's privacy and present its fashionableness to society.

The investment of money and effort in the domestic interior was usually meant to be obvious. This was the age of the period room, of bibelots, fabric walls, wainscoting, and the overly laden tables and cluttered mantels that we associate with Victorian taste. By the 1880s the interior was likely to be a jungle of objects that required a guide, and there were guides aplenty,

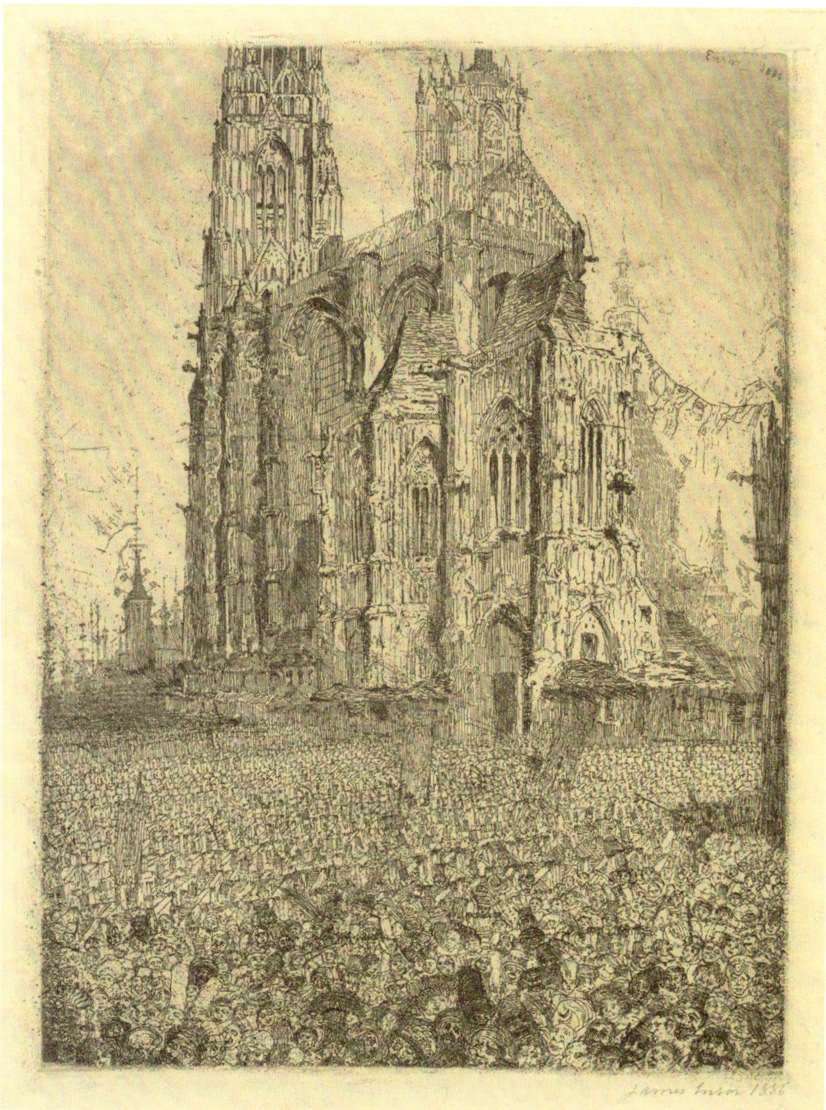

9 James Ensor, *The Cathedral*, 1886, etching, 23.5 × 17.6, National Gallery of Art, Washington, Rosenwald Collection

from a spate of new illustrated magazines to books like Falke's. Women were among the regular visitors to art exhibitions and browsers in furniture stores, print shops, and art galleries that cropped up to serve the passion for decor. This, too, reflected a change in socially respectable conduct. There had been a time when a woman's presence before the windows of a print shop provoked comment. In 1804, the English moralist John Corry wrote that "girls often go in parties to visit the windows of print shops, that they may amuse themselves with the view of prints which impart the most impure ideas."[22] Although Corry's concern doubtless lived on in some minds, images of print shops later on in the century indicate that women had become the preferred customers. This is certainly suggested by the many posters showing interested clientele published by Parisian lithography studios. Indeed, the old prejudice is given a mocking turn in Georges Bottini's depiction of a well-dressed woman looking disapprovingly at a lithograph of a prostitute displayed in a print shop window (fig. 10).[23]

Instructions on how to select, frame, and place pictures in the house were readily available, and the tastemakers generally agreed on what should go where, and why. In his *Hints on Household Taste,* the interior designer Charles Locke Eastlake discusses the choice of wallpapers, including what is suitable as a backdrop for paintings, watercolors, and prints.[24] An avid proponent of the Gothic Revival, Eastlake is nevertheless indisposed to clutter and knickknacks, especially in the sober context of a library, where plaster casts of classical busts should be preferred to "modern rubbish." Oil paintings ought to be grouped in a drawing room or a dining room so as not to distract from delicate watercolors, which are best hung in plain frames. For those of lesser means, metal engravings, wood engravings, and photographs are appropriate for sitting rooms or a library and suit the intimacy of these spaces.[25]

The rough plan was that paintings, if one could afford them, should be hung in social spaces. Watercolors were also suitable there and, in a pinch, prints, preferably landscapes and portraits. The comtesse de Bassanville proposed that engravings of "serious subjects, severely framed" should be hung in the *cabinet de monsieur,* but neither prints nor paintings in an antechamber.[26] Edith Wharton, however, deemed the entrance hall especially good for mythologies and architectural views—Piranesi, for example—but nothing requiring "thought and study," such as the symbolic complexity of an Albrecht Dürer engraving.[27] In Henri Béraldi's jaundiced opinion, the average household was too often burdened by prints of sententious historical subjects installed everywhere from the antechamber to the children's bedrooms.[28] A glaring exception to these stipulations, which would seem to prove the conventional rule, occurs in Joris-Karl Huysmans' infamous

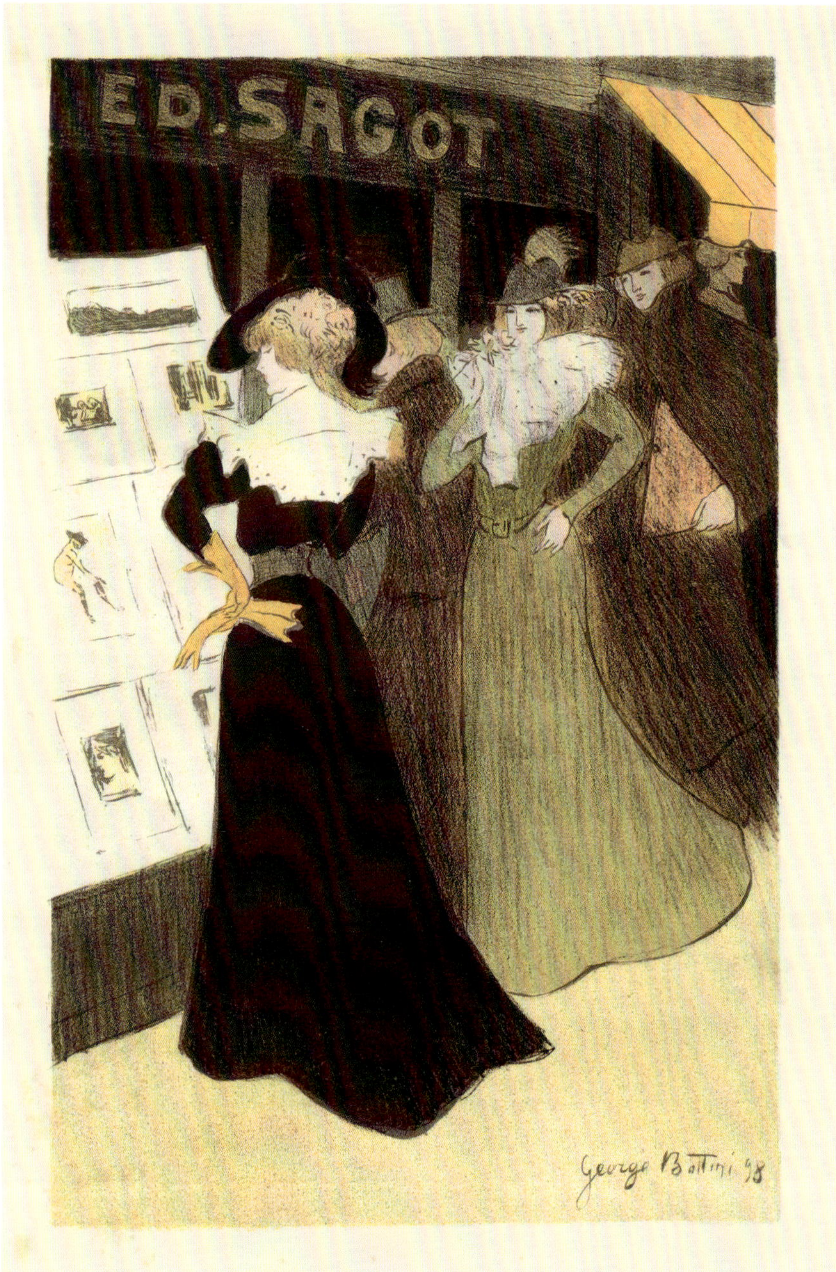
ED. SAGOT
George Bottini 98

novel *À rebours,* in which the main character, Jean Floressas des Esseintes, describes the entryway to his house as densely hung with prints by Redon and Rodolphe Bresdin (fig. 11), one case described as "dreamt up by an opium-befuddled mind."[29] It has been remarked that the brothers Jules and Edmond de Goncourt, model aesthetes in their art-packed house, the Maison d'Auteuil, were the joint inspiration for Des Esseintes.[30] It is certainly not coincidental that in both of these self-conscious departures from bourgeois convention the perpetrators are unattached men. Taste required discretion and care so as not to assert, much less offend.

Overall the patterns are consistent: try to display each medium separately. See that the content reflects the character of the room and the activities going on in it. Works of art hung on a wall or placed on a table or a bookshelf should serve as background, not centerpieces. Although they might provide occasions for conversation, they should not make much noise on their own. Or, if arranged in an overfurnished period manner, they should make sufficient noise to drown one another out. Managing these negotiations successfully was what constituted good taste, and good taste was regularly being held up for judgment. So far as contemporary art was concerned, the portfolios being issued by Cadart and etching societies elsewhere likely served in part as a guide to what was proper. The predominant blandness of the genre scenes and city views and the often narcotic picturesqueness of so many of the landscapes made for safe territory.

The manuals of Falke, Eastlake, and Wharton, like the endeavors of the etching societies, were addressed to an aspiring bourgeoisie seeking a guarantee of good taste. They were pitched at a level that both implied aspiration and accommodated beginners. Thus, while presuming to be social prescriptions for the educated professional classes, such handbooks were also fit for the attention of the lower end of the urban middle class and for provincial households such as that of Emma Bovary. Providing for those who could not afford fine watercolors and expensive reproductive engravings were the lithographic presses of Goupil, turning out inexpensive reproductive prints in color as well as black and white, often of usefully instructive subjects and often available framed.[31]

10 Georges Alfred Bottini, *Sagot's Lithography Gallery*, 1898, color lithograph, 28.9 × 18.6, National Gallery of Art, Washington, Rosenwald Collection

Although it must have involved just as much scouting and discrimination, interior decoration was not accorded the same rank as collecting per se. This venerable pastime was still regarded as the superior purview of the male. Men were seen to collect objects, whereas, as Falke saw it, women surrounded themselves with them. This is a principle that could be extended to the proposition that a household, including its mistress, constituted a kind of collection in itself, acquired and supervised by the master.[32] But within the domestic sphere there were retreats reserved for each: the boudoir and the study. In his book on the proper design of a residence, published in Paris in 1884, Henry Havard drew the distinction. "If the boudoir is, par excellence, the sanctuary of the mistress of the house, the *cabinet de travail* is the sanctuary of the master of the dwelling—but a sanctuary considered in a more elevated sense... and with a purpose altogether less trifling."[33] With the transfer of responsibility for the household to the mistress, the study, or *cabinet de travail,* was defined in opposition as a male preserve.

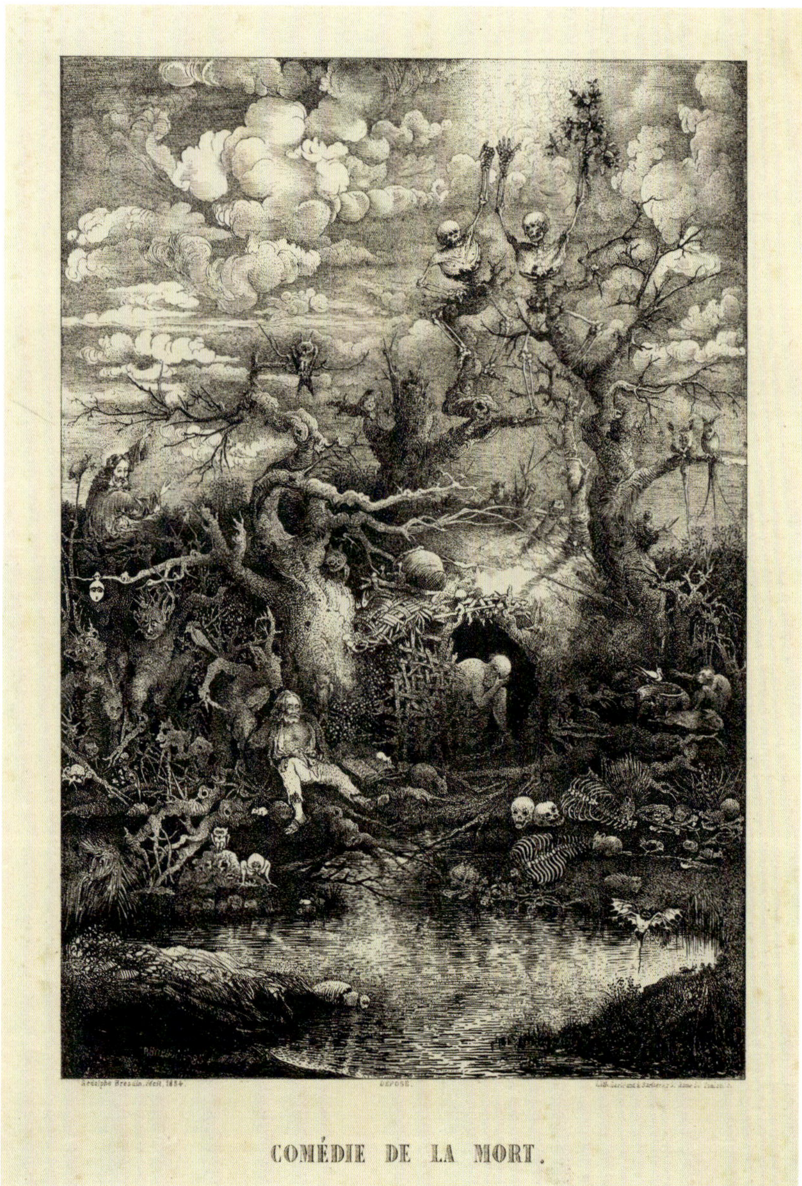

11 Rodolphe Bresdin, *Comedy of Death,* 1854, lithograph, 21.8 × 15, National Gallery of Art, Washington, Rosenwald Collection 1958.8.22

The literature on interiors describes the study as a relatively intimate space, not so cluttered as to be unsuitable for work and often, as in a drawing room, with a large table in the center, sufficient natural light, and bookcases if necessary. An independent library was a luxury found only in grander houses, more often in England. Books meant to be kept away from women and girls would have been in locked cases or placed on the top shelves in the drawing room. The study was for silent reading, contemplation, and managing one's affairs, for receiving close acquaintances or people on business. In contrast to the salon or drawing room, it was not a space normally given over to the run of the family. The *cabinet de travail* constituted the antithesis of the street and the public experience of Baudelaire's much-discussed "flâneur." Here was where a serious print collector leafed through his portfolios, either alone or in consort with invited family or friends.[34]

PRACTICALITIES

How did the print collector collect? The ways of acquiring prints, drawings, and books in the nineteenth century were many. The stalls along the quays of the Seine had long purveyed inexpensive books and prints. Booksellers, stationers, and art dealers included prints in their inventories, and of course, there were the auction houses.[35] There were also the independent print publishers like Cadart, who had an art gallery in Paris. He regularly issued prints by subscription, adopting a practice that had earlier produced income for clubs of amateur printmakers such as the Society of Painter-Etchers in London and similar groups in Berlin, Vienna, and Brussels.[36] Newly released single prints and suites of prints available over the counter or by subscription were announced in periodicals and newspapers, by the societies themselves, and by small publishers and dealers.[37]

Etching societies and print publishers supplied a significant portion of the market for fine prints, and at least in England and probably elsewhere, both men and women were among the subscribers.[38] An etching by Adolphe Martial Potémont advertising Cadart's Paris gallery shows a group of well-dressed couples staring avidly at the prints displayed in the windows, an indication that shopping could be a family affair (fig. 12). And throughout the Belle Époque, the highpoint of popular lithographic production, women are represented as connoisseurs evaluating the proverbial *belle épreuve*. The ubiquity of this motif suggests that they were indeed regular purchasers of prints and that for promotional purposes they were being recruited in their traditional supporting role as muses.[39] Private collecting was not altogether the male's exclusive province.

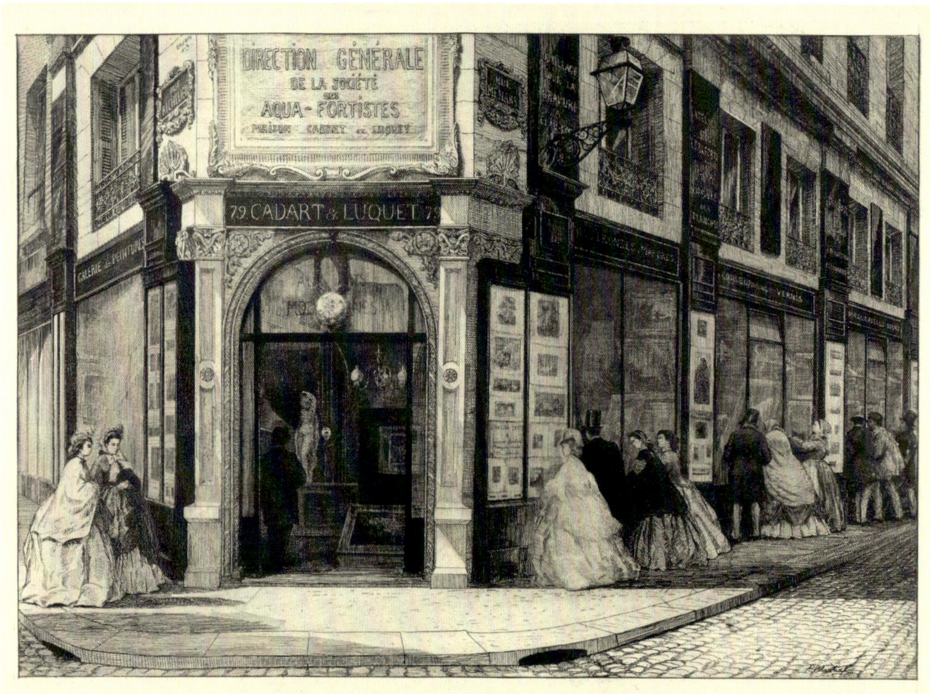

12 Adolphe Martial Potémont, *Seat of the Society of Etchers, 79 rue de Richelieu,* 1864, etching, 25 × 36, Baltimore Museum of Art, The George A. Lucas Collection, purchased with funds from the State of Maryland, Laurence and Stella Bendann Fund, and contributions from individuals, foundations, and corporations throughout the Baltimore community 1996.48.2436

Seeking out prints was likely to have been a frequent, if not feverish activity carried on in less rarified conditions than would have been true for more highly priced objects such as paintings and furniture. Acquiring prints demanded a lot of time and active ferreting; the discovery of a particular state or impression amid the piles of dross must have been a matter of special satisfaction. The daily comings and goings of the American collector and agent George Lucas, who lived in Paris from 1857 to 1909, illustrates the situation vividly. For example, on Thursday morning, November 3, 1887, Lucas went first to Georges Petit's gallery and then to the art dealer Paul Durand-Ruel. He drew cash from his accountants, bought spectacles, and proceeded to a print publisher, probably Delarue fils, where he bought animal studies (etchings?) by Félix Bracquemond for fifteen francs (see fig. 4) before heading to the auction house Hôtel Drouot. Two days later Lucas visited the photographer Nadar to order photos for the collector Frank Frick, with whom he had been spending time, and proceeded to the quay along the river in search of prints. He made three more calls and then went elsewhere for engravings after François Boucher. Next Lucas stopped by an exhibition of Léon Lhermitte, and after that he went to see a painter about etchings by Jules Ferdinand Jacquemart. He made two more calls before buying three etchings and two statues for a hundred francs from the printmaker Charles Courtry, after which he continued to the Hôtel Drouot in search of more etchings. Some days later he records visiting the collector, painter, and printmaker Léon Bonnat, going on to a bookseller and then to the print publisher Sagot (see fig. 10) to look at etchings, then to the art dealer Dupont to give a commission for three Meryon etchings (see figs. 16, 19) that were coming up for sale at Drouot's, where he went next and purchased a single lot of eighty etchings for forty francs.[40] Such busy days were by no means atypical. Lucas visited many artists, buying prints and drawings from them directly. His connections with dealers and publishers were obviously extensive, and he seems rarely to have been idle, except for the recorded days off to soothe his recurrent headaches. Although we should note that Lucas was an agent first and a collector second, his peregrinations give us a clear sense of what the paper chase could be like in the capital of European printmaking.

Advice to those interested in establishing and storing a collection of prints could be found in treatises written early on by collectors for collectors and later by curators and professional printmakers. This had begun in the seventeenth century with John Evelyn's landmark treatise *Sculptura,* composed for the Royal Society in London, and continued in an unbroken tradition through the nineteenth century.[41] These histories and handbooks touch on topics ranging from detailed accounts of technique to disquisitions

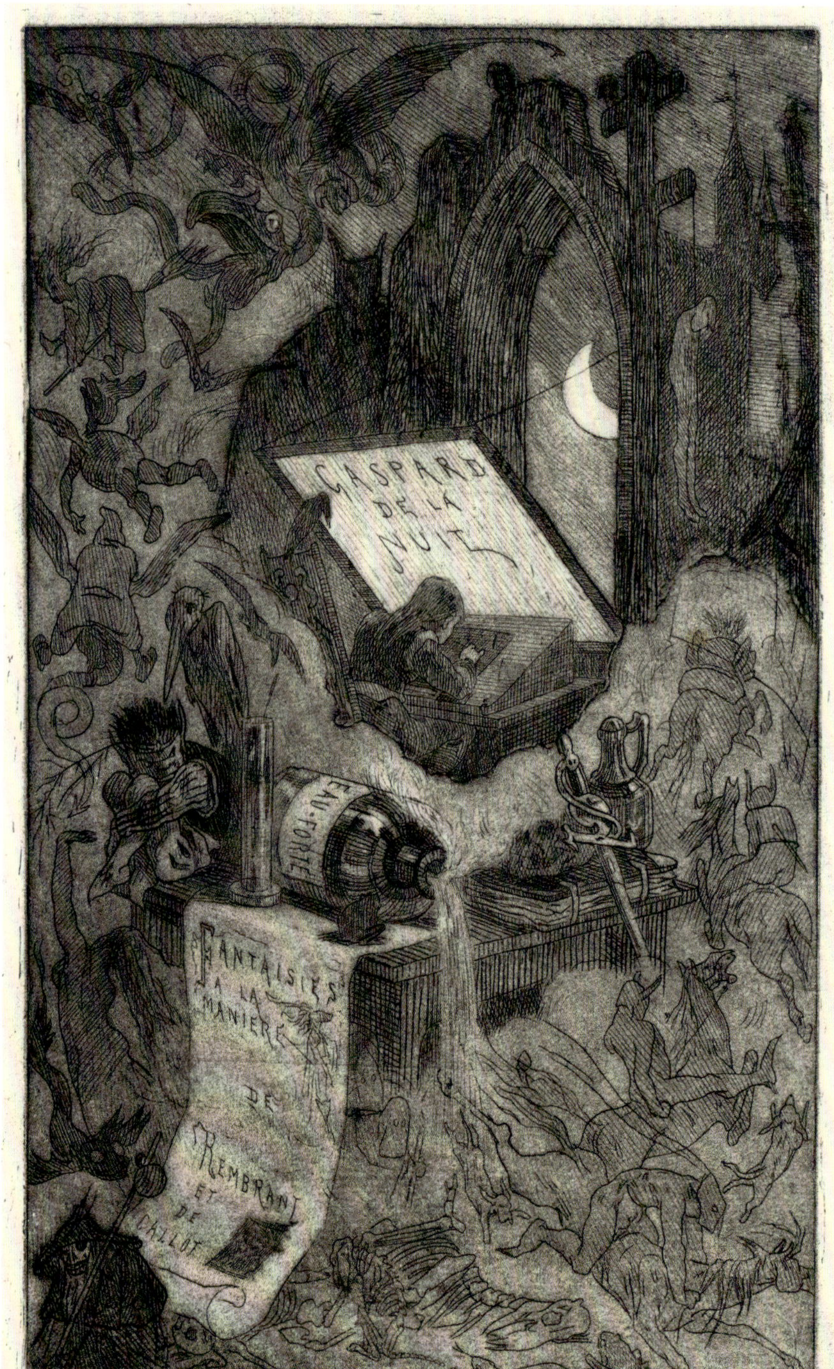
GASPARD DE LA NUIT
EAU-FORTE
FANTAISIES À LA MANIÈRE DE REMBRANT ET DE CALLOT

on the aesthetic properties of each medium, the importance of states and condition, and worries about forgery.[42] They often include short accounts of significant collections, always those on a grand scale that were unlikely to offer the reader a viable model, and they typically recommend artists whose works they deem worthy of purchase. Rarely do these treatises mention buying current work, confining themselves instead to the secure territory of the old masters.[43] In this respect they provide a conservative backdrop to the wider practice of collecting in the nineteenth century, which, judging from the remarkable level of production, must have been vigorous.

These manuals, along with pictorial evidence, collectors' diaries, and magazine advertisements, detail how prints were kept. Those not meant for the wall were stored mainly in portfolios and possibly, at a more advanced stage of collecting, in specially designed solander boxes. Noting the risks of keeping and studying prints in portfolios, experts encouraged mounting and matting for conservation. Exposure to light was an acknowledged problem.[44] There is occasional advice about furniture, for example, making provision for cabinets with deep storage for portfolios and supplying artificial light to study the works. In all of this an association between a print collection and the engagements of the library is implicit.[45] Literary culture provided a climate fully consistent with the growing enthusiasm for acquiring prints. The parallels between the act of reading and the study of prints are self-evident, and in theory as well as practice the historical relation between them merits further attention.[46] Collecting art was presumed to be a part of the life of a cultivated middle-class family, and prints were the most available art to collect.

13 Félicien Rops, *Gaspard de la nuit: Fantasies in the Manner of Rembrandt and Callot*, 1868, etching and aquatint, 14.2 × 8.7, National Gallery of Art, Washington, Rosenwald Collection

THE ODDITY OF PRINT COLLECTING

Privacy brings with it unspecified latitudes for indulging in oddity, and print collectors accordingly have long been singled out for their eccentricity. The reasons for this dubious honor are worthy of consideration. Among the proclivities associated with print collecting are an obsession with classification, an often fetishistic pursuit of rarity, and a temptation to achieve completeness in a chosen category. Each tendency relates to how prints came to be valued as collectible objects on the European art market. Once Adam von Bartsch published the twenty-one volumes of *Le Peintre-graveur* in 1803, collectors could identify and describe most old master prints with reference to an authoritative source.[47] By implication they could also determine whether a print remained undescribed and thus whether an impression was rare, perhaps unique. Last, because prints were made in multiple impressions, the hope of acquiring a particular work could be sustained indefinitely.[48] Each of these factors arises from the nature of the print as a replicated object and the resulting imperative

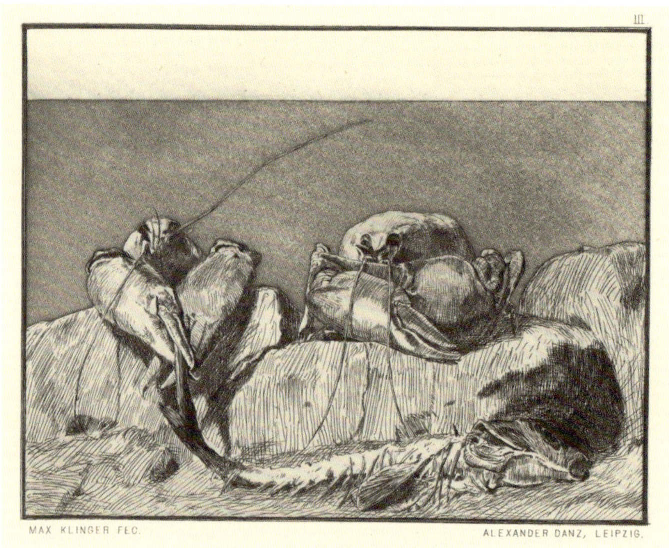

14 Max Klinger, *Siesta I,* 1879, etching and aquatint, 8.6 × 11.4, National Gallery of Art, Washington, Gift of the Epstein Family Collection

15 Max Klinger, *Moonlit Night,* 1881, etching and aquatint, 36 × 26, National Gallery of Art, Washington, Gift of the Epstein Family Collection

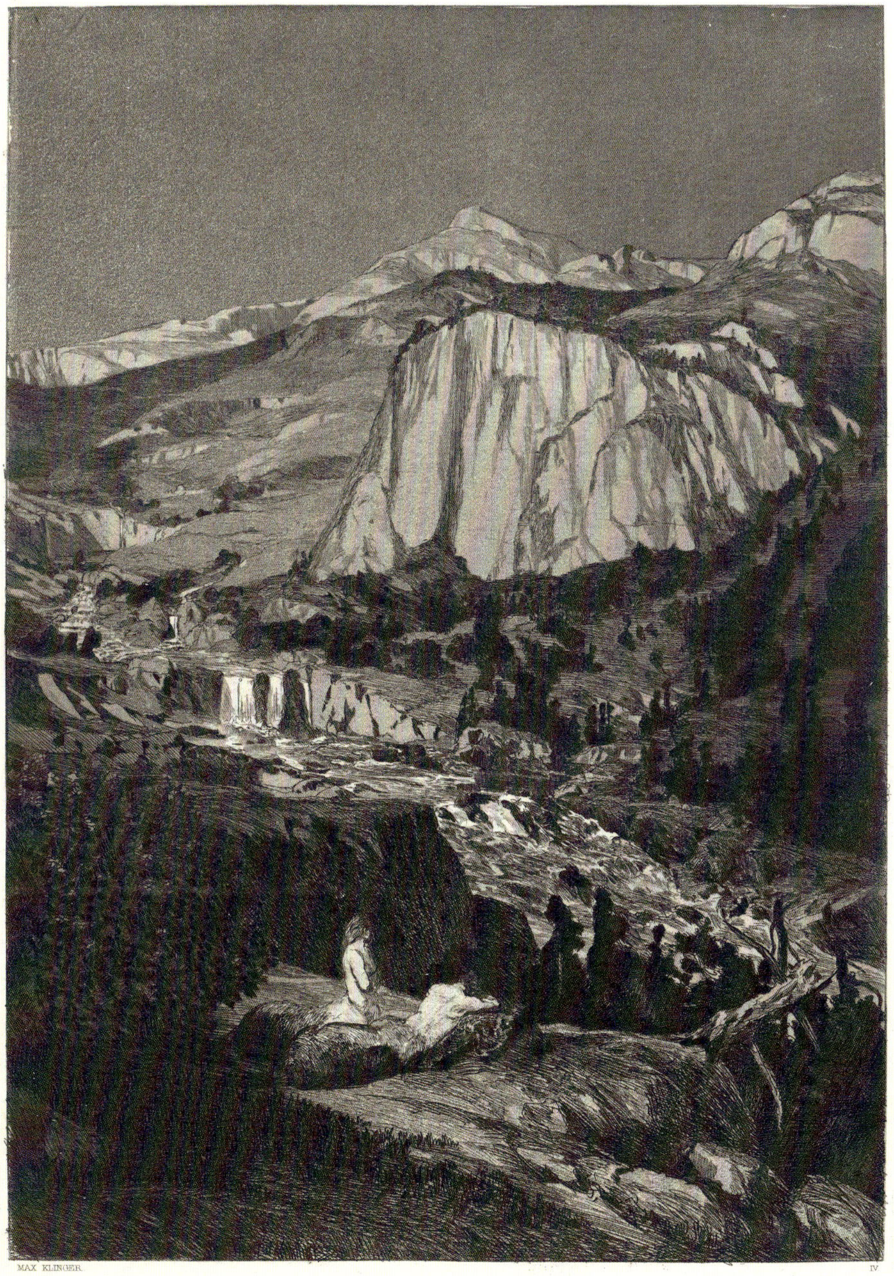

MAX KLINGER. IV

to compensate for its secondary status in a culture devoted to the exceptional. Rarity in prints differs from rarity in most other media.

The first substantial print collections—those running into the thousands—were formed in the Renaissance. They were generally compiled in albums and ordered by subject: mythological, historical, and scriptural subjects, ancient and modern architecture, ornaments, and so on.[49] In this respect they were not print collections per se but rather collections of printed images usually accumulated to serve as pictorial encyclopedias or reference books. Although this topical system of organization persisted in some cases until the nineteenth century, by the early seventeenth century portfolios and albums of prints were more likely to have been arranged by artist and national school, the scheme later recommended by most advice books and still followed in most museum print rooms.[50] Thus, for three centuries the system for organizing a private collection of prints has been art-historical, based on formal, chronological, and geographical rather than topical criteria.

With the shift from the encyclopedic motive for print collecting to the desire to acquire the canon of great masters, connoisseurship and the pursuit of rarity emerged as primary criteria for acquisition. Print collecting became like other kinds of collecting, which paradoxically led to a reputation for unconventionality. Already in the seventeenth century print collectors were pilloried by the French satirist Jean de La Bruyère for their obsession with rare states and impressions, and by the eighteenth century printmakers and print publishers were devising ingenious and sometimes outright fraudulent schemes to satisfy it.[51] Rarity began to be controlled artificially, and in the second half of the nineteenth century signing individual impressions by hand, and dedicating them to a friend or a patron, became common practices.

Printmakers' antics in search of their quarry were often a joking matter, and from the time of the romantics printmaking has been repeatedly associated with mischief. In Félicien Rops' frontispiece to the fantastic poetry of Aloysius Bertrand, the fumes rising from a spilled bottle of acid conjure a legion of demons who ride off into the night; printmaking is conceived as a form of alchemy and the etcher's acid bath becomes Pandora's box, ready to spread trouble throughout the world (fig. 13). The collector's obsession, by contrast, was more often regarded as merely risible. For example, in his novel *The Woman in White* (1859), Wilkie Collins caricatures the infirm Mr. Fairlie in silent repose in his secluded room, trembling feverishly over his album of Rembrandts, a pathetic old fool lost in his private pursuits.[52] We might take the lampooning of print collectors as little more than hyperbole were it not that the follies described are precisely those being fed by the market and simultaneously warned against in the books on collecting. Hamerton

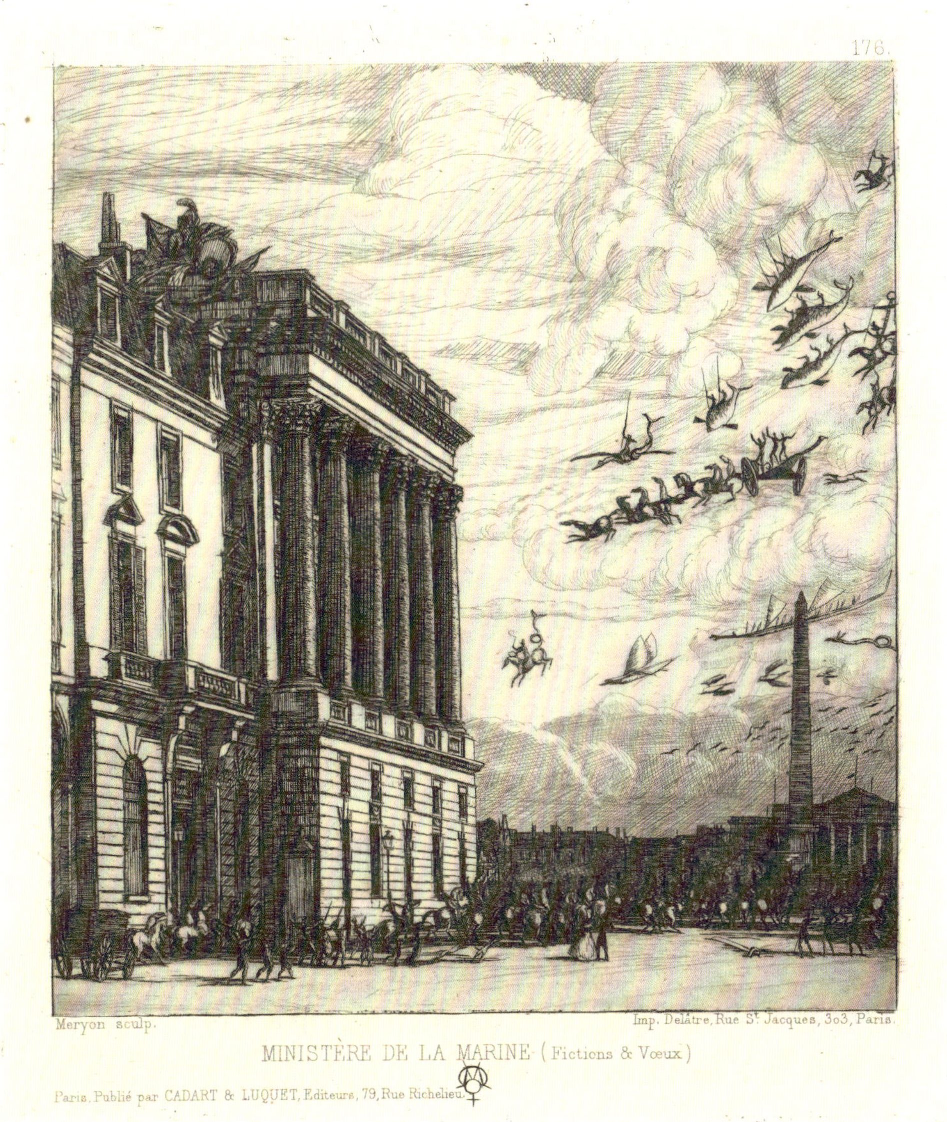

16 Charles Meryon, *Ministry of the Marine, Paris,* 1865, etching, 14.1 × 13, National Gallery of Art, Washington, Gift of Mrs. Harold Ober

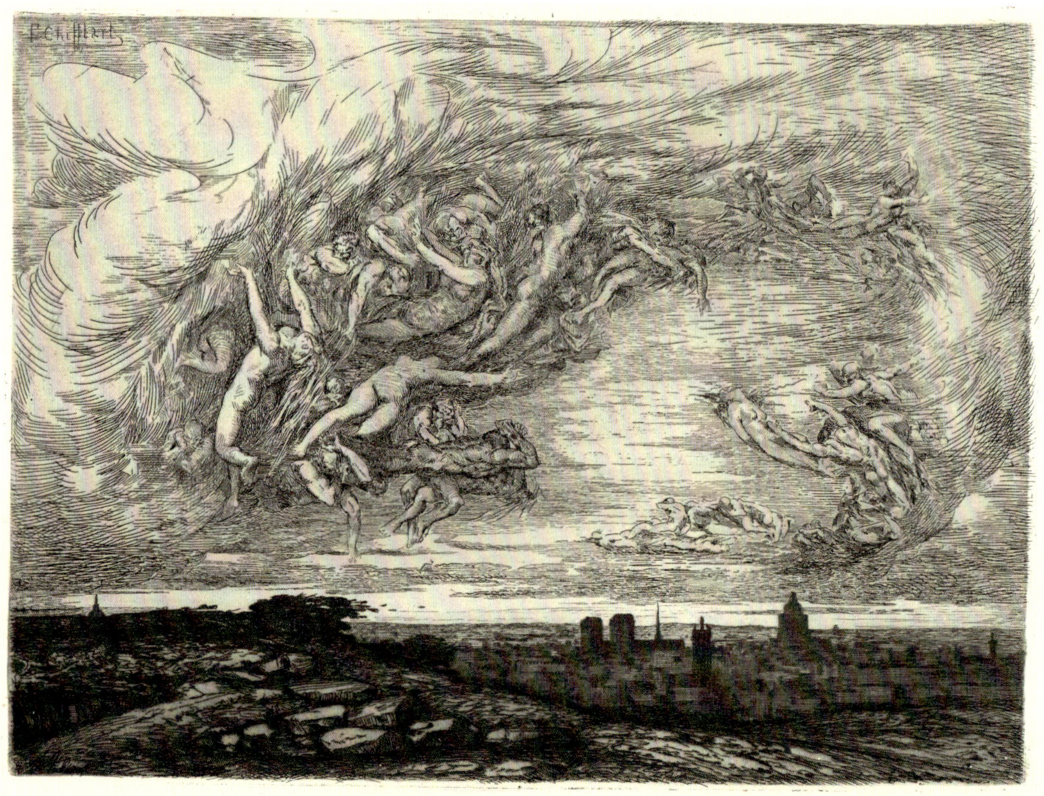

17 François Nicolas Chifflart, *Cholera in Paris,* 1865, etching with drypoint, 22.7 × 31.3, National Gallery of Art, Washington, Ailsa Mellon Bruce Fund

characterized the syndrome as a degeneration into "curiosity madness," in contrast to the genuine passion of the "amateur," who seeks out art for the sake of art.[53] For him the Mr. Fairlies were a stain on the noble tradition of "the curious," those venerable men of means who in their pursuit of knowledge had founded the great scientific academies and antiquarian societies of Europe. These men understood that curiosity was properly motivated not by an object but by what could be learned from it.

If this manner of collecting was in many ways a world unto itself, it was also a shared experience. Medals, coins, bronzes, and often prints were among the first significant collections of art and antiquities to be formed in early modern Europe. The earliest known document recording a collector's engagement with a print comes from a letter written in 1520 by the Nuremberg humanist Johann Cochläus reporting a visit from the mayor of Frankfurt. It tells how the two carried on a discussion of Dürer's master engravings *Melencolia I* and *Saint Jerome in His Study*.[54] Private or otherwise, collectors had long formed associations, and behind their concern with competition for exceptional impressions there lay another, perhaps equally important sensation peculiar to owning a replicated object. Possessing a print or a cast medal carries with it the presumption that somewhere someone else possesses it, too. That awareness in itself constitutes a silent fraternity related to but different from the affiliation of learning that arises from having read the same book or having stood before Raphael's *Sistine Madonna* in Dresden. The print collector's sense of affinity need not have been just competitive; it was also rooted in the mutual possession of an object. The community of Renaissance humanists was built in part on this understanding of a collection, and nineteenth-century bourgeois pride of ownership may not have been so distant from it.

THE NEO-ROMANTIC SENSIBILITY

Historians typically approach the modern concept of privacy as an aspiration of the bourgeoisie, defining it first as a social condition and then as a matter of individual experience. The experience of privacy, however, is best described by those who construct it for themselves, and here artists and writers provide the most eloquent testimony. Certain of the more recurrent themes adopted by the artists of interest to us here carry over a romantic sensibility, but it is a sensibility inflected by a secular redefinition of the world very much in terms of a new generation. The image of nature is no longer that of the terrible sublime but something closer to a mechanism out of which the human species emerges as an eventual product. Nature is perceived anthropomorphically and sometimes ironically, for example in Max Klinger's witty portrait of two crabs perched like a pair of Majas resting on

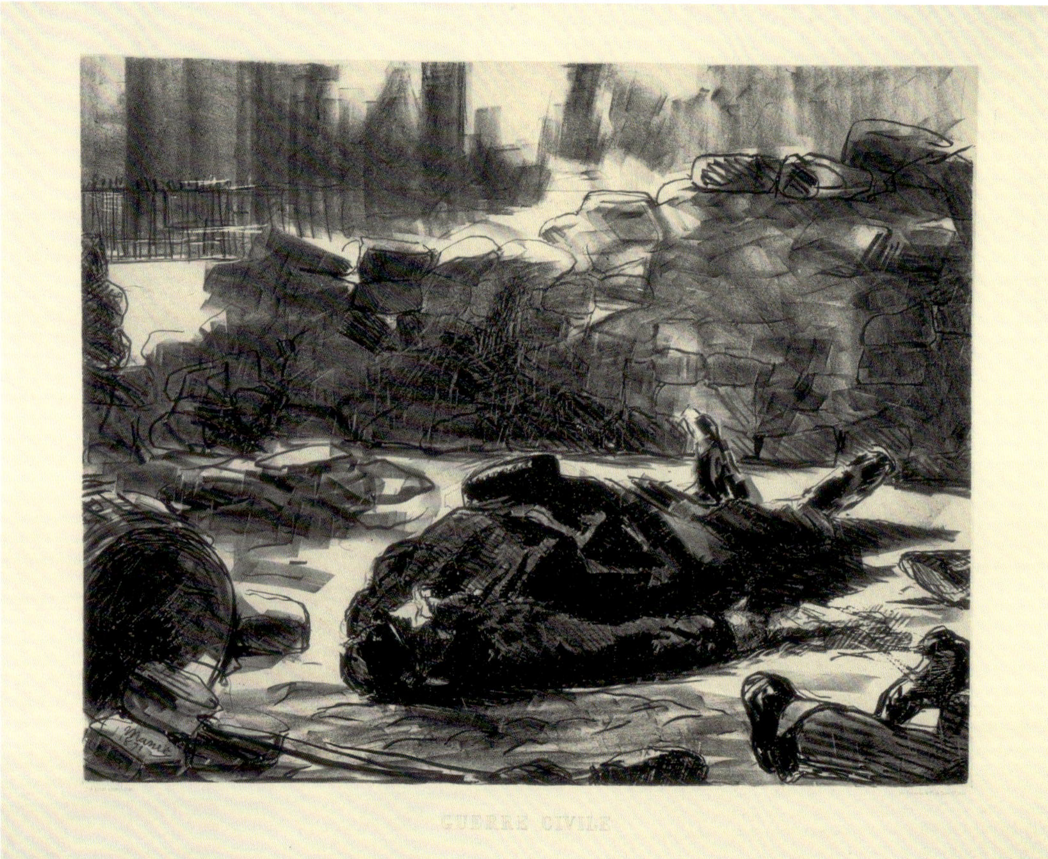

18 Edouard Manet, *Civil War,* 1871, lithograph, 39.4 × 50.7, National Gallery of Art, Washington, Rosenwald Collection

19 Charles Meryon, *The Clock Tower, Paris,* 1852, etching with engraving, 25.5 × 18.2, National Gallery of Art, Washington, Gift of R. Horace Gallatin

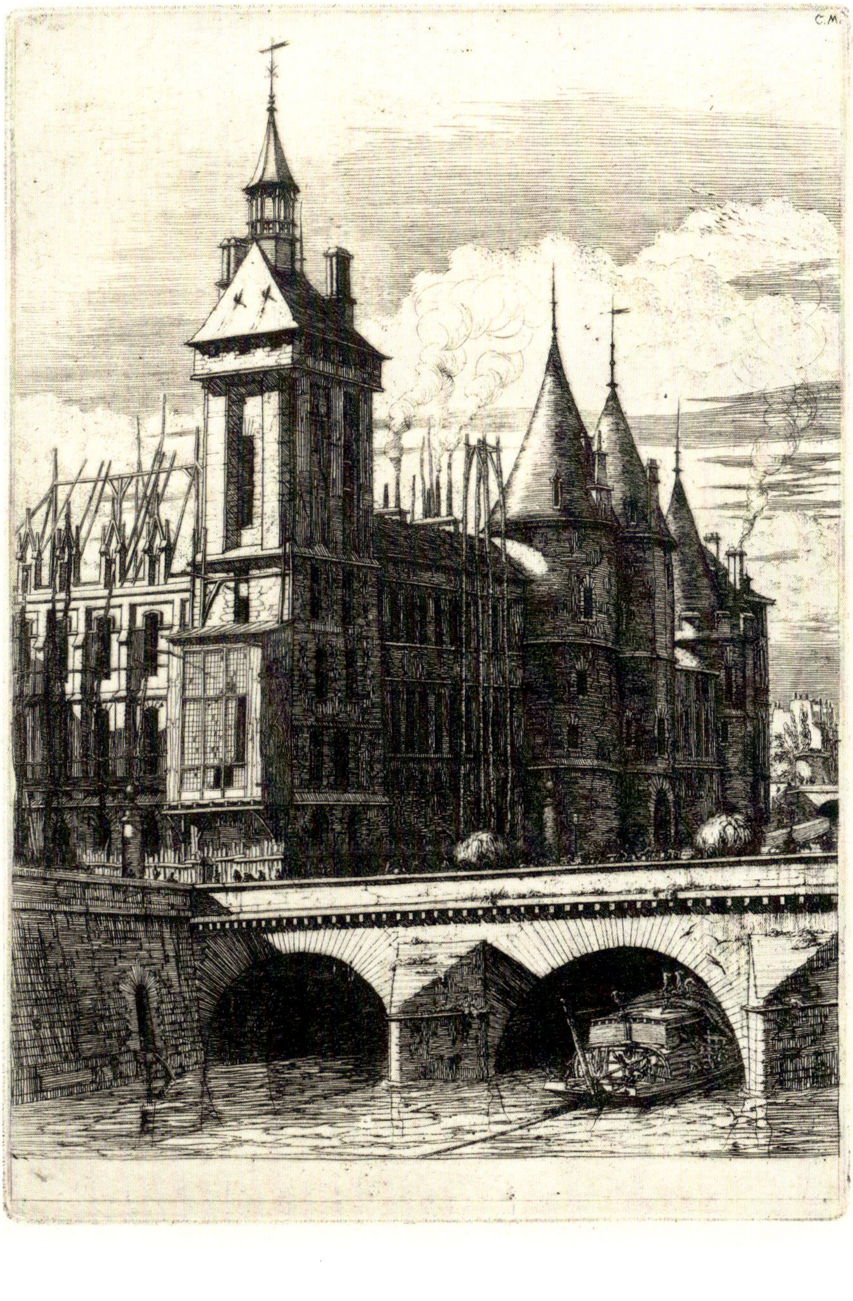
C.M.

a balcony after their midday meal (fig. 14). This blurring of boundaries also surfaces in Klinger's parodies of romanticized classicism, such as the wistful image of a centaur couple resting on a bluff and admiring the magnificent mountain valley (fig. 15).

Klinger put forward a concept of integrity to medium that portends high modernist theory and assigns all that we might consider flights of the bizarre and fantastic to species of the real. In his lengthy discourse on drawing published in 1891, Klinger insistently condemns fantasy, allegory, and the novelistic as diversions from the essential artistic task of addressing reality.[55] This position at first appears radically inconsistent with the bizarre and fanciful elements that pervade his work. It is a question not only for the art of the symbolists. Baudelaire likewise regarded fantasy and caprice as unsuitable forms of digression from the experience of modern life, but he was nonetheless a great proponent of Meryon, who depicted the Ministry of the Marine in Paris being assaulted by a flotilla of Hieronymus Bosch–like monsters (fig. 16). The truth of these phantasms lies in the integrity of the artist's vision—in the working of Meryon's imagination, both witty and paranoid, but free of capricious invention. In essence, Baudelaire's argument, like Klinger's, is rooted in the proposition that art must remain true to the mind of the artist, admitting no reference external to itself, and that content should arise naturally out of the artist's own formal language.[56]

Introspection, rapture, abjection, and a preoccupation with death became familiar themes in the neo-romantic repertoire of printmaking. In one of Edgar Degas' obscure black monotypes of a low-lit interior, a nude woman is curled up tightly on a couch reading a book, a vision of privacy that overturns the conventions of brothel imagery in a covert challenge to unwanted prurience (but see Clayson, fig. 10). Alongside the daily bustle of the streets and evenings at the café concert and the circus, a darker vision of the city surfaces in Chifflart's vision of the cholera epidemic of 1865 (fig. 17), Manet's blunt acknowledgment of the carnage resulting from the rise of the commune in 1871 (fig. 18), Buhot's vision of a city of spirits (see fig. 6), Meryon's renderings of scaffolded buildings that were admired by Baudelaire for their "paradoxical and arachnean beauty" (fig. 19).[57] And there are images of abjection in extremis such as Besnard's suicide balanced on the railing of a bridge, the psychologically drifting young men and women in Edvard Munch's prints, and the gentle pathos of Henri de Toulouse-Lautrec's confounded figure of a village madman (fig. 20). Subjectivity was everywhere being given a social context.

20 Henri de Toulouse-Lautrec, *The Madman*, 1895, lithograph, 24.3 × 14.5, National Gallery of Art, Washington, Rosenwald Collection

Much of this imagery is rooted in conflict and meant for something other than what passes under the rubric of entertainment. Although far from

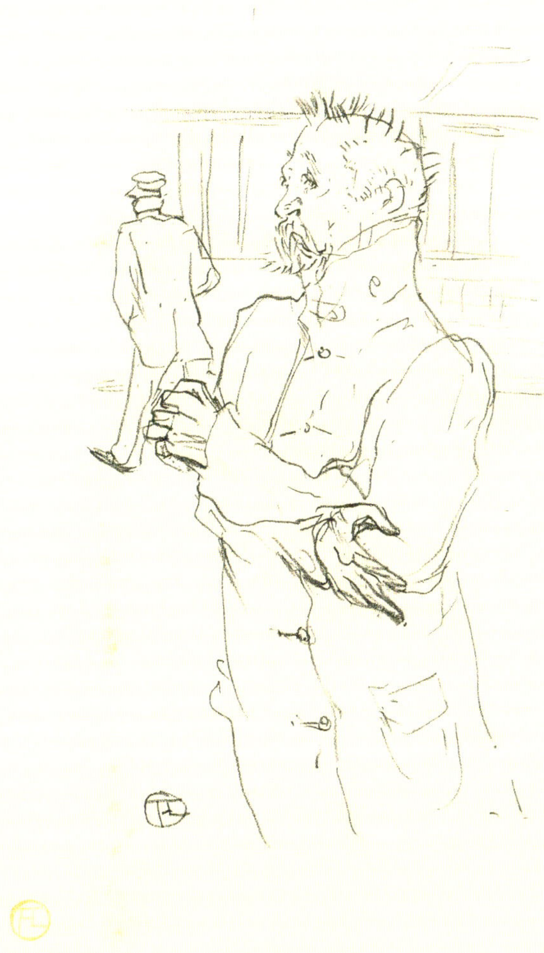

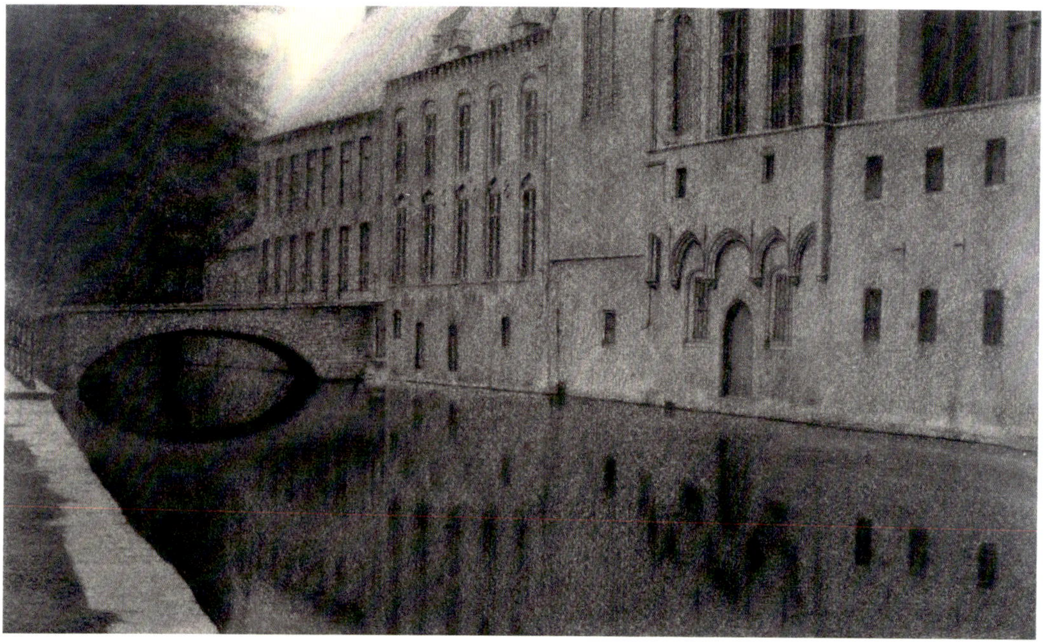

21 Fernand Khnopff, *Memory of Flanders: A Canal,* 1904, conté crayon over graphite, 25 × 41.5, Hearn Family Trust

a new range of subject matter for the visual arts, images like these with their deromanticized emotional texture, their social indictments, and their pathos are very much of their time. It was a language of black and white evolved to generate an ambivalent and compromised world of gray. The critical rhetoric that churned up around the promotion of the original print was initially engaged with its potential as an unfiltered mode of individual expression, a creative ideal inherited from the romantics and especially invested in intimate content. This was Baudelaire's ambition for the etching revival. By the 1880s the status of the original print was well established, and the writing in support of it was turning rapidly to a more conventional aesthetics of beauty: the enshrinement of the belle épreuve, the perfectly tailored product of a finely printed etching plate or lithographic stone. Claims for the print as a medium of subversion able to violate the expectations of public conformity had begun to fade. Nonetheless, the more adventuresome printmakers continued to follow the pathway that had opened to them.[58] The later stages of symbolism and then expressionism were the inheritors of this ferment. Among the deepest and most mesmerizing realizations of this aesthetic are drawings such as Fernand Khnopff's nostalgic visual meditations on the embalmed medieval city of Bruges (fig. 21).

Of course, print collecting did not comprise a culture entirely unto itself, nor should it be seen in opposition to the more retrospectively privileged artistic movements at this pivotal stage in the history of European avant-gardism. In much the same way, the metaphor of light and dark should not be overstressed, nor should the divide between public and private be seen as absolute. Nonetheless, the importance to modernism of the culture that evolved around the original print has been underestimated. The aura of privacy and the experience it was meant to evoke offered an arena for artistic experiment specific to the moment: avant-garde subjectivity had a disctinctively private world as well as a public one. It is arguable, however, whether this manner of bourgeois collecting survived the self-conscious triumph of modernism in the twentieth century. Eventually the limited edition suite of prints and the artist's book became well-staged events, and the collectors for whom they were intended bore a more formal and also less eccentric stamp. In this respect, the terms of aesthetic experience cultivated by these late nineteenth-century printmakers and enacted by their clientele composed the final chapter in a long history of private collecting as an endeavor of pure seclusion.

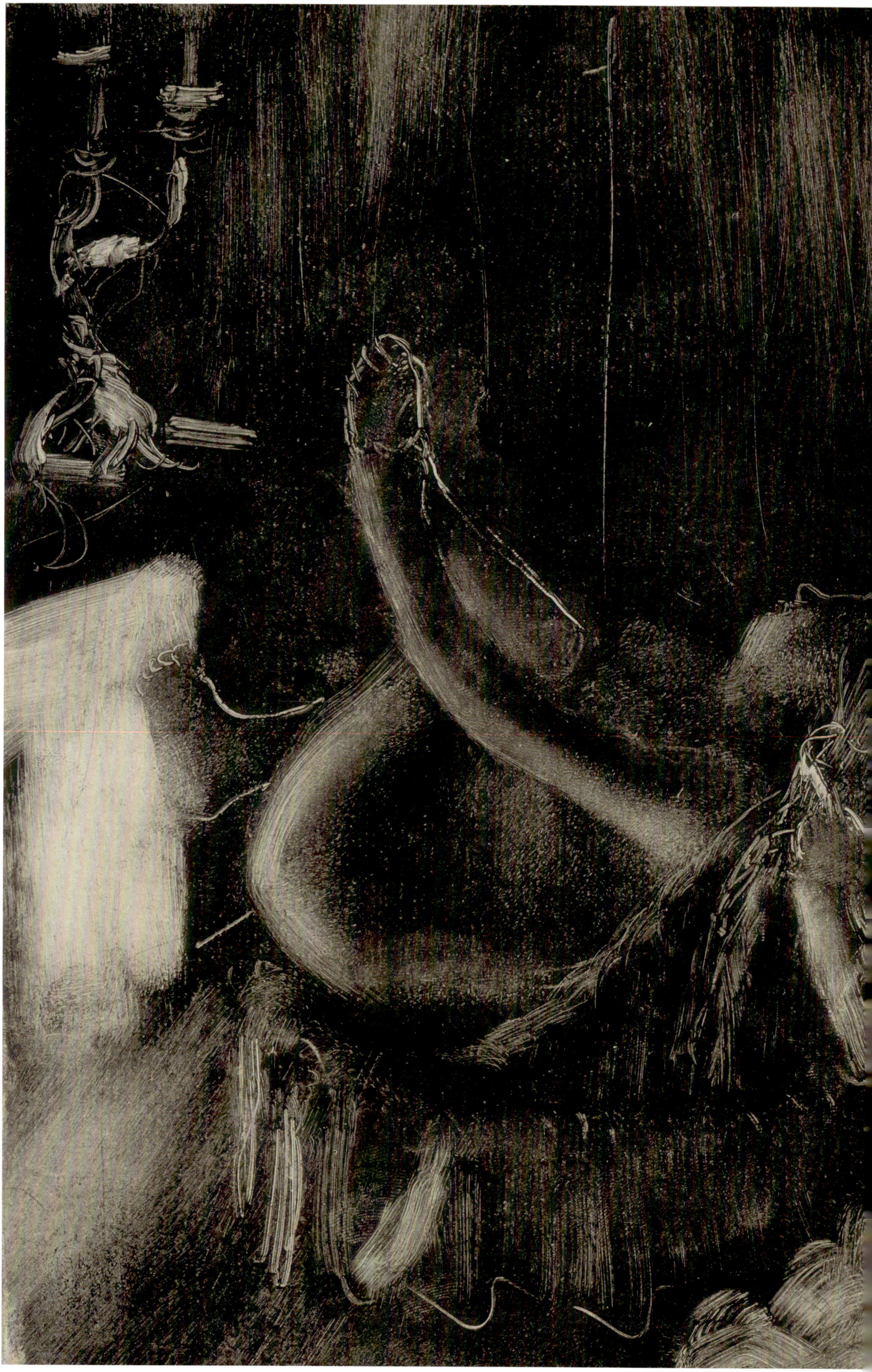

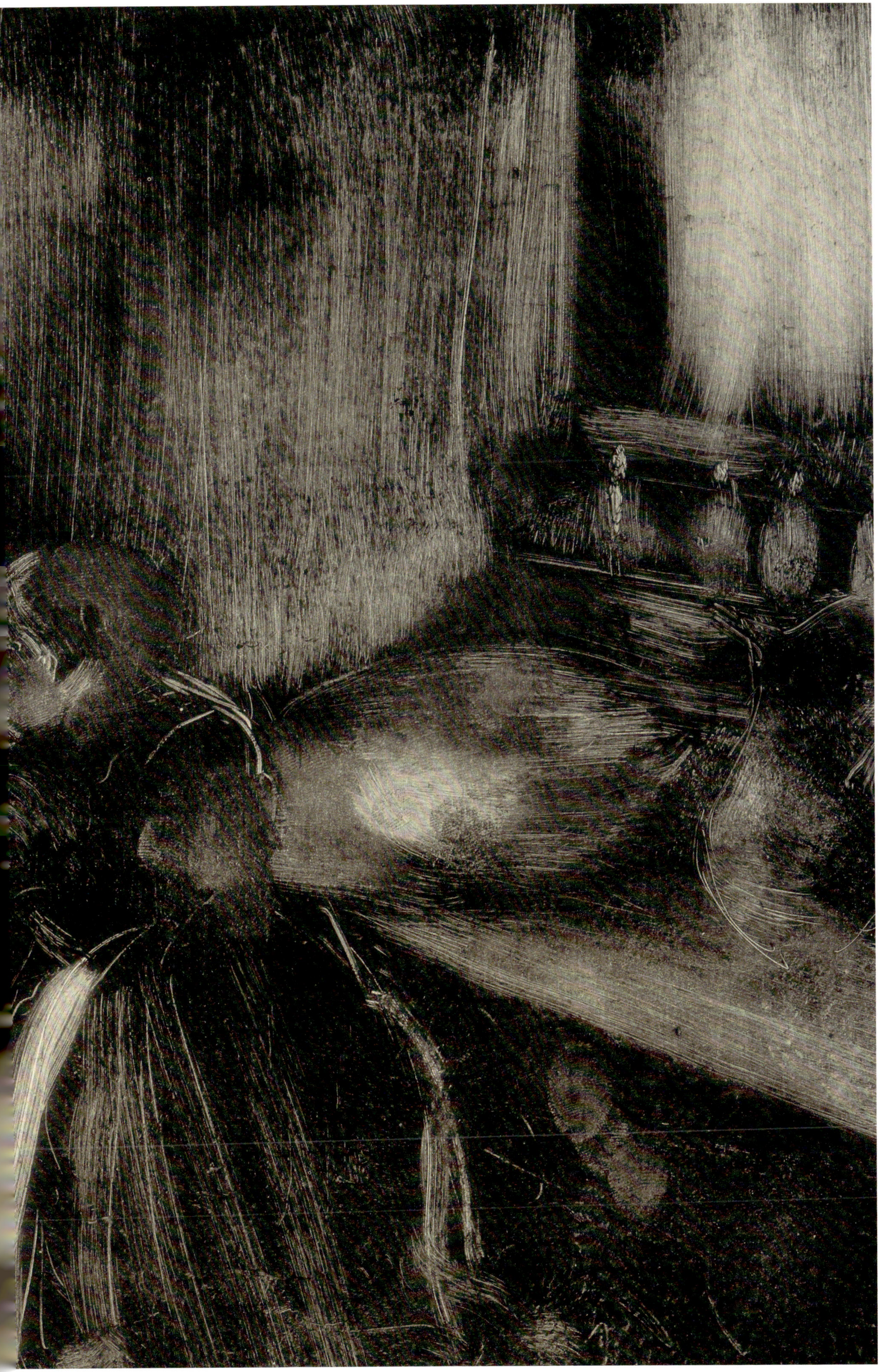

LOOKING WITHIN THE CELL OF PRIVACY

S. Hollis Clayson

THE NINETEENTH CENTURY IS THE CENTURY OF THE *INTERIEUR*. . . .
[IN THE PAST] ISOLATED CELLS OF PRIVACY WERE UNNECESSARY.
— *Christoph Asendorf*

The ambitious mid-nineteenth-century rebuilding of Paris, known as Haussmannization, transformed the city, but is usually construed as a radical refashioning of public, not private, space. Yet it evidently did shape private space insofar as the transformation of the capital coincided with the discovery by many French writers of the interior as domestic ideal. Though the average "home" in the French capital was an apartment, the English house became the model of a new and desirable mode of domesticity: private, comfortable, and homey.[1] A new era of concentration on the interior ensued. Indeed, the imagining and practice of private life became inseparable from fussing over the domestic interior, the paradoxical modern anchor of both personal well-being and discontent.[2]

The distinctive interior that emerged was both a space and an image.[3] It entailed the creation of enclosed, private spaces through changes in both architectural form (actual living spaces) and cultural values.[4] The architectural historian Sharon Marcus stresses the historical specificity of this "discovery" of the interior: "The equation of interior spaces with the political, social, and subjective characteristics of privacy does not inhere in the spaces themselves, but constitutes a possible interpretation of them."[5] In other words, the saturation of this particular space with the values of domesticity was not inevitable, let alone natural. Walter Benjamin, the influential German literary critic, agreed.

He made a powerful case for the historicity of the nineteenth-century interior and its link with privacy. With the emergence of the interior, he stated, "The private individual makes his entry into history."[6] Further, as Marcus observes, "'interior' no longer marked a space whose physical difference from the exterior was neutral, obvious and thus trivial; it became identified with *le foyer,* the family home and hearth."[7]

Inventive artists working in the print media (most of them *peintre-graveurs,* painters as well as printmakers) explored and bolstered the pre-occupation with intensified subjectivity that accompanied the period's signature exaltation of private life and space. Works of art certainly helped to instate the mania for interiors and interiority by figuring domestic space as the context par excellence of the newly passionate desires for privacy and home-based comfort. The investment in the interior is a thematic hallmark of nineteenth-century art, a conspicuous presence in both painting and the graphic arts.[8] The monochromatic palette of prints—and thus their superiority to painting in delineating tonal and spiritual darkness—suited them for investigating the quirkier, often darker, sides of private life.[9]

The center of emotional intimacy for well-heeled and upwardly mobile urbanites, the modern interior, whose use was usually determined by men, was nonetheless repeatedly merged with women *tout court.*[10] This conflation arose from a perceived link between bourgeois women, consumption, and the bibelot-filled private space, an interior thereby enhanced to emulate organic nature outdoors, to which "they" were thought to be especially close.[11] Manichaean thinking about gender and private space—that the interior concealed and belonged to the dreamy woman while the empowered man felt at home in the street—gave rise to many figurations of women alone indoors. That women were construed as the equivalent of hot-house plants, perfectly attuned to the comforts of the well-upholstered, even hermetic, private world, is evident in period prints. So is the dystopic underside of the same association: imagining the modern *bourgeoise* confined to a haunted house. The intensity and contentiousness of beliefs in circulation about the modern interior led artists to imagine it as a site of serenity and balance, or a place of excess, disequilibrium, puzzlement, and fracture. Print media were especially suited to probing the darker side of solitude and privacy. Printmakers frequently used (in some cases, elaborated and redefined) long-standing tropes: woman asleep, at her toilette, reading, and in reverie. The most interesting images envision a female protagonist at home as a full-blown subject—self-absorbed, unobserved, and markedly pensive and cerebral.

But the dichotomy of man as producer (headquartered out in the world) versus woman as consumer (affiliated explicitly with domestic space) is problematic.[12] Certain later nineteenth-century prints maintain discursively that maleness—encompassing masculine well-being and equipoise as well as gloom and excess—was a part of the modern interior. Indeed, many later nineteenth-century tracts that address the new interior as a woman's natural habitat explicitly argued for the convergence of interiorization and masculinity by urging men to join domestic space—getting more involved in the life of the family and the ornamentation of household spaces.[13]

WOMEN ALONE

Asleep James McNeill Whistler's *Weary* (fig. 1), an 1863 drypoint, is an exemplary image of modern repose embodied by a solitary young woman nodding off in an interior. Made while the expatriate American artist was an influential young Paris naturalist, the linearly bold print of an attractive, long-haired woman collapsed in an expansive chair or couch appears at first glance to capture an authentic yielding to fatigue—in both body and spirit.[14] Close inspection, however, reveals a contradiction. Indeed, the linear and spatial differences between the upper and lower parts of her body create a telltale fracture that speaks to the diffculty of imagining a woman fully self-absorbed and alone in her cell of privacy.

The linear venturesomeness of the roughly contoured convexities of the skirt and the weary woman's swirling hair, as well as the crisscrosses comprising the wall surface, are noteworthy for their looseness and lack of inhibition. That the lightly conjured but ample skirt models a pair of casually sprawling legs is certainly striking. As indices of relaxation, they bear comparison with the unself-consciously flopped-out lower extremities of Mary Cassatt's petulant girl sprawled in a blue chair, *Little Girl in a Blue Armchair,* 1878 (National Gallery of Art).

Whistler's *Weary* is a striking drypoint. Its zone of maximum interest and complexity (if not utmost graphic force) is undoubtedly the woman's head—both its drained yet alert expression and vexing profile positioning. The pale head is set off against the dark, tightly described garment that clads her torso and arms, and her head's rigidity interrupts the upper body's nesting into the concavity of the scoop back of the broad chair. The backward and sideways tilt of her head carries the fatigue invoked by the title and denoted by the abandon of her legs, and her wide-eyed gaze off to the side endows her with a perceptible measure of self-absorption. But rather than creating a look of reverie in isolation, her studiously arranged pretty face has been engineered to please a male onlooker through its explicitly rigged display. The presentation of an attractive woman's visage would

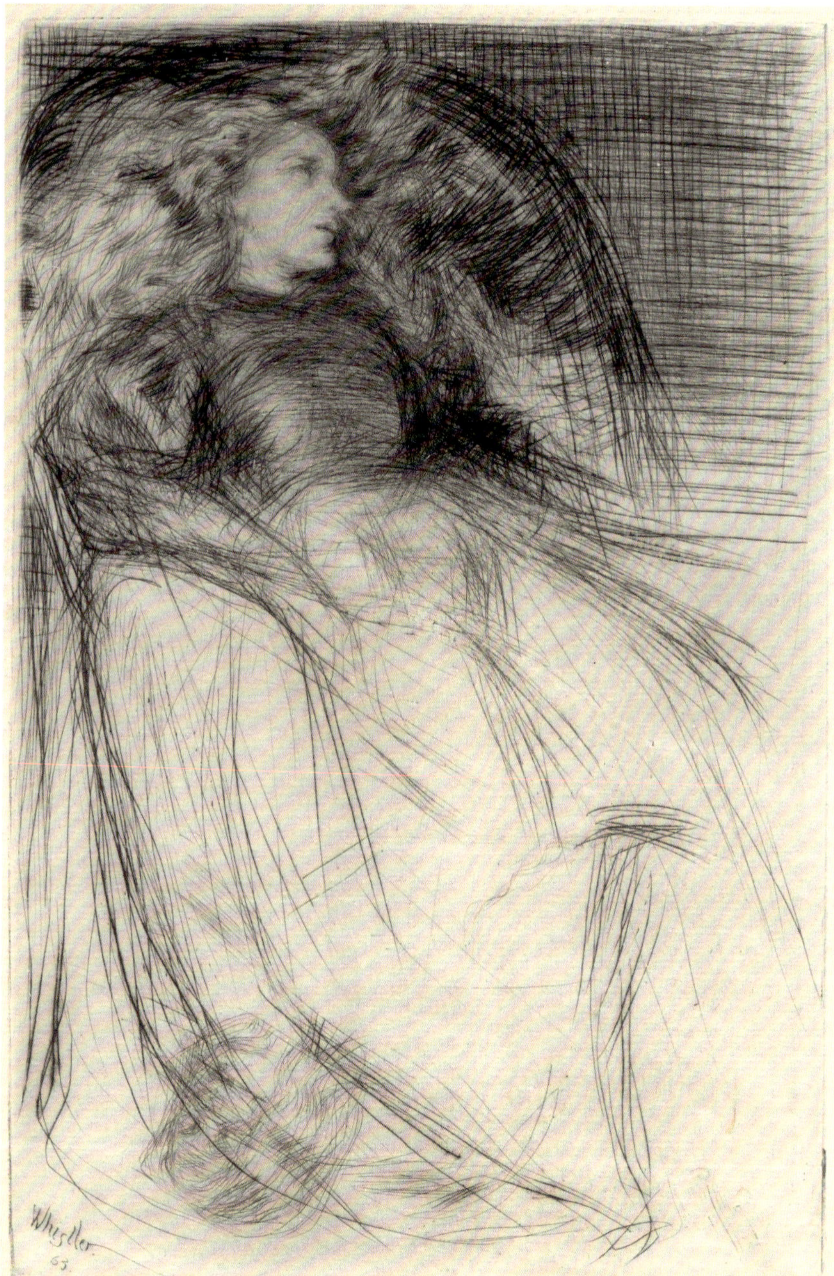
Whistler
63.

appear to clash with the undistracted self-regard connoted by her slumped deportment, a carriage that suggests a body yielding to exhaustion.

The drypoint is a generally convincing portrayal of a woman enjoying genuine solitude, but the head's rigidity, pretty features, and profile placement defer to the interests of a beholder. She is undeniably prettified in her collapse, if less explicitly so than the considerably more dainty reclining sleepy woman of Whistler's later color lithograph, *Draped Figure Reclining* (fig. 2). But in *Weary,* beautification coincides paradoxically with rigidity. The tautness and uprightness of the head insinuate the unsettling possibility that its tensions go beyond figuring an unsettled or hyperconcentrated state of mind to suggest gingerly that the pose is involuntary, that she was obliged by another to assume and maintain the position. The head's stiffness and the discomfiting implication of force bring to mind a famous example of a parallel if much more extreme situation: the violently incommoded woman in the right foreground of Eugène Delacroix's *Death of Sardanapalus,* 1827 (Musée du Louvre, Paris). Or to reference an image closer in time and milieu, the tension at the expressive center of Whistler's print adumbrates the fin-de-siècle eccentricity of the theatricalized, uncomfortable pose "assumed" by the model in the Austrian artist Maximilian Kurzweil's color woodcut *The Pillow,* 1903 (fig. 3), an image whose contorted pose and concealed face deform and decisively undermine the trope of the woman dozing cozily at home. Whistler's *Weary,* too, is defined by disparity: she is withdrawn into the orbit of private exhaustion yet still in some measure on offer to a viewer—psychically via her face and bodily via the legs and skirt.[15] But whereas Whistler's drypoint operates within the domain of naturalism, Kurzweil employs narrative quirks borrowed from a willfully idiosyncratic Nabi and symbolist repertoire.

1 James McNeill Whistler, *Weary,* 1863, drypoint (state iia/iii), 19.7 × 13.2, National Gallery of Art, Washington, Rosenwald Collection 1943.3.8458

La Toilette Albert Besnard's arresting *Woman with a Vase,* 1894 (fig. 4), puts an eerie slant on the customary toilette scenario. The governing conceit of this genre is its provision to a privileged spectator of an unobstructed peek at an exposed body caught up in self-adornment in an extremely private space. At its most extreme, the woman is presented as vain even as she is displayed for the gratification of a judgmental spectator. The down-to-earth qualities of toilette scenes accelerated during the second half of the nineteenth century thanks to the bracing frankness of naturalist bathing scenes by Edgar Degas, for example.

Besnard's etching, a classic of the weird interior idiom of the 1890s, is certainly a toilette picture that seeks to record an observed moment, but it nonetheless operates in thrall to the subjective intensities of the new interior.

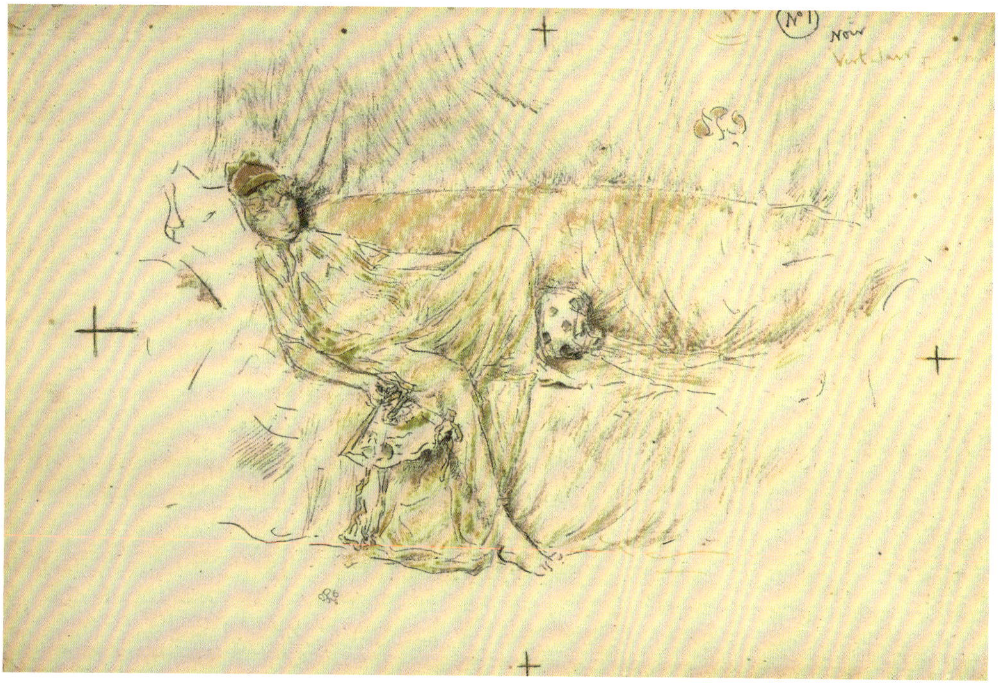

2 James McNeill Whistler, *Draped Figure Reclining,* 1892, color lithograph (state i / ii), 21.8 × 28.5, National Gallery of Art, Washington, Rosenwald Collection 1943.3.8800

3 Maximilian Kurzweil, *The Pillow (Martha Kurzweil Sitting on a Divan),* 1903, color woodcut, 28.7 × 25.9, National Gallery of Art, Washington, Ailsa Mellon Bruce Fund 1972.66.30

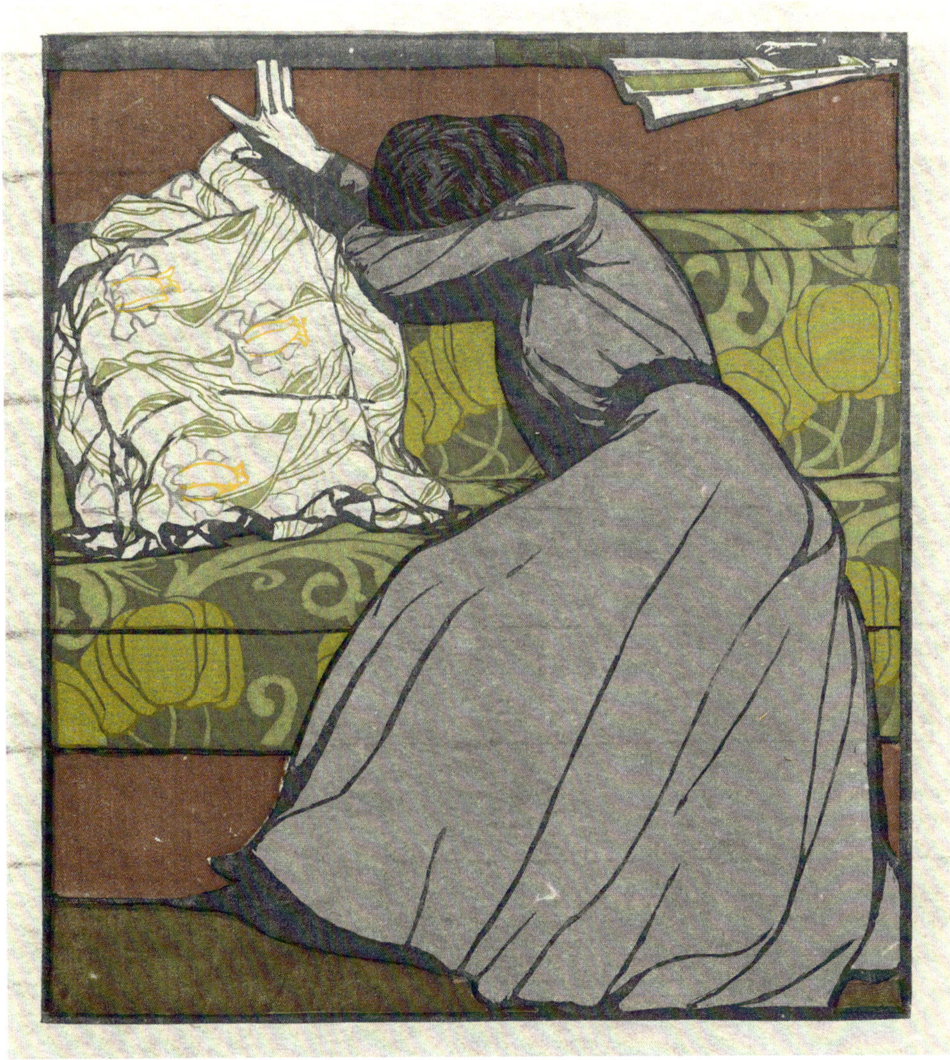

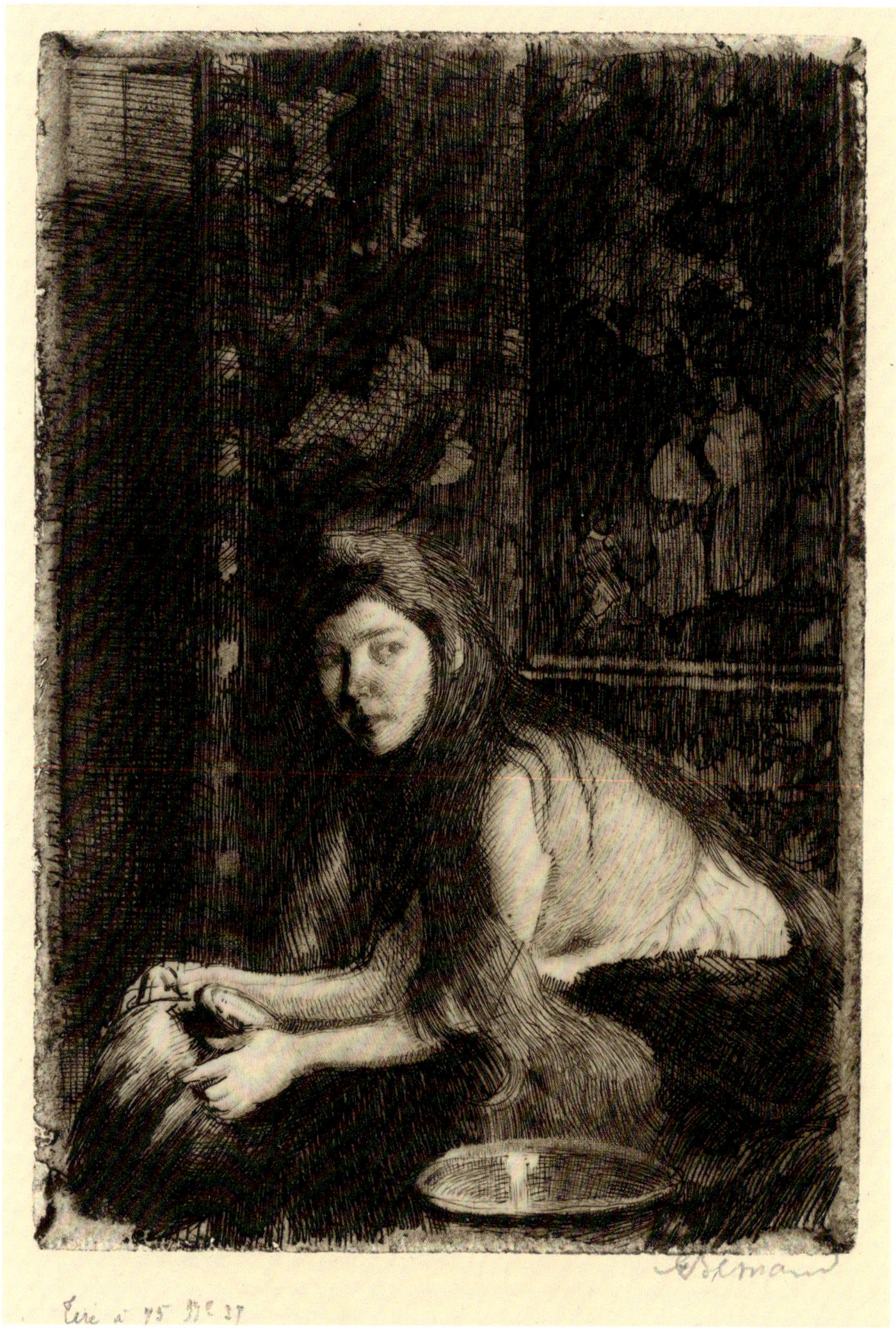

Because the young woman with the flowing long hair is only half-clad, we read her (otherwise puzzling) clutch of the handles of a bulbous earthenware vase in a difficult-to-define space as preparation for grooming.[16] Getting to that conclusion requires some concentrated if not convoluted interpretative work, arriving via educated guess at the assumption that she will transfer water from the vase to the basin at her left side for washing. Her elusive, even troubled facial expression works against an easy sorting out of the picture's temporalities, further upsetting the protocols of *la toilette*. Because she looks out of the picture to one side, she is neither completely absorbed by her preparations, nor, as her oblique glance denotes, is she vainly preening before a spectator. She is surely not hailing the attention of a servant, but her expression unmistakably indicates that she is seeking guidance or permission. This intimation of alertness to someone nearby in such a moody space proposes, albeit gingerly, that the other may be powerful, frightening, or simply unsettling by virtue of being unexpected. The woman's inchoate awareness of an invasion of her privacy enhances the moodiness and idiosyncrasy of Besnard's decidedly murky, even claustrophobic, interior.

As it turns out, the vigilant ceramic-vessel–clutching model was posing for two artists at once. Anders Zorn, a cosmopolitan Swede who worked in Paris from 1887 to 1896, was at Besnard's side in the studio, as shown by his etched description of the scene, *Albert Besnard and His Model,* 1896 (fig. 5).[17] Zorn's etching is an extraordinary document, laying bare and testifying to the conditions of studio art production. The artist-model power relationship at its core is the circumstance of both prints, but Zorn's record of the studio event strips it of mystery. His print injects light and air into Besnard's gloomy space and, with supreme ease and clarity, provides an obvious focal point for the model's eyes: Besnard himself. The furtiveness is also gone from her facial expression, and her haunting face has been softened by being plumped up. Has she dropped her script and stopped acting? The emotional quirkiness and shadowy atmospherics created by the French artist—the sly and unsure focus of the model's gaze, the dark closeness of the narrow space hemmed in by the dark figured panels of an Indian textile—are completely, even flippantly, dispersed by Zorn's "documentary" portrait of Besnard at work. Zorn's etched portrait demolishes Besnard's meticulously contrived illusion of a haunted domestic interior. The efficiency with which Zorn's image undermines the fragile illusion of mystery constructed by his friend underscores the singular eeriness, idiosyncratic character, and notable inventiveness of Besnard's etched illusion.

4 Albert Besnard, *Woman with a Vase,* 1894, etching and aquatint, 19.8 × 13.9, National Gallery of Art, Washington, Gift of Mr. and Mrs. Daniel Bell, in Honor of the 50th Anniversary of the National Gallery of Art

Graphic work by Mary Cassatt, likewise devised in the shadow of interior mania, also heightened the complexity and interest of the toilette genre.

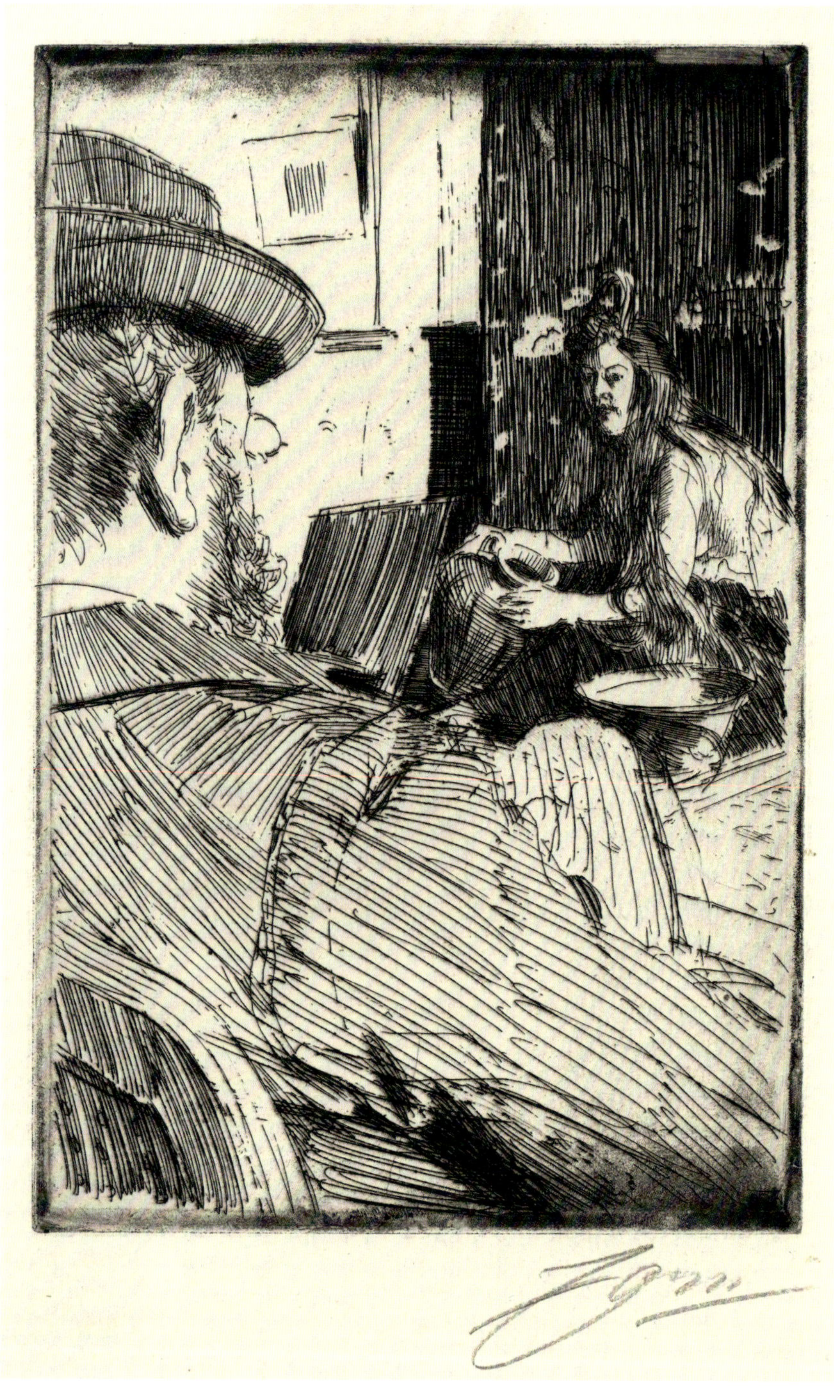

Her extremely *japoniste* print *The Coiffure,* c. 1891 (fig. 6), was exhibited at the Galerie Durand-Ruel in Paris in April 1891, after she had been excluded from the third exhibition of the Société des Peintres-Graveurs Français (Society of French Painter-Printmakers) because she was not French. (The organization previously had been named, much more broadly, the Society of Painter-Printmakers.) Cassatt's image belongs to the series of ten highly inventive color prints (drypoint and aquatint) that she produced in the annus mirabilis of her work as a peintre-graveur. *The Coiffure* is well known, if not exhaustively analyzed as an image.[18] More interesting than the color print is a drawing of the toilette, also entitled *The Coiffure,* c. 1891 (fig. 7), and considered to be a study for the more famous print.[19] The drawing is fascinating, not least because of the paucity of female nudes in Cassatt's oeuvre. The adult male nude was out of the question for her, and she had attempted the adult female body in a merely inchoate and evasive fashion in several earlier prints.[20]

In the color print, the breasts are described in the most generalized —one is tempted to say squeamish—way. They are effectively conjoined into an abstracted mono-bosom. In the brown-toned drawing, by contrast, a convincing effort has been made to describe the curves and volumes of breasts, one of which is doubled by its mirror reflection. The image marks an altogether less recalcitrant grappling with the anatomical hallmarks of a woman's body. But the most interesting element of the drawing is the character of the model's face reflected in the mirror. It is a void, a cipher, a blank overlapped and almost crowded out of view by the primping woman's sharp left elbow. Imagining a face for the coiffing woman was evidently a tall order and, in the end, one that could not be filled. The voluptuous drawing had no successor in any medium.

5 Anders Zorn, *Albert Besnard and His Model,* 1896, etching, 23.6 × 15.9, National Gallery of Art, Washington, Rosenwald Collection 1943.3.8845

After all, the conventions of the toilette picture provided no template for a facial expression that could convey womanly self-absorption and the denial of an onlooker when naked and exposed. Albert Besnard also tackled this challenge in his moody *Woman with a Vase* of 1894. In the case of Cassatt's fascinating drawing, it is reasonable to assume that the blank spot registers the difficulty that the artist experienced imagining an unconventional face for such a shapely primping woman. Devising the face may even have struck her as impertinent or intrusive—a potential invasion, as it were, of the privacy of her invented women. In her refusal or inability to provide an appropriate face (the face in the subsequent color print bears a wholly schematic and oblique set of features), Cassatt—sharing many but not all points in common with her cross-town contemporary Besnard—recognized that the codes of privacy that ruled the newly secluded interior posed substantial challenges to innovative peintres-graveurs mining the themes of the private everyday. Such artists

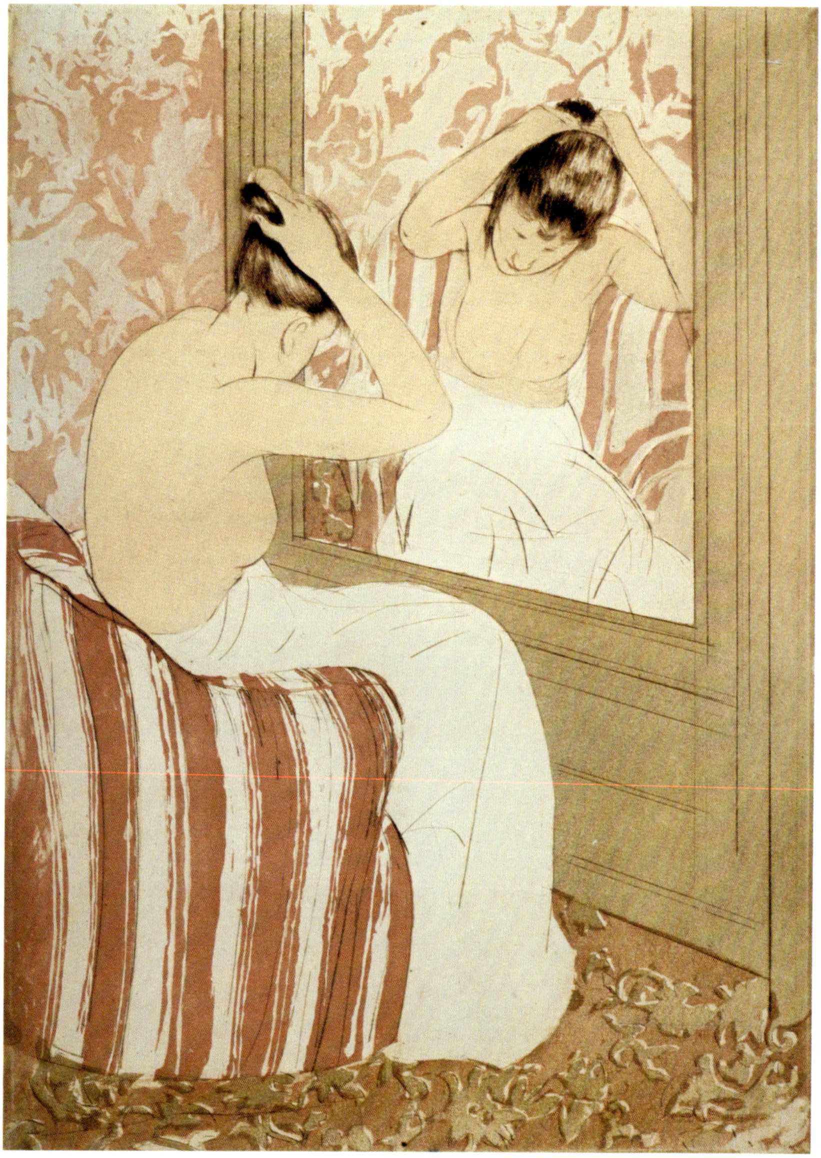

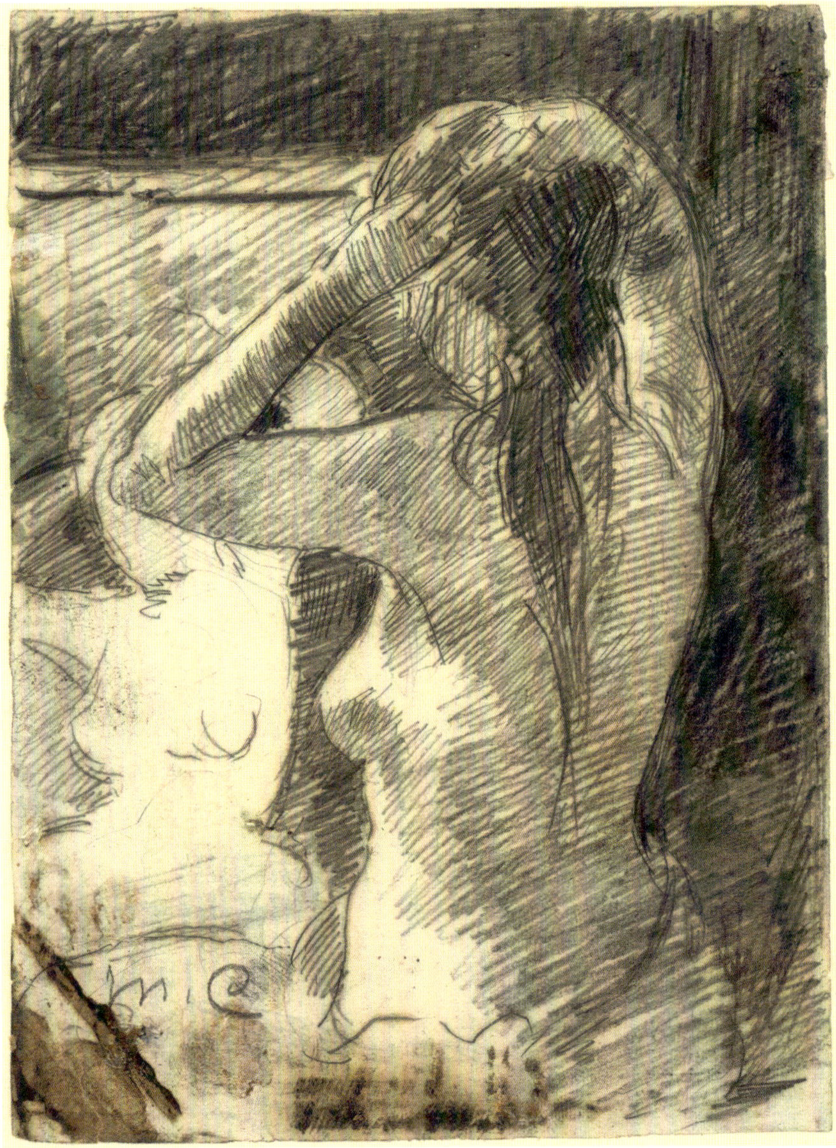

6 Mary Cassatt, *The Coiffure,* c. 1891, drypoint and aquatint (state v/v), 36.5 × 26.7, National Gallery of Art, Washington, Chester Dale Collection 1963.10.257

7 Mary Cassatt, *The Coiffure,* c. 1891, graphite and watercolor, 14.8 × 11.2, National Gallery of Art, Washington, Rosenwald Collection 1954.12.6

sought to align their weariness over the protocols governing eroticization with a fascination with the recesses and rights of the new privacy. Indeed, artists who became enmeshed in the codes and spaces of Parisian interiority in the late 1800s were forced to rethink the representation of solitude and the cohabitation of interior space by those shown within and beyond the frame. This was one of the most consequential effects of the new interest in privacy in the visual arts.

Reading A defining feature of the new regimes of indoor privacy was the privatization of reading. Unlike the old era of recitations, reading became almost insular, an act undertaken in isolation from one's literate comrades.[21] Representations of women reading alone outdoors in public by such artists as Edouard Manet and James McNeill Whistler were constitutive of the new art of modern urban life, but the resonances among the new interior, the modern woman, and nineteenth-century reading practices were frequently exploited in the indoor genre images that proliferated in the 1880s.

Two etchings by Besnard, *The Reader by the Window* and *News,* associate the female reader at home with behavioral restraint (or bodily dignity) and ensconce her in an atmosphere of quietude and equipoise. In *The Reader by the Window,* 1888 (fig. 8), the sitter's clothing and ladylike posture correlate the solitary and absorptive pursuit of reading (a cultivated form of indolence as self-improvement) with social privilege: Besnard's well-bred subject wears an elegant fur-trimmed dress of a sort worn exclusively at home. Sidled up to the window to profit from the muted daylight streaming through the sheer draperies on the French doors, she is certainly engaged by her book, but she is also arranged to model an exquisite feminine demureness at the same time, as though her internalization of codes of deportment can never be let go, even when alone. It is tempting to call her restrained engagement with her book an instance of "absorption light"—analogous to a low-calorie confection selected in place of the rich and heavy original. The etching appeared in one of the albums published by *L'estampe originale,* and the print's circulation in that publication shored up a definition of the modern bourgeois interior as a peaceable female realm, free from anxiety.[22]

In the case of *News,* 1889, Bernard profits from an evening mise-en-scène to exploit the domestic poetry of the high tonal contrasts of backlit conditions. According to André-Charles Coppier, Madame Besnard modeled for the plate.[23] The light streaming in though the window, supplemented by the table lamp, illuminates her newspaper while casting her face and upper body into a dark silhouette that flatters her pretty features. The complicated patterning of surrounding textiles and crenellated wood furniture, presumably part of the

Besnard household, creates the enfolding embrace of a strongly decorative, homey atmosphere. The etching thus brings into being a soothing world of domestic comfort, centered on an elegant *femme du foyer* reading by lamplight, a marker of well-being as such. When it appeared in the January 1887 issue of the *Revue Indépendante de Littérature et d'Art,* the print did not bear Madame Besnard's name and was therefore not made and published in order to display the qualities of the artist's own home.[24] With its exceptionally sensitive record of subtle lighting conditions, the print instead promoted a particular feminine role in a categorical sense.

In sharp contrast to Besnard's etchings of reading women, Cassatt's *Interior: On the Sofa,* c. 1883 (fig. 9), is a riveting examination of the complexities of solitude and the dreaminess fostered by reading.[25] (This is "high-calorie absorption.") Lacking any sentimentality or sweetness, the black-clad woman in Cassatt's intriguingly asymmetrical composition, dominated by a patterned couch, leans back into the cushioned surface. Her hands, placed atop her temporarily ignored reading material, are folded in a merely instrumental way, as opposed to signifying a particular type of femininity. She looks up and off to her right but barely shifts position. The simplicity of her facial features and posture conveys the solemnity and inwardness of text-inspired woolgathering. The contemplative woman is endowed with a gravitas that enables her to hold her own—both psychically and volumetrically—even above the decorative and aesthetic excitement of the patterned fabric. Cassatt's reader simply does not melt into the adjacent floral motifs the way Madame Besnard is engulfed by a moody, patterned, and tonally gradated atmosphere.

The position of Cassatt's figure at the far edge of the couch does nothing to diminish her solemnity and contemplative force.[26] In fact, her compositional marginality actually strengthens her presence. The dark tone of her form visually bolsters her psychic credibility. The experience summoned up by Cassatt's minimal denotation of human expression is persuasive not only because it is subtle but also because it is both familiar and encouraging. Female cerebration in the well-upholstered interior remains an ideal for the private quotidian in modernity—especially for female readers and art viewers.

Edgar Degas' monotype *Woman Reading,* c. 1885 (fig. 10), could hardly differ more starkly from Cassatt's and Besnard's etchings. Dedicated to his friend and fellow artist Vicomte Ludovic Lepic, with whom he made his first monotype, Degas' entrancing dark print is an exceptionally bold representation of faceless and hideous female bodily absorption in reading set in an interior.[27] Degas' uninhibited naked monster is an arresting foil to Besnard's restrained readers. The twisting of the woman's torso, the wild extension of her left leg and awkward foot, and the deformation of her high-crested,

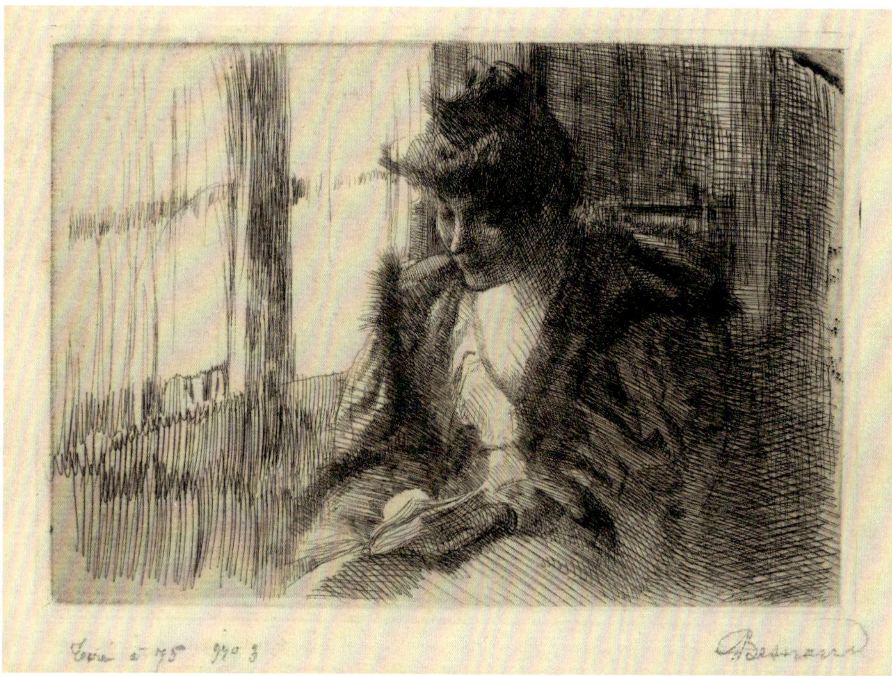

8 Albert Besnard, The *Reader by the Window,* etching, 1888, 19.8 × 13.8, Museum of Fine Arts, Boston, Bequest of Janet H. Stevens 1978.346

9 Mary Cassatt, *Interior: On the Sofa,* c. 1883, soft-ground etching, 14 × 21.4, National Gallery of Art, Washington, Rosenwald Collection 1949.5.469

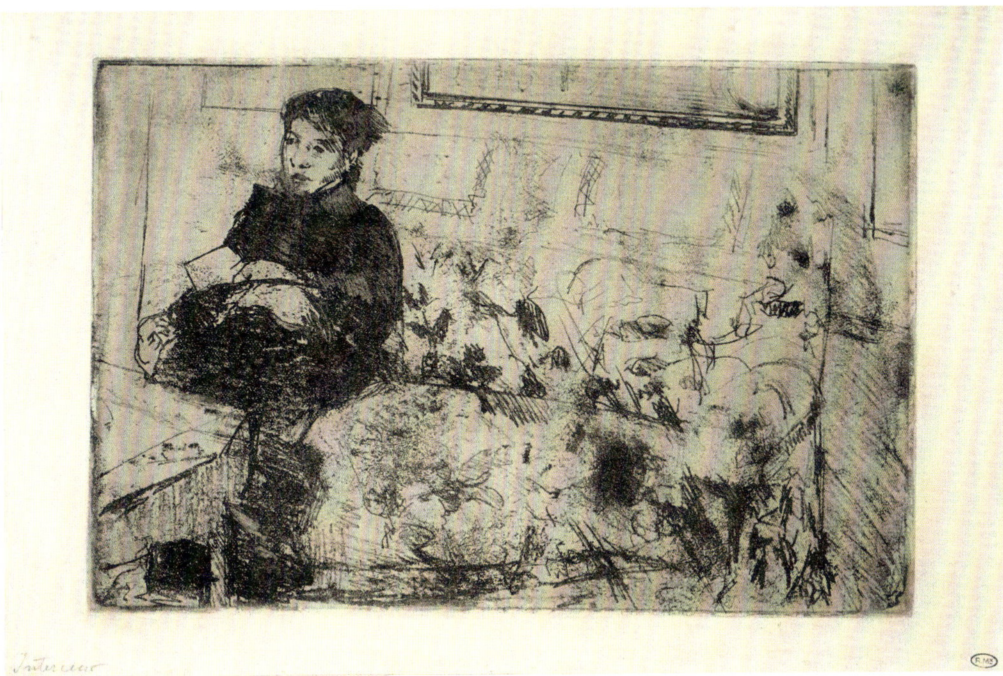
Intérieur

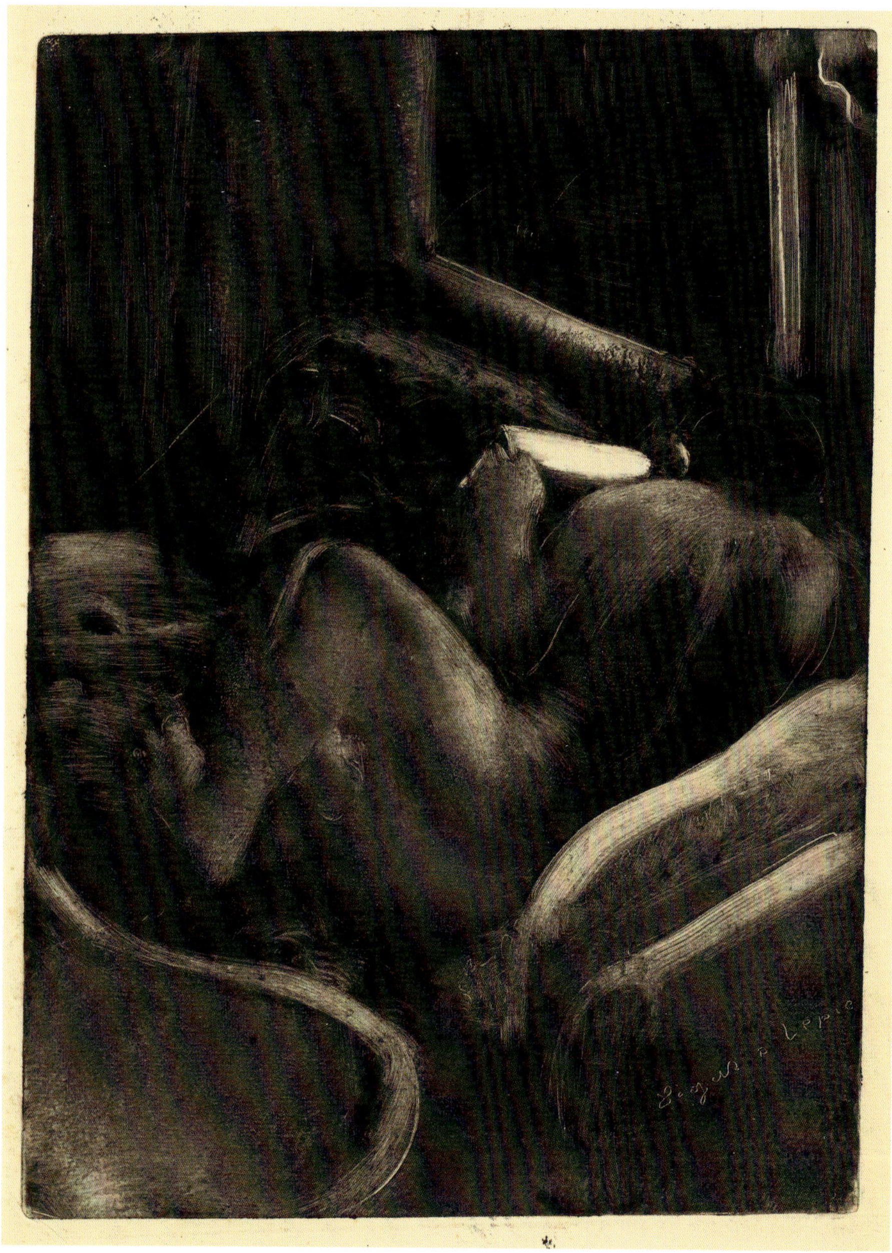

incipiently hunched upper back define a confrontation of reader and book of exceptional somatic intensity. Degas' inky bookworm does not hold back; the contours and twists of her seated, faceless body seen from above and behind index a particularly vigorous engagement with the text in her hands. Reading is staged as a somatic rather than a cerebral event by Degas' dynamically conceived *liseuse,* by contrast with, for example, the kind of intense thought communicated by Cassatt's deep-thinking and motionless reader. Degas' reader might also be described as throwing off the restraints of etiquette that govern the appearance of Besnard's ladylike subjects.

Do the aesthetic and ideological unorthodoxies of this monotype deserve applause? Is this streaky and dark-toned print of a distorted woman who appears somewhat more animal than human—hunched over a book in an armchair near the hearth with caricatured limbs akimbo and torso askew—a kind of aesthetic and philosophical triumph over cliché and meretricious *politesse?* Is it a plus that, unlike the etchings described earlier, this print alone insists that reading is a preponderantly physical engagement rather than an intellectual event? The degree to which the reader's body registers a ferociously dynamic engagement with the book in her solitude is impressive. It claims the interior as a space of incomparable freedom, both physical and psychic. The image would thus seem to deserve our approbation for having invented a language that speaks the utter *je m'en foutisme* of a woman lost in what she is doing. It is that unusual female body in visual representation of the era that is imagined to ignore and disdain any thing or any body beyond (or other than) its replete self.[28] (Of course, the woman's facelessness and her disinterest in the nearby tub buttress her keenly single-minded fascination with the book and supreme disregard for others. Seen in this light, the work of art is also a twofold repudiation of the scenario of a toilette picture: the bathing equipment is idle and no grooming is performed, or, rather, the tub is ignored and the mirror bears no reflection.)

10 Edgar Degas, *Woman Reading,* c. 1885, monotype, 38 × 27.7, National Gallery of Art, Washington, Rosenwald Collection

Another approach to the print might realize less enthusiasm, insofar as Degas' monotype also suggests that a woman becomes physically monstrous or at least misshapen when she becomes intellectually absorbed. It proposes that a woman left alone with a book loses her behavioral compass, coarsening her femininity and social distinction by her surrender to the life of the mind. Domesticity and propriety could go awry within the cell of privacy, and women were evidently particularly vulnerable to the erotics of solitude in the interior, as in the eighteenth-century conventional depiction of sensual abandon fostered by reading.[29] In Degas' imagination, by contrast, an intensely self-directed mode of passionate reading unfurls in the private opacities of the modern interior.

Reverie Besnard made two quirkily innovative etchings on the theme of female reverie, and they are two of his best: *The Cup of Tea* and *In the Embers*. *The Cup of Tea,* 1883 (fig. 11), a striking figuration of stringently correct social bearing and ramrod posture, is exceptional in two ways. The fashioning of the young sitter's manner and the placement of a hat on her head would seem to reflect the obligations imposed on a young Victorian woman by an encounter in the public sphere, and the print was done in London (not on the Continent); witness the signature at upper center right. The resolute primness of the subject's facial expression is created in part by the bright light that limns and highlights the contours of her profile. It endows the impeccably proper (even excessively correct) young woman with an almost metallic edge. The tonal scheme of the sheet overall, which places a crystal-clear figure in nebulous surroundings, is unusual for Besnard. Note that the contrast between the young woman and her imprecise surroundings was of such interest to the artist that he altered the inking of the plate to yield six distinct versions.[30] The version reproduced here is particularly highly tailored by Besnard, who used heavy, monotype inking on the plate and then wiped it as one does a monotype. This helps explain the print's uncommonly painterly qualities.

But is this avatar of supreme social correctness and refined deportment, elevating her delicate porcelain cup in one hand and saucer in the other, to be imagined sitting in a teashop? Insofar as the space she occupies is fuzzy and indistinct, it is hard to be sure, but the Besnard scholar Coppier has identified some of the room's murky furnishings: he reads the squared-off shapes at the right as picture frames stacked up against an English-style fireplace that runs across the back of the otherwise indistinct room.[31]

These details become suggestive when we note that, counter to sartorial custom of the day, the young tea drinker is not wearing gloves. If she had purchased her hot drink commercially, her hands would be covered. Her bare hands conflict with the enclosing carapace of her fussily contoured dark jacket and feathered hat. Surely the gloves would have come off only in a home, if then.[32] Is Besnard's *anglaise* a visitor to a private interior—a home or a studio (which might explain the frames)? If she is a caller in such an environment, then this is a Frenchman's elucidation of a socially correct young female English guest. The sharpness of her features and confidence of her bearing guarantee, then, that she appears to uphold the fussbudget set of restraints governing the circumstance of being seen in company. But Besnard's decision to show her alone is a key thing, a supremely interesting move. The tension between her comportment and her solitude, and the friction between the precision of her description and the vagueness of the surrounding space

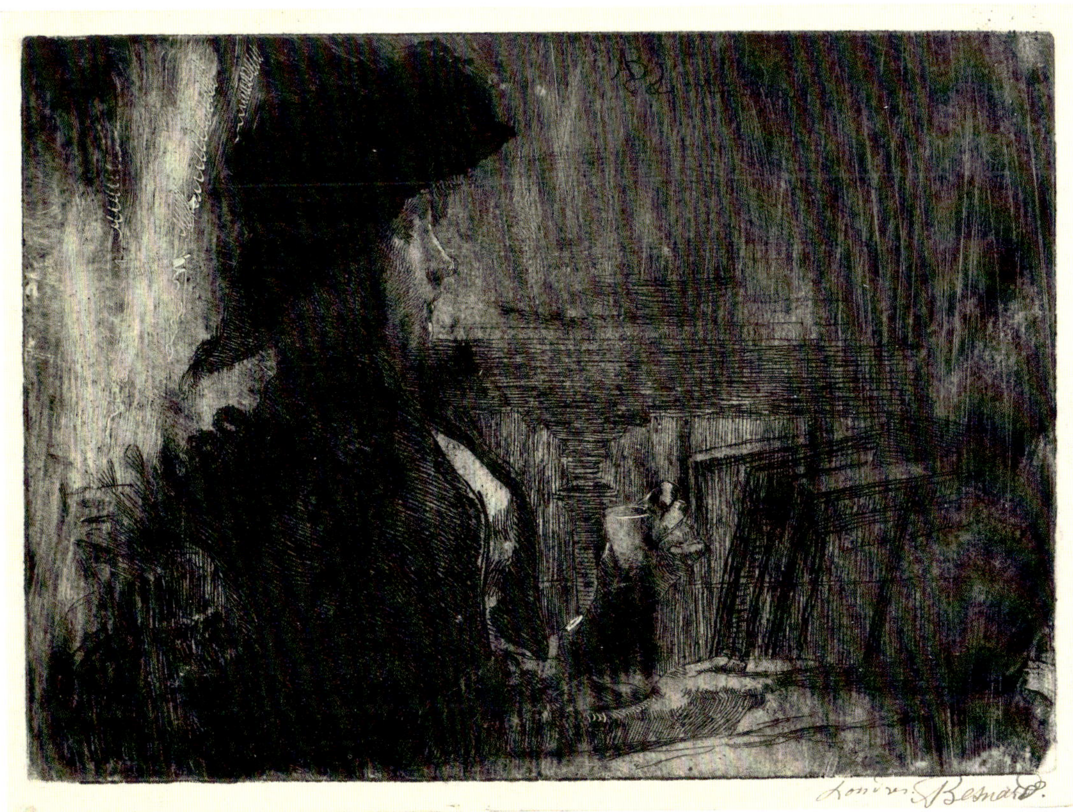

11 Albert Besnard, *The Cup of Tea*, 1883, etching with monotype inking, 17.6 × 25.1, National Gallery of Art, Washington, Ailsa Mellon Bruce Fund

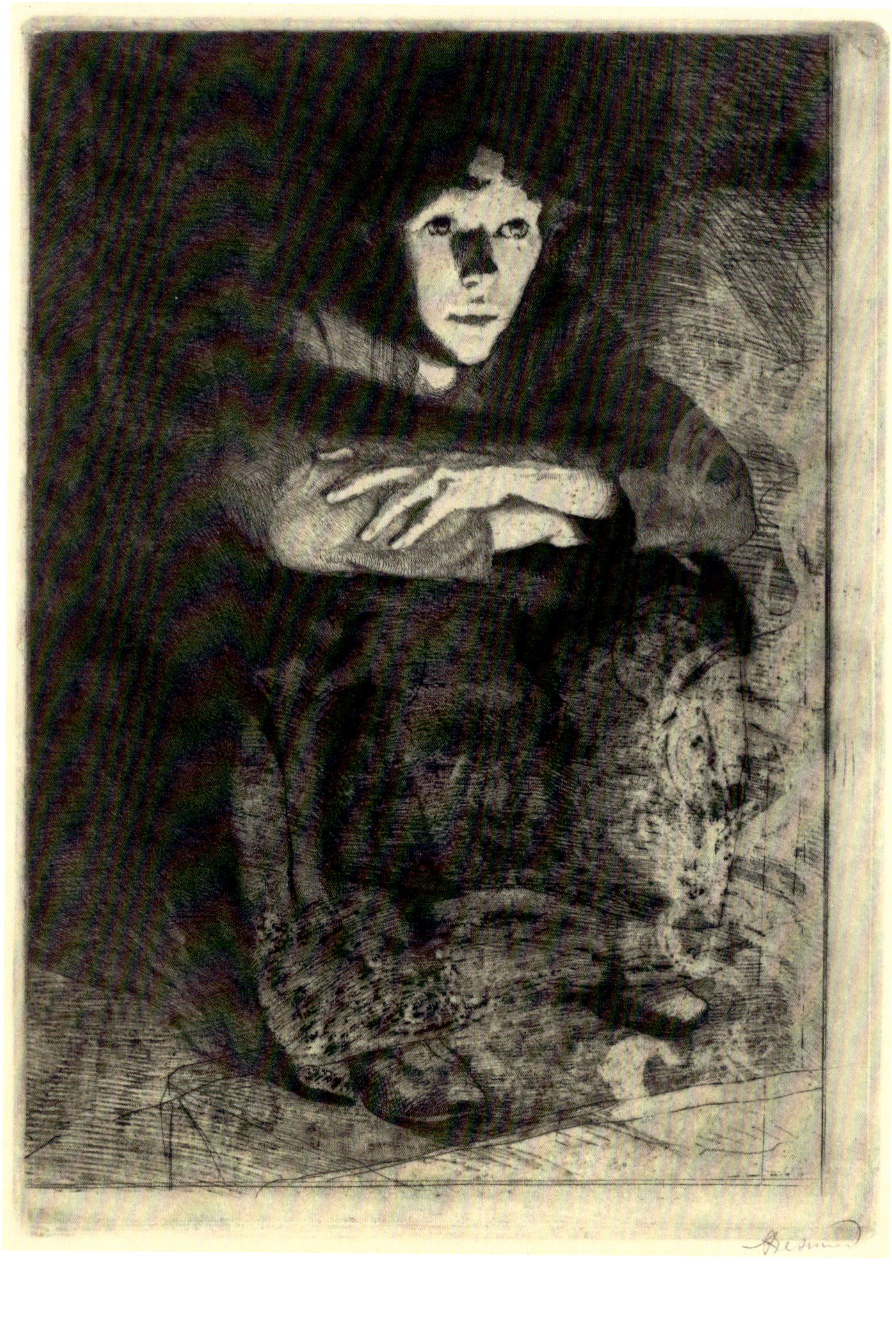

activate the image, turning it into a study of a woman in a daze, alone and brought up short—if only briefly—by her excessive obeisance to the social norms of etiquette when no one is present to assess her appearance and performance. We are witnessing her no doubt ephemeral discovery that the script she was following was not written for the emotionally "authentic" encounters that unfold within the (new) interior. She thus appears distracted from her tea drinking.

In the Embers, 1887 (fig. 12), was dedicated to Auguste Rodin and underwent a radical transformation from state to state. (It was greatly reduced in size sometime before the turn of the new century, when a standing second figure at left was excised.)[33] The etching won a grand prize at the Exposition Universelle of 1900 in Paris.[34] Understanding the now solitary figure's ostensible context requires no guessing game this time: the etching is an atmospherically rich depiction of an exemplary, all-encompassing daydream, activated and sustained by the unseen, but smoky, fire nearby just beyond the sheet's right margin.[35] The bold handling of the plumes of smoke (or are they flames?) as snaky and variegated white striations—essentially as absences—is extremely effective and inventive, further enchanting the thinker's stare. The concentration of the young sitter's gaze directly into the hearth severs her persuasively from the surrounding space, and the compactness of her knees-up, informal position echoes and reinforces her containment in and by her thoughts. The woman's perfectly symmetrical limpid eyes, shockingly blunt nose (its dark cast shadow and reductive shape both visually bracing), and brightly lit face embed her in the fire's residue and enmesh her in the pensive ambiance of rumination.

12 Albert Besnard, *In the Embers*, 1887, etching and roulette with drypoint, 42.8 × 31.5, National Gallery of Art, Washington, Rosenwald Collection

A third solitary female meditation etched by Besnard, *Rêverie*, January 1887, a small (8 × 4.8 cm) study for a menu, throws the special intensities of feminine consciousness figured by Besnard in *The Cup of Tea* and *In the Embers* into sharper relief.[36] A daydreaming but smiling woman with eyes half-closed leans back delicately into a bentwood rocking chair. Draped in a collared coat opened to reveal a blouse and pale vest (neither clearly indoor nor outdoor clothing), the sitter has a decidedly cheerful demeanor.[37] Identifying the interior as a restaurant would align with the print's purpose. The woman's pleasant face and relaxed body contrast sharply with the edginess of the young fashionista caught in her tense masquerade in *The Cup of Tea* and the haunted, unflinching gaze of the firelit young woman in *In the Embers*.

Anders Zorn's *An Irish Girl*, 1894 (fig. 13), was apparently a product of one of the Paris-based artist's first trips to the United States.[38] The print's sizzling yet subtle projection of outward-directed female regard, perhaps passion, that originates within the cloistered murk of an interior is extraordinary. According to an astounding piece of critical analysis published in Sweden in 1902: "This is a woman that belongs to the family of Baudelaire and Edgar Allan Poe—the woman who arouses the hottest desire, the most lethal horror, the bitterest hatred (in a word), the woman as chalice containing the sweetest and most dangerous poison."[39] The ferocity, even potential danger, of the mesmerizing young woman's look (intensified by her shadowed face, the arresting dishevelment of her copious jet-black hair set

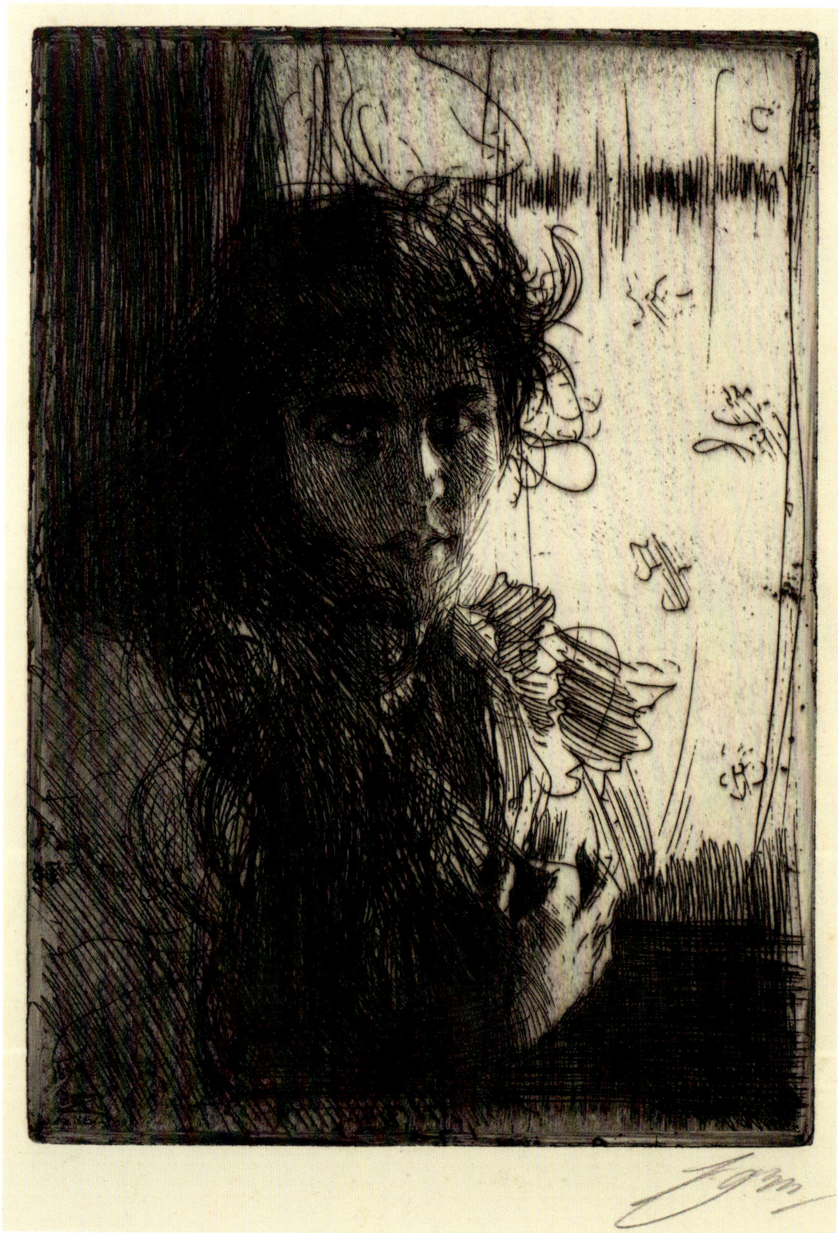

13 Anders Zorn, *An Irish Girl*, 1894, etching, 27.3 x 19.8, National Gallery of Art, Washington, Rosenwald Collection

off against the diaphanous curtain, and the self-regard instanced by her hand gesture) contrasts sharply with the rare figurations of the other extreme: solitary women in the domestic interior possessed of inwardness and self-sufficiency in exceptional prints by Besnard, Cassatt, and Degas.

In Company *Reading (Mr. and Mrs. Charles Deering),* 1893 (fig. 14), by Zorn, achieves an effect of considerable rarity. The print imagines a tension-free and fully equilibrated, indoor male-female intimacy, cemented via reading, and the result it achieves is entirely unfractured and persuasive. As in the link between Zorn and Besnard that shaped Zorn's image of the studio (see fig. 5), this etching grew out of an alliance between the artist and his sitters. Zorn met the Chicagoan Charles Deering in 1893 during the artist's first visit to the United States, where he was commissioner for the Swedish art section of the World's Columbian Exposition.[40] They became close friends, and the Deering family eventually owned the largest collection of Zorn's work in the United States.[41] This etching is set in the Deering home in Evanston, Illinois, where Zorn was a houseguest (while he worked on his oil portrait of the redoubtable Mrs. Potter Palmer, today in the collection of The Art Institute of Chicago). Shortly before Zorn was scheduled to leave Evanston, Deering injured his eye; apparently Zorn decided to help him convalesce.[42] In this print, undertaken presumably for his and his friends' pleasure (Zorn would not take etching commissions), he has endowed his recuperating friend with the panache and hauteur of a well-to-do gentleman despite the black eye patch.

Deering's wife also evidently fostered her spouse's recuperation by reading to him. Her profile combines traits that we have learned are hard-won: she is conventionally pretty and feminine while also convincingly absorbed in the text she shares with her one-eyed, temporarily incommoded husband. (Charles Deering's downward gaze also meshes the couple in a secure psychological loop.) The tonal darkness of her head enforces her gravity. But Zorn does not allow the solemnity of her engagement with the text to coarsen her feminine attractiveness.

The easy atmosphere and convincing rapport between the Deerings may be explained in part by Zorn's fondness for Americans, about whom he wrote: "Their frank, straightforward manner suits my nature. I've never really been able to stand European city folks' ceremonious way and artificial customs.... (in America) when they say 'He is all right,' all doors open to the foreigner, which Europeans cannot understand."[43] This declaration by a Swedish artist living in France evokes the specifically European perception of the uneasy interior that we see fashioned in numerous prints made on the right bank of the transatlantic art world.[44]

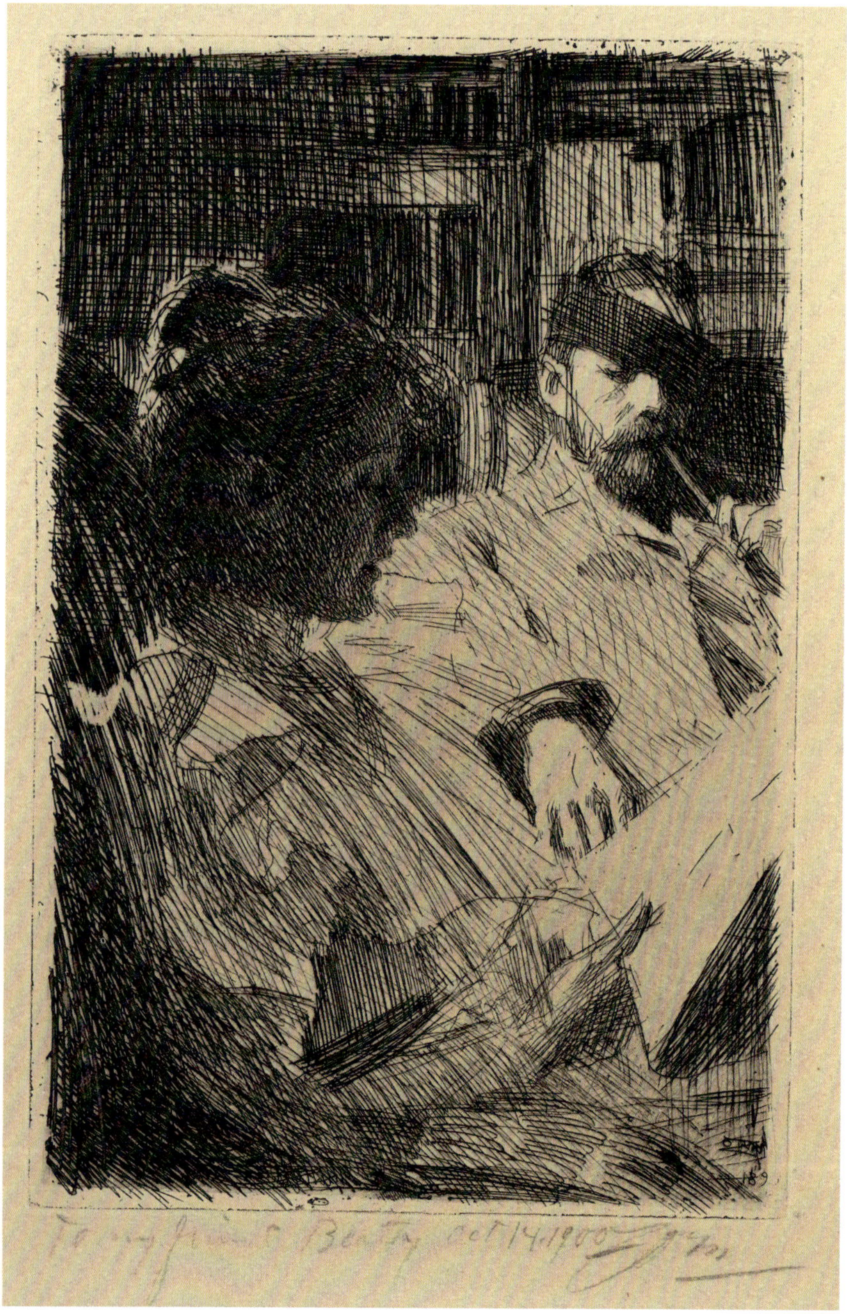

Indeed, when prints of modern European domestic interiors were populated by more than one person and where social and psychological harmony was an ostensible goal, complex, even troubling effects frequently emerge. In Whistler's etching *The Music Room,* 1858 (fig. 15), for example, every effort appears to have been made to build a congruent and organic trio of the busy folks seated in the evening at a table within the perimeter of its enabling lamplight. But the artist's effort to array the members of the group taking their ease instead generates considerable strain. Indeed, the composition is obviously deliberate: its evenly spaced figures give it the clockwork quality of a diagram. As a result, an organic and pressure-free bond among the people is missing.

The components of Whistler's design procedure evidently were these: put one figure at left (check), follow up with one placed dead center but slightly back (check), and complete the impeccably neat array of figures with one over at the right while preserving the even spacing (check). The man at left leaning back in his chair with legs stretched forward, gazing on a section of newspaper, is, on his own, a consummate marker of stress-free after-dinner activity. But when inserted in company, he shifts to signify the preplanned and artificial. The woman sewing at right is also problematic. She is positioned in profile so as to "point back" across the space toward, and link up with, the newspaper-reading man across the table. Though she was surely designed to convey the look and secure an atmosphere of engrossed activity, she appears tense and stiff, as though *performing* engagement in a creative pastime in company rather than experiencing and enjoying it naturally. Thus her cramped (and crabbed) posture and arrowlike function in the composition actually isolate her from the two men. Indeed, the intensities of the body and face of the second man, at the center back, secure the conviction of his interest in his task—an order of engagement commensurate with that of his intensely sewing female colleague. But he, too, seems exaggeratedly positioned. Because of these points of rigidity, even the inky black pools of tonal darkness in the print enhance the disconnection among the three adults rather than pulling them together. A final and crucial compositional detail warrants highlighting: the sharp downward-pointing tablecloth slices through and divides the space like a knife, stepping up the unease that dominates the room.[45] The edgy tenor of their coexistence contrasts strongly with the easy feeling engineered between the Deerings (see fig. 14). In Whistler's etching, strain and tension prevail.

14 Anders Zorn, *Reading (Mr. and Mrs. Charles Deering),* 1893, etching (state iii/iii), 23.6 × 15.8, National Gallery of Art, Washington, Gift of John W. Beatty, Jr. 1964.4.19

Besnard's etching *Intimacy,* 1889 (fig. 16), appears soothing and convincingly trouble-free by comparison, especially because the tranquil indoor scene is lit naturally, by faint sunlight filtering in through transparent panels of

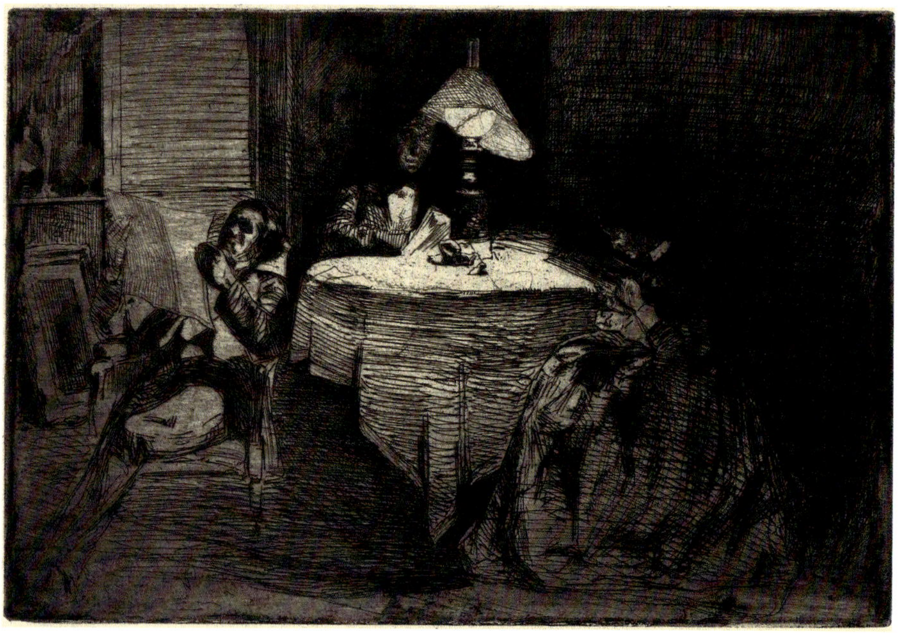

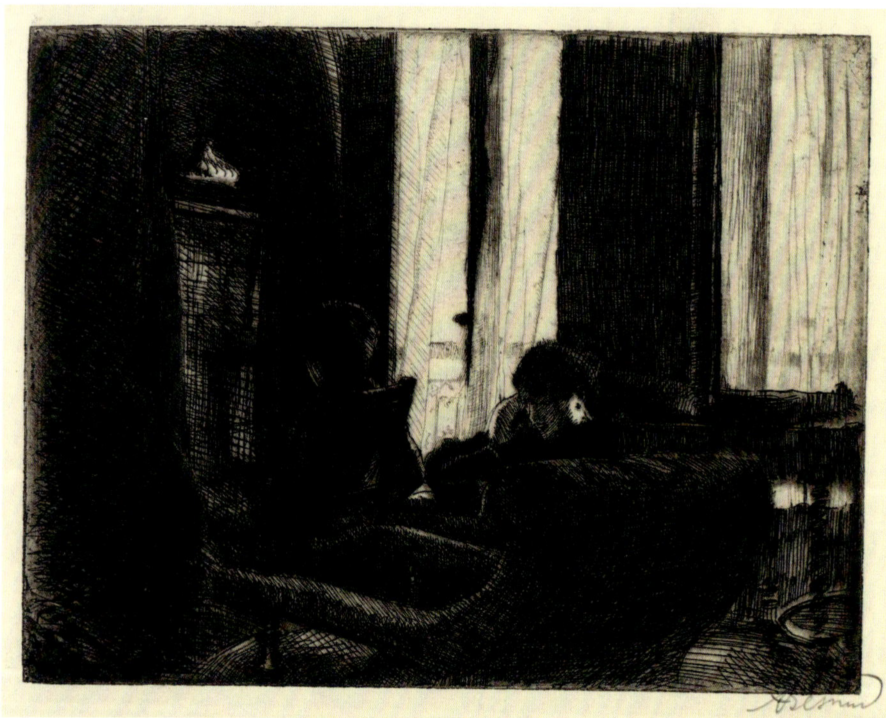

mousseline. But that restful impression does not survive close looking. Again we encounter the trope of reading in company in the bosom of a dim, upholstered interior, but in this case, pace Coppier, the imposing body and limbs of a large foreground chair disturb the print's serenity.[46] Trouble is inchoate in the room, latent in the piece of sprawling furniture that poses a vague threat to the two inhabitants. This menace can be effectively captured using a term theorized by Sigmund Freud: the "uncanny" (*unheimlich*). The uncanny conveys the eeriness or weirdness of a threatening presence in a private interior; it captures the sense of unease, even threat, when it is right there in the family foyer, within the very space that was designed to exclude it.[47]

Anthony Vidler has written helpfully that "the uncanny [which reflects the sense in which a newly established class was not quite at home in its own home] might be characterized as the quintessential bourgeois kind of fear.... The uncanny was, in this first incarnation, a sensation best experienced in the privacy of the interior."[48] Freud's concept encourages us to concede that the large size and confident foreground sprawl of the English armchair create the equivalent of an unwelcome third being in the room. Some may argue, to the contrary, that the chair is merely the benign marker of the absent father, but its scale in the picture and the angle of its placement make plausible a more baleful assessment of its role. The armchair's lateral foreground placement (note its plainly outstretched arms) not only parallels that of the body of the boy warming himself at the fireplace, but the tentacle-like outstretched limbs also reach out toward the vulnerable back of the distracted young man. When read as a creaturely presence in the room, the chair can thus be seen to haunt, even threaten, the sheltered space of the home and its unsuspecting occupants.

15 James McNeill Whistler, *The Music Room*, 1858, etching (state ii / ii), 14.4 × 21.7, National Gallery of Art, Washington, Rosenwald Collection 1943.3.8418

16 Albert Besnard, *Intimacy*, 1889, etching, 18.1 × 23.8, National Gallery of Art, Washington, Rosenwald Collection

In the world of Besnard's etching, the boy is particularly exposed to the probing of the fiendish chair because his companion—his sister or mother—is reading aloud from her book and unaware of the peril. But let us observe at the same time, looking at the chair from a more practical perspective, that Besnard was undoubtedly also attracted to its rich cushioning and the protective feeling and muffling of sound that an upholstered chair in the foreground of the room provided. That the chair simultaneously instances protection and alien invasion shores up the ideological conundrum at the heart of conceptions about the interior at the time: its pleasures and delicious seclusions were haunted by fretfulness over its potential insufficiency and vulnerability to contamination.

Other prints also speak to anxieties about the discomfort of, even peril triggered by, the penetration of the interior by outsiders. Cassatt's *The Visitor*, c. 1880 (fig. 17), stages an awkward encounter between the (seated) right-

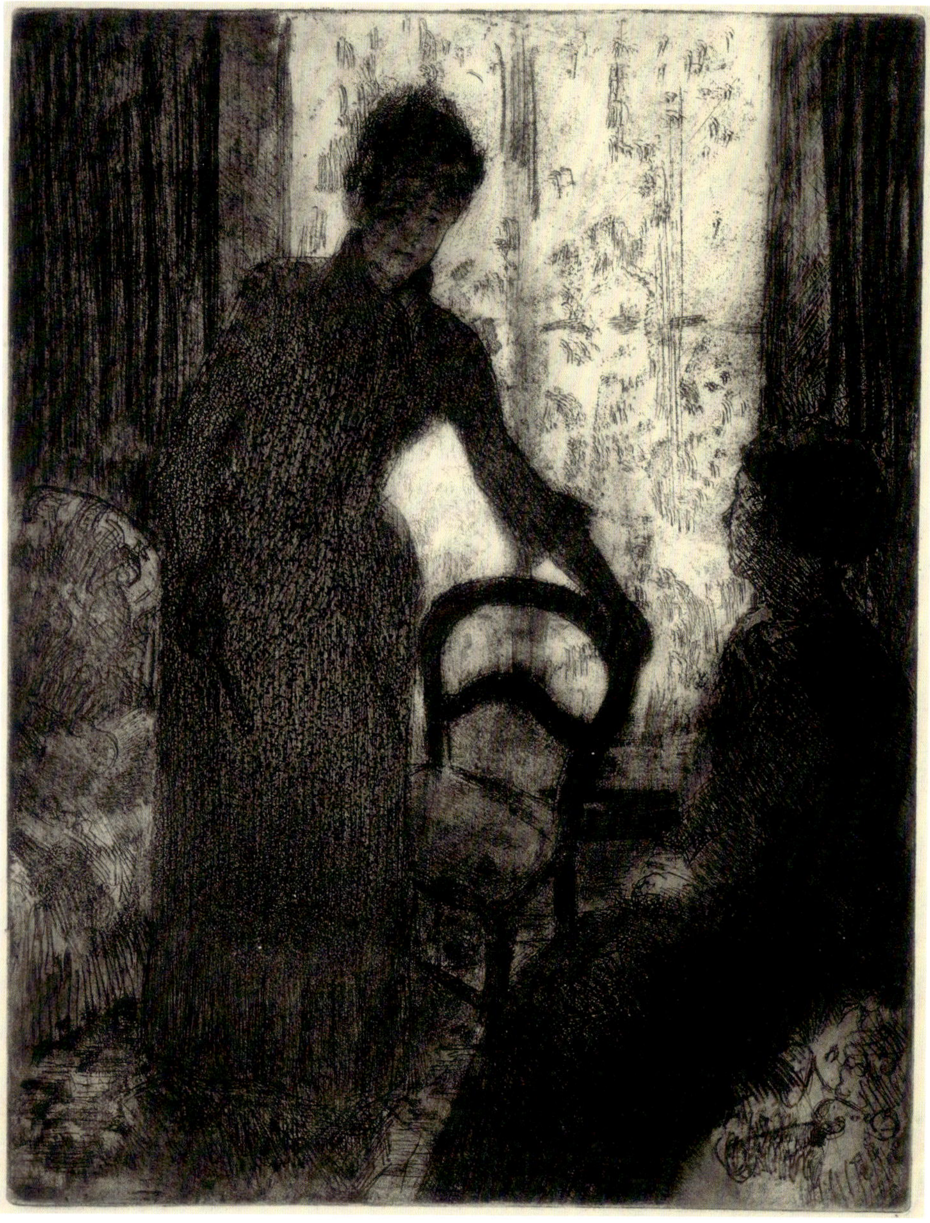

ful occupant of the room and the extremely stiff and awkward visitor who stands. That they are both barely illuminated by the sun filtering through the patterned curtains guarantees that the encounter is shadowy in content as well as atmosphere. Although nothing more complicated than the visitor's acceptance of an invitation to draw her chair closer to her hostess may be described here, Cassatt nonetheless maximizes the subject's complexity and suggestiveness by her rendering. The visitor's grip on the chair is surprising, even arresting, because it is off-kilter and eccentric (why grasp its back all the way over to the opposite side?). The peculiar position of hand and arm combines with the visitor's apprehensive, albeit simplified, facial expression, to hint that the outsider has brought unease into the shadowy salon.[49] What matters most—and note that the print is simply but suggestively entitled *Interior Scene* in French—is that what is represented here, a cornerstone of bourgeois social life, the welcoming of a visitor across the threshold and into the private foyer, is pictured through the self-conscious lens of belief in the fraught quality not just of the modern interior but of encounters between American hosts and French guests in the sequestered spaces of the female domestic sphere.[50] The patterned scaffolding created by the forms of the chair back combined with the visiting woman's arm and sharply defined body contours (crisply legible in *contre-jour* lighting conditions) create one of the most arresting spidery grids to be found in etchings of this period and are a strong and inventive marker of intersubjective and spatial tension.

Both Degas' monotype *Woman by a Fireplace*, 1880 / 1890 (fig. 18), and James Tissot's mezzotint *Morning*, 1886 (fig. 19), represent the infiltration of the private interior by a female domestic servant—an invasion that could be vexing.[51] In *Woman by a Fireplace*, a complex spatial and intersubjective scenario unfolds. The sprawling woman of the house, whose class and moral status are admittedly difficult to pinpoint, daringly and languidly pokes her serpentine leg into the air in the direction of the fire's warmth. Degas elsewhere combined bathing women and their female servants in his graphic work, but the closeness and oddity of the interaction between the women is especially striking here.[52] The maidservant is dauntingly close to her mistress, and the simian character of her face is unmistakable, highlighted as her features are by the firelight. The servant's attentions appear to license and facilitate the extravagant bodily expansion of Madame, but the closeness of her ministrations gingerly suggests an impertinent interest in and control of her employer's unfolding body. By placing her so close to her employer's head, Degas seems to imply that the pleasures of the interior may be shaped in unanticipated, even uncontrollable ways by the interests of the alien invader, in this case the serving woman who is preparing her mistress' bath (imple-

17 Mary Cassatt, *The Visitor*, c. 1880, softground etching with aquatint, and drypoint (state v / vi), 39.7 × 31.1, National Gallery of Art, Washington, Rosenwald Collection 1946.21.94

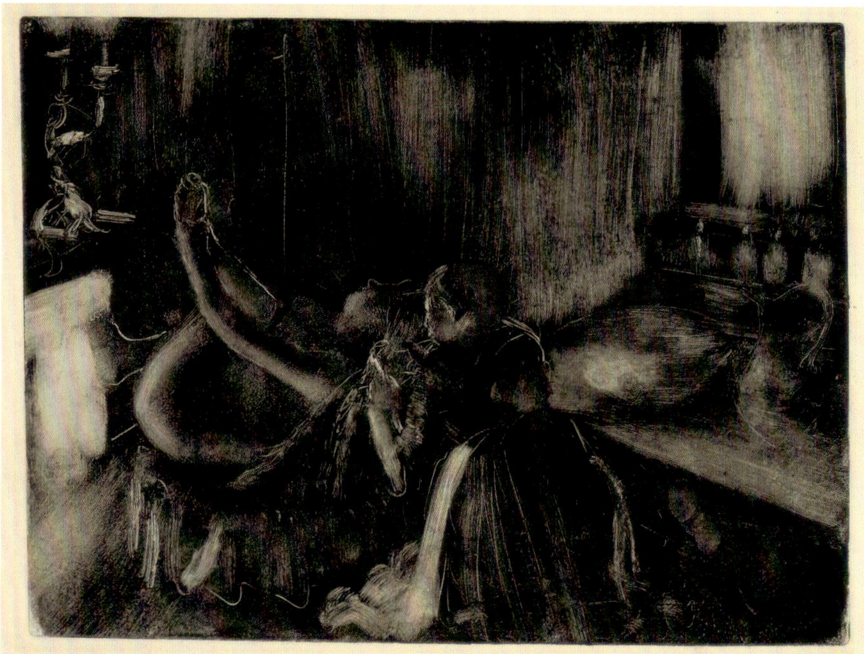

18 Edgar Degas, *Woman by a Fireplace,* 1880 / 1890, monotype, 27.5 × 37.7, National Gallery of Art, Washington, Collection of Mr. and Mrs. Paul Mellon

19 James Tissot, *Morning,* 1886, mezzotint, 48.9 × 26, Art Gallery of Ontario, Gift of Allan and Sondra Gotlieb

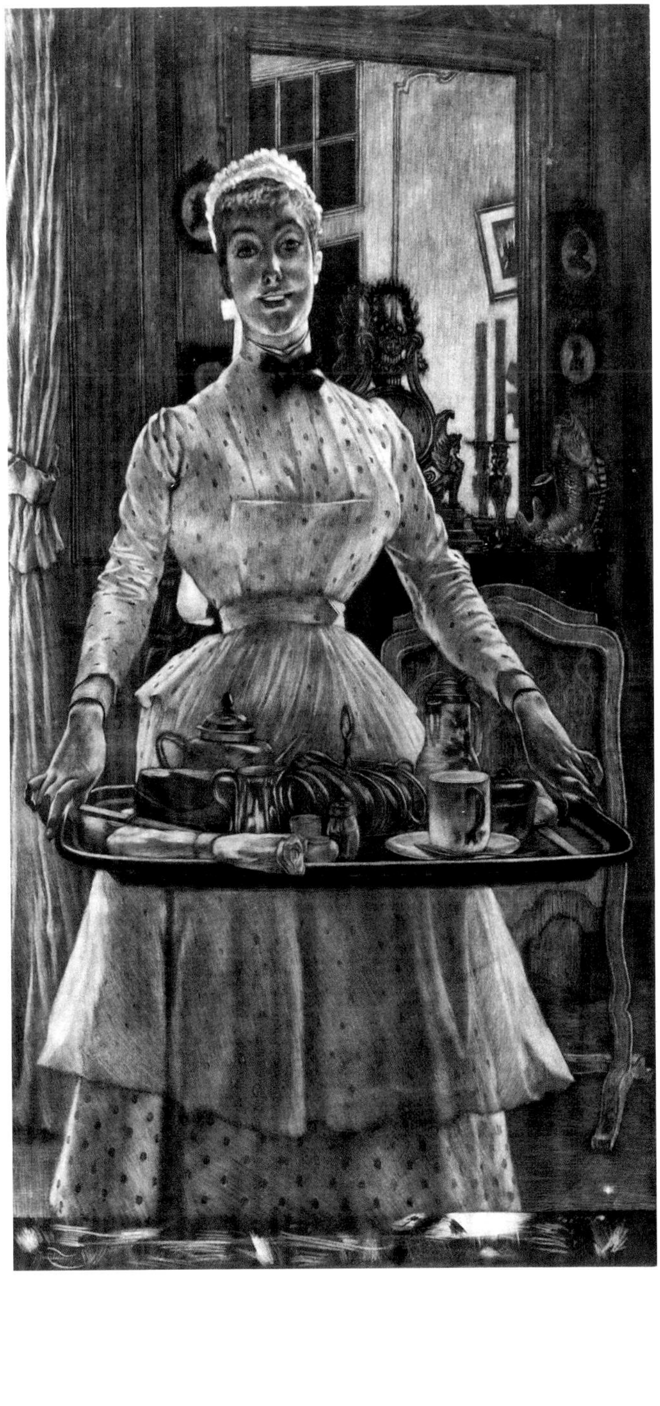

ments are laid out at right). The insect quality of the candelabrum on the hearth also promises trouble by tilting toward the uncanny.

Tissot's mezzotint ushers us into a contrasting visual economy of crisp details, middle tones, and rational space, in which we directly confront a leering and troubling female servant's face. *Morning* exemplifies what Elizabeth Prelinger considers to be Tissot's courting of "a deliberate strangeness."[53] She writes: "Lit from below, the maid's face, teeth bared, glows demonically. Improbably elongated fingers curl around the tray like serpentine instruments of arcane erotic torture. Imposingly, even menacingly frontal, the figure wears a slightly glazed expression."[54] The apposite conclusion is that this representation of the maidservant, the sine qua non of the cosseted bourgeois life, inscribes the social and psychic cost of such a dependency and calls attention to the uncanniness of cohabiting with strangers in order to live the most comfortable kind of private life—an eerie quality, the print suggests, that may be bracketed from thinking about the satisfactions of the interior but at the cost of delusion, even possible hazard.

James Ensor's peerless renditions of the Seven Deadly Sins go farther in this direction. They overflow with wildly imaginative explorations of the modern interior imperiled by the household employee. In *Gluttony,* 1904 (fig. 20), the skeleton of death serves a ghastly meal on a tray—like any food—to two disgusting, excessive diners who vomit while at table. The victuals include terrible animated crustaceans, an undead featherless bird, spilled wine, and a severed head. More familiar edibles—huge hogs—are being savagely prepared outside the window, echoing the stuffed hog whose head is displayed on the wall. Ensor thus imagines the domestic servant as the great unwanted visitor himself, death.

Man and Bird Edouard Manet's second illustration for Edgar Allan Poe's "The Raven" (1845), *The Open Window ("Open here I flung the shutter"),* 1875 (fig. 21), is a fitting stopping point for this study of the imagination of the cell of privacy in the print media, because although the lithograph represents an invaded interior space, it is of a divergent sort. By engaging an explicitly male interior, it takes us onto new architectural terrain: the male preserve of the *cabinet de travail.*[55] Manet's interest in Poe—the leading nineteenth-century specialist in the uncanny, especially the topos of the haunted house—was shared by his friends Stéphane Mallarmé and Charles Baudelaire.[56] Indeed, Manet's illustrations for "The Raven" were a collaboration with Mallarmé, whose translation of the poem had appeared in 1872.[57]

Manet's image illustrates Poe's lines: "Open here I flung the shutter, when, with many a flirt and flutter, / In there stepped a stately Raven of the

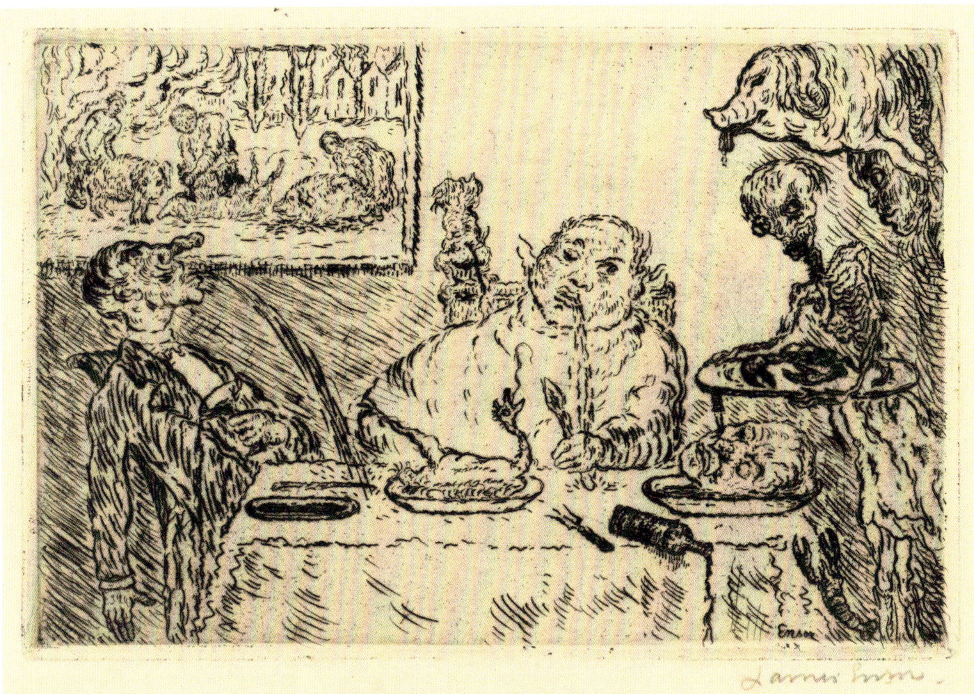

20 James Ensor, *The Deadly Sins: Gluttony,* 1904, etching, 9.8 × 15.1, National Gallery of Art, Washington, Rosenwald Collection 1964.8.2758

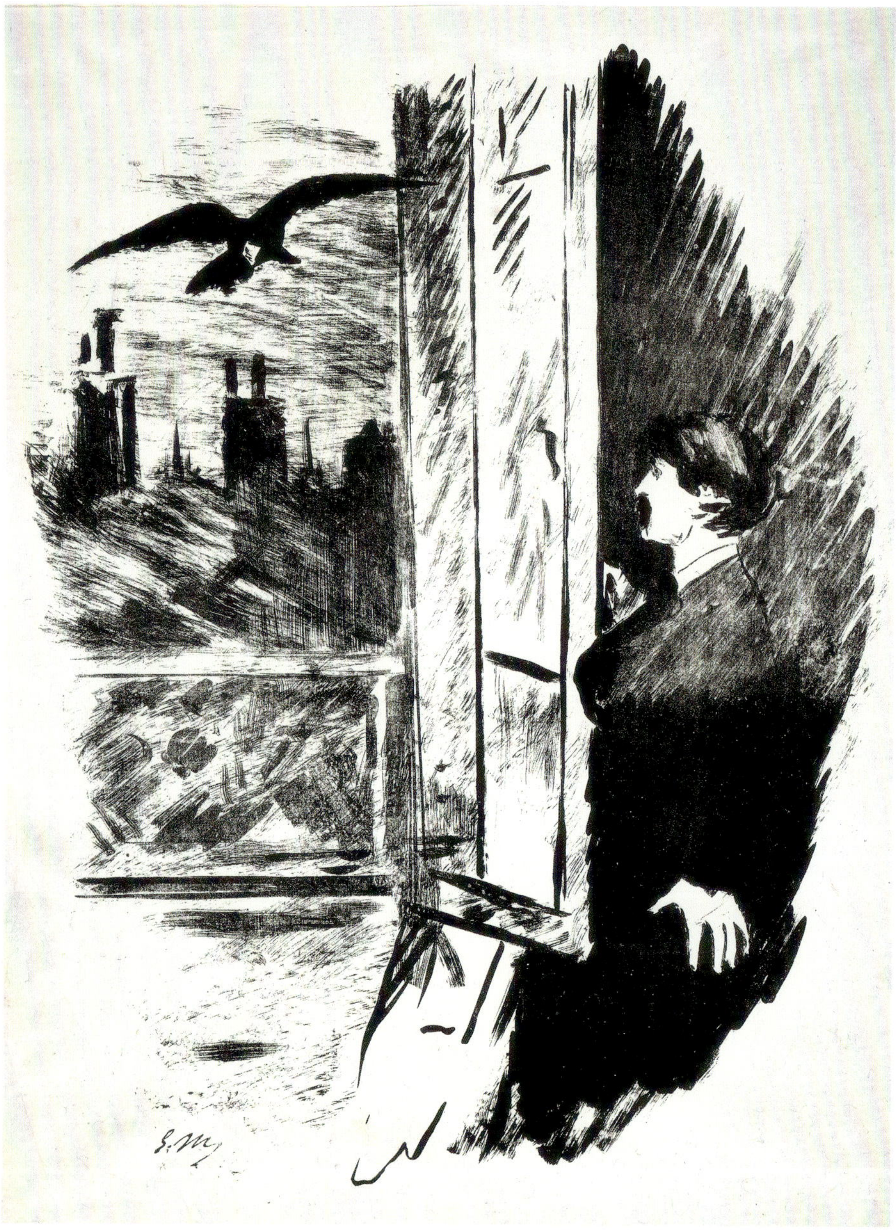

saintly days of yore," but with several modifications. The study is a locus of mournful intellectual activity in Poe's poetic text, but Manet shifts the emphasis somewhat by staging the sleek black bird's arrival as a clear, even dramatic interruption or invasion of that space. Jay McKean Fisher notes a further divergence: "Manet departed slightly from the text in having the raven fly through the window, whose shutter opens inward, not outward as in the poem."[58] The topicality of the modern urban interior—its privacies and fragilities—surely prompted the artist's reorganization of the action and space. The mustachioed narrator observes the arrival of the raven (whose angular, foreshortened pale beak amplifies the portentous quality of the bird's intent focus) with mild surprise (the tensed left hand). But it is he who has flung open the shutter (his right hand touches the window frame) in preparation for the unavoidable bird—emblem of his destiny.

The question that hovers over Manet's illustration is whether the artist succeeded in summoning up a worrisome invasion of a protected space of thought and writing, thus acknowledging the inescapability of the despoiled interior and the haunting of the private house in urban modernity. Or does Manet disenchant the bird and its menace through the generalizing, offhand, and sketchy nature of the draftsmanship? In the hands of a modernist like Manet, we are left wondering whether the bird that arrives from the realm of fate to trouble the narrator in his lair, as well as the finely detailed, industrialized city beyond the barrier of windows (this is the first depiction of an open window discussed in this essay), is proof of Manet's awareness of the vulnerable contemporary home mirroring Poe while also deploying the raven as a symbolist cipher of the intellectual's interiority.

21 Edouard Manet, *At the Window ("Open here I flung the shutter")*, illustration from Stéphane Mallarmé's translation of Edgar Allan Poe's "The Raven," 1875, transfer lithograph (state iii / iii), 42.2 × 31.5, Baltimore Museum of Art, The George A. Lucas Collection, purchased with funds from the State of Maryland, Laurence and Stella Bendann Fund, and contributions from individuals, foundations, and corporations throughout the Baltimore Community 1.33.53.18047

According to Anthony Vidler's discussion of the *unheimlich* houses of Poe: "The house provided an especially favored site for uncanny disturbances: its apparent domesticity, ... its role as the last and most intimate shelter of private comfort[,] sharpened by contrast the terror of invasion by alien spirits."[59] Vidler's insight helps us understand the preoccupation with the domestic interior in modernity and allows us to position our valedictory example, Manet's Poe-based lithograph, with its disconcerting airborne raven, securely within the compass of this essay: the imagination of the spatial and emotional insides of private space in the era of the interior. Manet's use of the trope of the invaded interior in this lithographic illustration showcases his circle's attachment to Poe's haunted literary imaginary, but it also aligns his interests as an inquisitive and inventive painter-printmaker with those of his artist contemporaries, including those discussed here, who also probed the psychic and atmospheric qualities of the introverted domestic interior during the heyday of its veneration.[60]

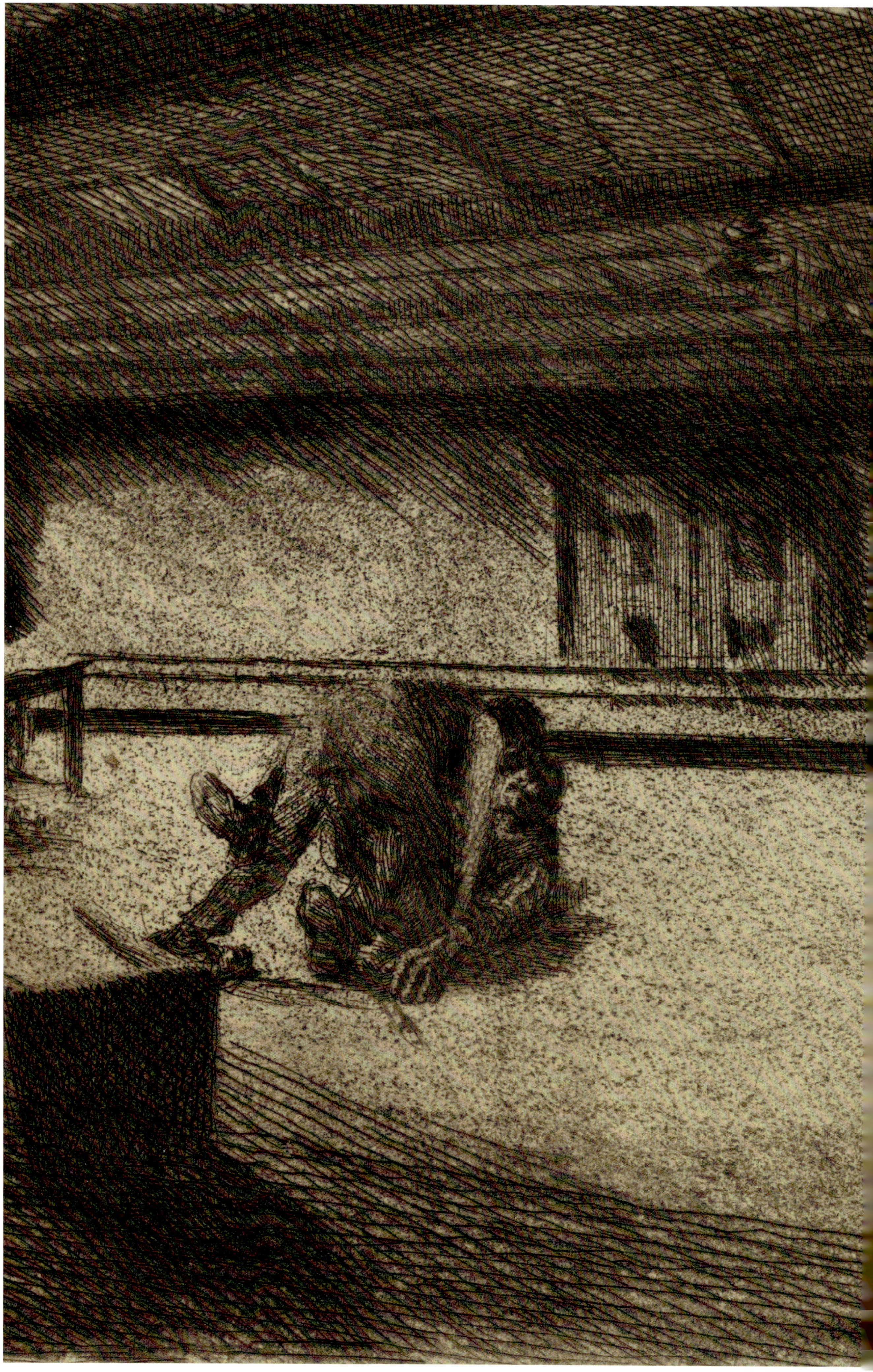

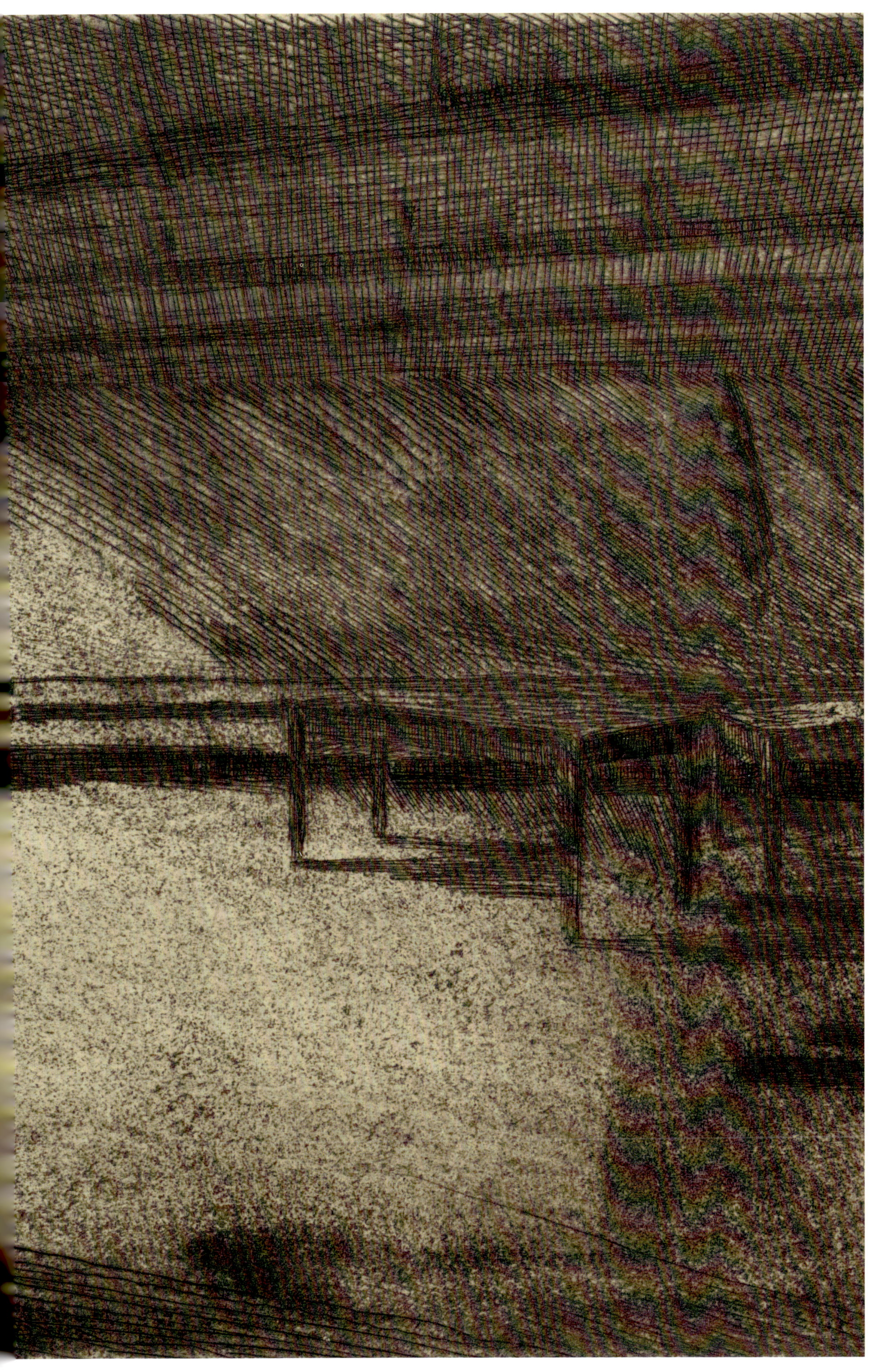

THE WORLD INSIDE: PRIVACY ACCORDING TO KLINGER, LIEBERMANN, AND KOLLWITZ

Christiane Hertel

"Just now someone has died!"
"Yes, but in foreign lands."
"Now something is turned INSIDE OUT!"
"Yes, but in foreign lands."
"Now something goes CRACK!"
"Yes, but because we can talk about it, it is a dream."

—*Peter Handke, "Distinctions," from* The World Inside of the World Outside of the World Inside, *1969*

Privacy, we might still say, is the right to be let alone.[1] In the later nineteenth century, German printmakers such as Max Klinger, Max Liebermann, and Käthe Kollwitz explored the world of privacy—"the world inside."[2] By "the world inside" I mean interiority, its representation as experience from within a personal and subjective perspective. Artists working on prints and drawings can be considered as working in privacy for a private audience, for themselves, their friends, and their supporters—collectors, art dealers, subscribers to art journals, and art association members looking forward to the annual gift of a print.[3] This semiprivate, or semipublic, segment of the art world is a not entirely risk-free sphere of artistic experimentation, expression, and reflection. The risks are private in part in an economic sense, but more important, they are private in a personal sense. Here we should not think solely of self-portraiture, though all three practiced it, Kollwitz with a Rembrandt-like intensity, Liebermann frequently, and Klinger occasionally by casting himself in a dramatic role. There are also the personal risks of embarrassment, offense, uncertainty of tone, and the disappointment of misunderstanding, or, in contrast, the fear of too deep an understanding. In turn, the most public side of their prints, the artists' choices of styles and techniques of graphic representation, appear inseparable from a kind of personal handwriting and therefore an embodied seismographic rendering of self. This exposure is not a symptom of a latent identity; it is evident on the surface of the sheet.[4]

The final stanza of Peter Handke's prose poem "Distinctions," quoted above, distills the intense exploration of that semipublic, semiprivate sphere, the burden and the freedom of interiorizing the outer world, whether it be reflected, judged, interpreted, made one's own, or in the end disowned. Here the two poetic voices in dialogue go back and forth, one accepting as close, all-important, and inescapable what the other tries to place in the distance. The dynamic of inside and outside, and closeness and distance, ends with a compromise and with an insight: we can speak about the dangerous, disturbing, or uncanny in the form of a fiction, a dream, a work of art.

The concept of "the world inside" has a long history.[5] What in the sixteenth century began with the Lutheran idea of religious freedom as a matter of personal conscience had developed in late eighteenth- and early nineteenth-century German idealist philosophy and romantic art and literature into a freedom of subject and self.[6] This freedom was attended more often by a lingering religious notion of conscience and accountability than by social-political responsibility and activism.[7] In the mid-nineteenth century, however, Karl Marx's interpretation of German idealism, along with the revolutions of 1848 and 1849, led artists to embark on different paths with the burden and treasure of this heritage. This legacy was still, if precariously, held in balance with a modern realism in Alfred Rethel's treatment of the revolution of 1849 in *Another Dance of Death* (1849), in which political conflict appears driven by the late medieval personification of Death joined and equipped by the Greek Harpies, who devastate the land with their evil powers.[8]

When Kollwitz, Klinger, and Liebermann intended to ground their work in reality or in nature, each meant something quite different. Of the three, Liebermann put his conviction most succinctly: "For all art is grounded in nature and all that endures in it is nature."[9] In Kollwitz' oeuvre, the exploration of self and a deep social-political engagement in the world exist side by side. Both were mediated by family life, her husband's working-class patients, and the literary naturalism of Émile Zola and Gerhart Hauptmann. Klinger's art is inflected by his reading of Arthur Schopenhauer. His print cycles mix styles and allegiances (naturalism, neo-romanticism, and symbolism) without clear commitment to one and without a preference for topics from one social class, but also with striking experimental imagination and technical skill. These endeavors are backed by his thoughts on printmaking in the treatise *Painting and Drawing* (1891). Liebermann's early etchings and lithographs focus on charitable institutions and on leisure, work, and home in the preindustrial or agricultural countryside, an approach that goes beyond the heritage of German interiority and art by openly avowing models in modern French and Dutch art. And yet, in his essay "Imagination in Painting" (1904), Liebermann insisted on the primacy of imagination and the artist's phenomenal rather than cognitive perception of the outer world.[10]

In Wilhelmine Germany, privacy also had a political meaning. The right to be let alone applied to the emperor traveling "en particulier" (privately) as much as to the established artist working in the studio. The emperor's private travels were known, not secret, yet they suspended certain obligations of ceremony for him and for those he met along his way.[11] Similarly, the artist could choose among a range of venues to show or share works created in privacy. In this sense privacy and publicity are acknowledged modes of being an emperor or an artist, and they coexist perhaps with inner conflict but without external challenge. However, the question of when external challenge is appropriate is something the monarch could decide for the artist, as happened to Klinger, Liebermann, and Kollwitz more than once in the early decades of their careers, when their privately created work entered into annual academic art exhibitions that were subject to scrutiny by state authorities or came under the monarch's veto.[12] Yet these were the exhibition venues in which the three artists first hoped to succeed. Success and failure had different implications and consequences for each artist.[13] Klinger's and Liebermann's families were established industrialists and propertied bourgeoisie (*Besitzbürgertum*) in Leipzig and Berlin, respectively, Klinger's well-to-do, Liebermann's wealthy. Kollwitz, by contrast, came from the educated middle class (*Bildungsbürgertum*) in Königsberg / Kaliningrad and, moreover, from a close-knit family whose members repeatedly sacrificed professional success to personal conviction.[14] None of them grew up surrounded by art or a pronounced interest in it. And if both Kollwitz and Klinger were apparently given considerable liberties to explore world and self, Liebermann grew up in strict discipline, sharing with his two brothers a room pierced by a glass door for paternal supervision.[15] All three spent years in Munich and, with the exception of Kollwitz, who studied there only briefly, Paris. Although Klinger and Liebermann achieved financial success as artists, Kollwitz remained solidly middle-class, her lifestyle modest. Like, and often with, Liebermann she had the opportunity to shape art institutions through teaching and participation in exhibition juries, but she made no major founding gesture. Klinger's activities included the endowment in 1906 of a residential fellowship for private artistic development at the Villa Romana in Florence, and in 1907 Kollwitz was one of its first recipients.

In 1913, the satirical journal *Kladderadatsch* published a caricature offering fictive "Sensational Vacation News: The Secession as the Emperor's Guest on His Nordic Trip!" The caricature shows Liebermann, president of the Berlin Secession for most of its existence, and the Kaiser both en particulier, seemingly suspending all differences between them.[16] This "sensational news" entered a long-standing debate in the art world regarding the importance of French naturalist and impressionist art and its influences on German artists, museums, and the art market in general. The debate eventually centered on the Bremer Kunsthalle's acquisition in 1911 of Vincent van Gogh's *Poppy Field*, 1889–1890, which prompted the landscape painter Carl Vinnen to publish *Protest of German Artists,* an attack on modernism that was cosigned by many, including Kollwitz.[17] This was soon refuted by museum directors, artists, art historians, and art dealers in *German and French Art,* which contains seventy-five contributions ranging from short protest notes to detailed essays. In his introductory essay, Gustav Pauli, director of the Bremer Kunsthalle, unmasks Vinnen's text as a nationalist campaign, denying modern French art's good influence on modern German art. Pauli and others saw through the cliché of pitching German spiritual depth and technical skill against French superficiality of mind and brush. In his monograph on Liebermann, also of 1911, Pauli suspected these nationalist sentiments of anti-Semitism directed against Liebermann and Paul and Bruno Cassirer.[18] Thus in 1913, the *Kladderadatsch*'s caricature "sensationally" closed a long-standing gap when it presented Liebermann, the Berlin Secession's leading artist and collector of French impressionism, together with the anti-French emperor intent on introducing the artist to his preferred "Nordic" realm.[19] Liebermann and others were disappointed when Kollwitz, to her later regret, sided with the nationalists in this debate. Klinger did not sign on, though he also abstained from contributing to *German and French Art.*[20]

Liebermann, Klinger, and Kollwitz were founding members of the Berlin Secession, which was organized in May 1898 to counter the imperial control of art and the generally stale status quo of the annual exhibition venues.[21] Liebermann, its president, was also professor and member of the art academy and a recipient of gold medals at official exhibitions in Berlin, Dresden, and Munich. An established artist in all media, Klinger was a corresponding member of the Secession and participated in its first spring exhibition. Liebermann welcomed Klinger's support of modern and internationally oriented art. Despite an official German boycott, both artists had participated in the 1889 Exposition Universelle in Paris celebrating the centennial of the French Revolution—although Liebermann reportedly found Klinger's art "atrocious."[22] Kollwitz was still starting out, and Klinger's influence on her early work is recognized. As she later wrote: "I *thanked* Klinger from all my heart, for I have *much* to thank him for."[23] When in 1898 the emperor vetoed the jury's proposal to award the Grosse Berliner Kunstausstellung's small gold medal to Kollwitz for her print series *A Weavers' Rebellion,* Liebermann, together with Max Lehrs, director of the print collection in Dresden and henceforth Kollwitz' unwavering supporter, secured for her the equivalent award there in 1899.[24] The three artists' relations fluctuated over time. Although they differed most in their practice of the arts of painting (Liebermann and Klinger) and sculpture (Kollwitz and Klinger), they shared much as printmakers.[25] Unlike the Secessions in Vienna, Munich, and elsewhere, beginning in 1901 the Berlin Secession featured solely works on paper in its annual winter exhibition, and it is in this context that Klinger, Liebermann, and Kollwitz exhibited together in 1901.[26] This, then, suggests their parity as paradigmatic modern printmakers.[27] Also important in this context is the artist Adolph Menzel, an artist of the previous generation to whom Klinger especially paid homage in image and Liebermann in print.[28] Menzel was among Liebermann's earliest supporters even as he chided him for what he perceived as his technical laziness, and he nominated Kollwitz for the gold medal in 1898. In turn, as printmakers, all three artists were indebted to Menzel and to his prints' narrative power, unflinching observation, and technical skill.[29]

TREATISES AND PRINTS IN DIALOGUE

In his widely read treatise *Painting and Drawing,* Max Klinger set out to define and explain "the special status of drawing as an art," coining the term *Griffelkunst,* or the art of the stylus, for "works of art restricted to the monochromatic portrayal of light, shadows, and forms."[30] His principal tenet is that, in contradistinction to painting, the graphic arts are free in their choice of topic. Often critical, *Griffelkunst* exposes the dark side of human life and cannot help being ironic:

> The most powerful emotions can be compressed into the most confined of spaces, the most contradictory emotions come thick and fast.... Drawing creates a piece of life with as many impressions as we can absorb. They may be of epic dimensions,

> they may take on a dramatic intensity, they may regard us with dry irony; mere shadows, they even embrace the monstrous without causing offense.
>
> The wealth of raw material that goes into drawings—the same material on which religions are based, for which nations annihilate each other, which we so gladly ignore..., a material kept in constant ferment by egoism and self-sacrifice—such wealth suggests that ideas and images shower upon the artist in abundance.[31]

Mentioning Hans Holbein's and Francisco José de Goya's "cyclical works" as examples, Klinger argues that the practice of drawing avails itself of three liberties: "[The] technical aspects of drawing further reinforce the ideational nature of drawing. The most important of these are: the unadulterated outline, the possibility of working without a definitive background, the ready amalgamation with ornament, and the combined forces of all these freedoms."[32] In this and other passages, Klinger's perhaps unexpected emphasis on the ready amalgamation of representation with ornament harks back not only to the romantic arabesque of Philipp Otto Runge and Eugen Neureuther but also to the rococo ornamental print, where this amalgamation had a subversive function.[33] Just as important here is what he writes about the expressive potential of "drawing":

> It is always the material nature of the subject that preoccupies painting: the air—light and luminous; the sea—moist and sparkling; the flesh—soft and silky. In the drawing all these materials can take on qualities that have less to do with the eye than with poetic attitudes and combinations. Now air suggests the notion of freedom, the sea that of power, and the human being is not a person contained within his individual form so much as a being that relates to and depends on all those external forces.[34]

Put differently, instead of depending on an iconography of conventional symbols that convey meaning in bounded form, the entire image is capable of metaphorical representation. If this is so, should works on paper not receive a different kind of criticism from, say, paintings or sculpture? Although periodicals such as Vienna's *Die graphischen Künste* focused on *Griffelkunst*, Richard Graul's appreciative essay there, "Max Liebermann" (1892), discusses his prints only occasionally. Where he does, Graul explicitly uses Klinger's treatise and his terminology to validate them, emphasizing less Liebermann's impressionist technique or effect than the prints' interiority, imagination, and psychological refinement.[35] Remarkably, Liebermann both edited and approved of this essay. His corrections include, among other

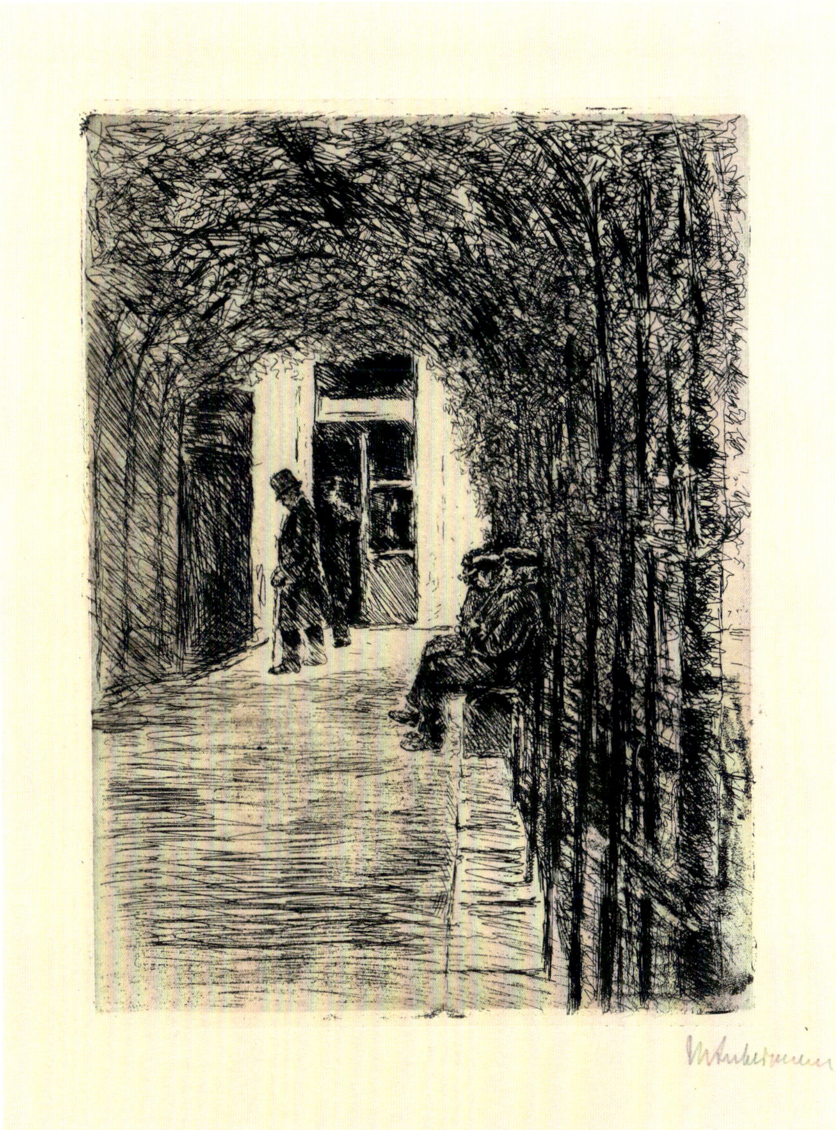

1 Max Liebermann,
Old Men's Home, 1890,
etching, 22 × 17, Schiefler
10, Fine Arts Museums of
San Francisco, Achenbach
Foundation for Graphic Arts
1963.30.34005

details, introducing the expression "inner emptiness" to characterize the nineteenth-century art he opposed and hoped to overcome.[36] As we explore prints by Liebermann, Klinger, and Kollwitz, we are thus well advised to suspend our assumptions about the differences among these artists.

Liebermann's early paintings representing industrial and agricultural labor and marginal social groups incensed critics in the 1870s and remained critical, even comical targets into the 1890s because of their perceived ugliness.[37] As an example we might think of his airy painting *Old Men's Home in Amsterdam,* 1880 (Staatsgalerie Stuttgart). The print *Old Men's Home,* 1890 (fig. 1), is an independent variant of this painting, exuding a much darker mood.[38] In both images brooding old men await death as they keep one another silent company. In the print, however, the tunnel-like arbor underscores the only exit ahead, through which a visitor, perhaps a doctor, is about to leave. At first sight, Liebermann's emphatically vigorous, sketchy style seems to defy each of Klinger's technical and representational freedoms in printmaking and looks unlike anything Klinger ever produced. But on closer examination, a subtle dialogue between them is visible. In *Old Men's Home* the arbor's steeply dropping ground, or groundlessness, inflects the boredom of old age with ominous foreboding. Its dense, flickering, and yet ornamentally rhythmic foliage is as claustrophobic as it is in many of Klinger's prints (see fig. 14). Here it combines with the merciless march of dark trellis poles into the unknown foreground. Not unlike Klinger in several prints (see fig. 12), Liebermann uses reflections on the glass door's panes in a faintly anthropomorphic way, suggesting a mask or skull or perhaps the collective face of the otherwise faceless men. Put differently, the entire image is a metaphorical extension and exposition of the old men's lives on the threshold of death. In *Imagination in Painting,* Liebermann calls the artist's imagination that which brings to life what he sets out to represent. It "is visible in every stroke," essential to the efficacy of art, and perceived solely by the beholder's "inner eye."[39]

The mere trace of symbolism in Liebermann's *Old Men's Home* seems barely comparable to its marked inflection of Kollwitz' early works. And yet it appears that she saw this trace, as the following comparison suggests. In both her lithograph *Need* from *A Weavers' Rebellion,* 1897–1898 (fig. 3), and Liebermann's *The Weaver,* 1883 (fig. 2), we see poverty, but only in one of them do we glimpse a privacy directly linked to privation. Both Kollwitz and Liebermann represent the weavers in their narrow, one-room living quarters and workspace.[40] The layout of this room and placement of figures and objects, such as the small mirror in the upper left-hand corner, suggest that Kollwitz was familiar with Liebermann's print. But whereas in *Need,* all

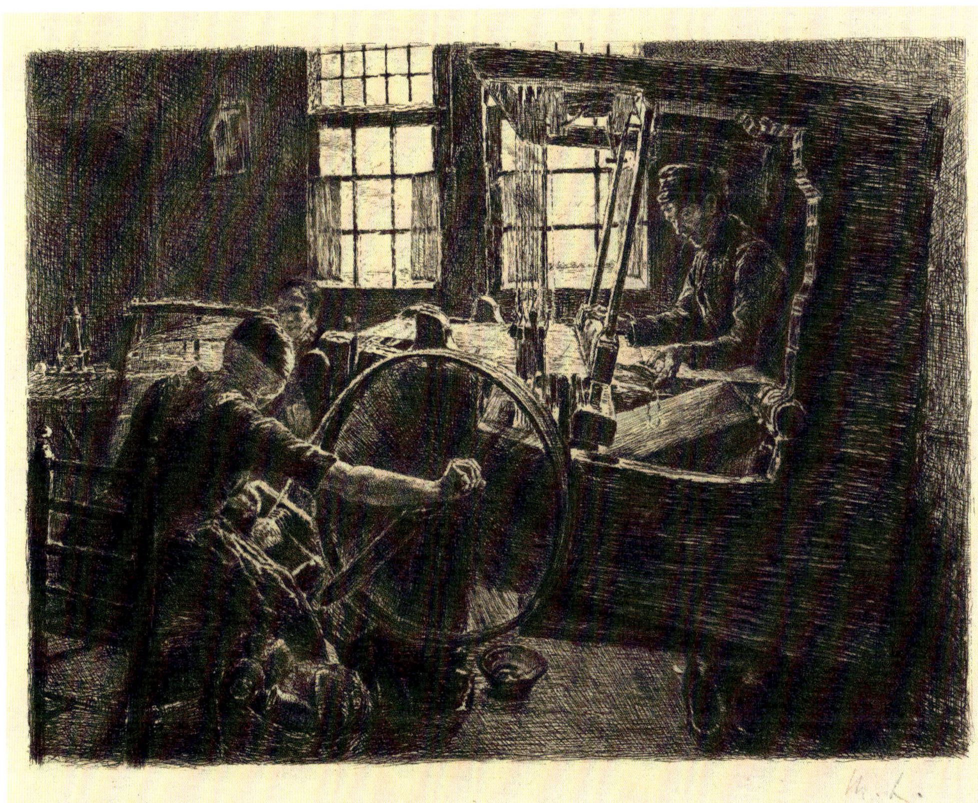

2 Max Liebermann,
The Weaver, 1883, etching,
14.3 × 19.5, Schiefler 2,
Hamburger Kunsthalle

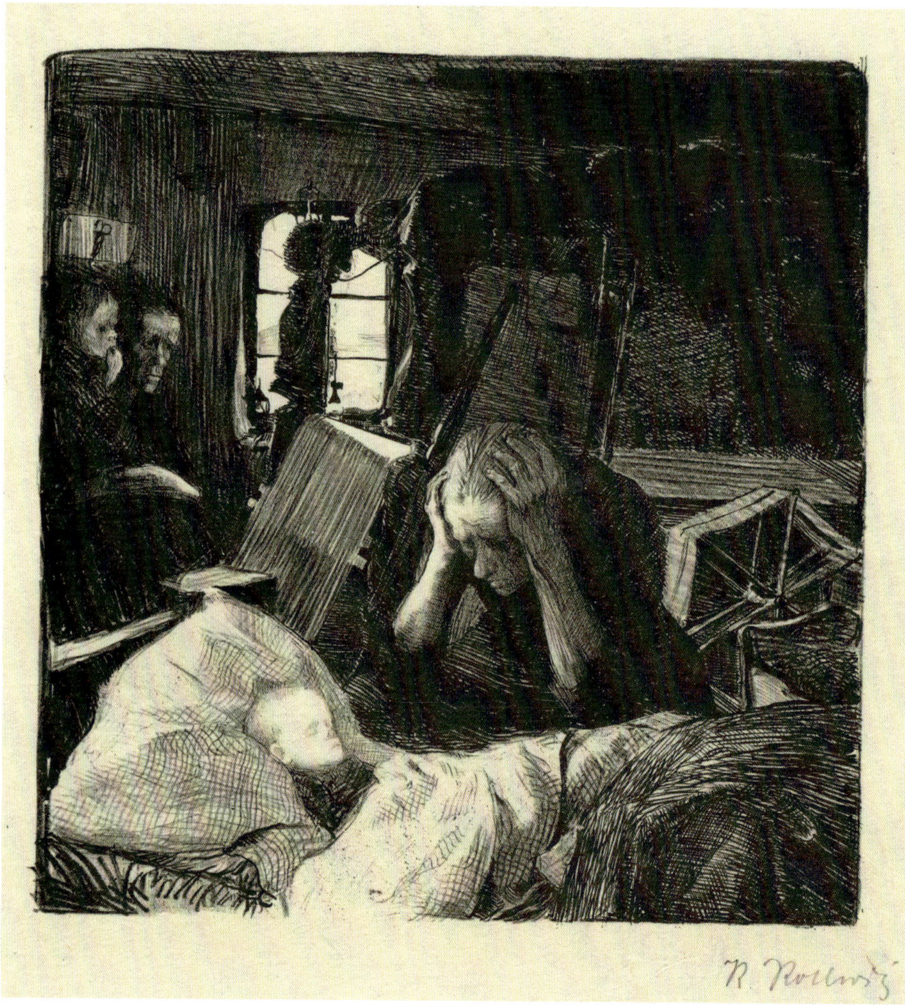

3 Käthe Kollwitz, *Need*, from *A Weavers' Rebellion*, no. 1, 1897, lithograph, 15.4 × 15.3, Klipstein 34, National Gallery of Art, Washington, Rosenwald Collection

work has halted and become pointless in the face of exhaustion, starvation, incurable illness, and hopelessness, in *The Weaver* we see a nuclear family harmoniously at work. Both man and woman are industrious and strong, in control of their simple machines and thus, seemingly, of their lives. Their work dignifies them. Whereas in *The Weaver* the loom is useful, in *Need* it is monstrous. Kollwitz' one small window cannot brighten the room; Liebermann's two bright windows need curtains. Both artists use strong chiaroscuro; Kollwitz, however, dramatically skips the middle range, suggesting a dark cell with indiscernible dimensions far from the world outside, whereas Liebermann lets the middle range predominate so that its variable tonality gives the room air to breathe and a place for its inhabitants in the larger world beyond this room. Both artists use crosshatching, but whereas in *The Weaver* it models figures, objects, and boundaries, thus defining their relations, in *Need* diagonal hatching suggests instability, as if line could follow the law of gravity and let everything slip away, everything except the dying child in the bed and the silently desperate mother at its side. In short, Liebermann's weavers are not forsaken, whereas Kollwitz' weavers are.

Following Kollwitz' perceptive and radicalizing interpretation of Liebermann, we understand how she uses the expressive potential in his print's two strange passages. One is the extreme simultaneous closeness and distance of the mother's and child's heads with their seeming mutual oblivion, even momentary indifference, enhanced by the woman's nearly blindfolding broad headband. The other results from Liebermann's effort to fit and even blend the loom's structure into the right window's frame so as to avoid its potentially disruptive heavy silhouette. Kollwitz takes up Liebermann's motif of close heads to present a woman and young boy at once closely huddled together and yet each alone in their fear and hunger. She matches his loom's light frame and diaphanous warp with the heavy silhouette of her loom's post, from proof to proof changing its shape from relative straightness to something grotesquely resembling a skeleton.[41] The loom is thus directly identified with Death, and Death is what in *Need* becomes of the self-assured male presence in *The Weaver*—hence now also the scissors on the wall. Kollwitz draws attention to the weaknesses and illusions of Liebermann's print and turns them into powerful elements of her own print. In so doing perhaps she inadvertently suggests that Liebermann struggled with his own illusory representation of a content working class far removed from the truth of nineteenth-century labor.[42]

If *Need* and *The Weaver* now conduct a mutually reflective dialogue in the eye of the beholder, Max Klinger's *Bear and Fairy,* 1881 (fig. 4), and

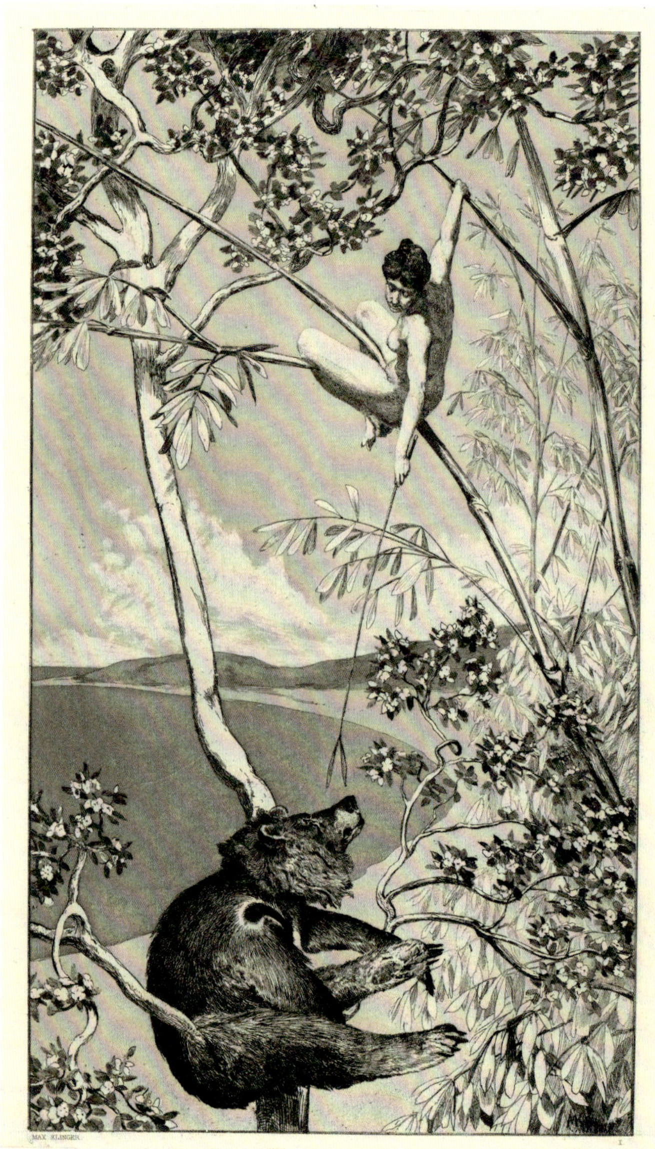

4 Max Klinger, *Bear and Fairy,* 1880, from *Intermezzi,* no. 1, 1881, etching and aquatint, 41.7 × 29, Singer 52, National Gallery of Art, Washington, Gift of the Epstein Family

5 Adolph Menzel, *Bear Pit in the Berlin Zoo,* from *Essays on Stone with Brush and Scraper,* 1851, lithograph, 24.8 × 19.7, National Gallery of Art, Washington, Rosenwald Collection

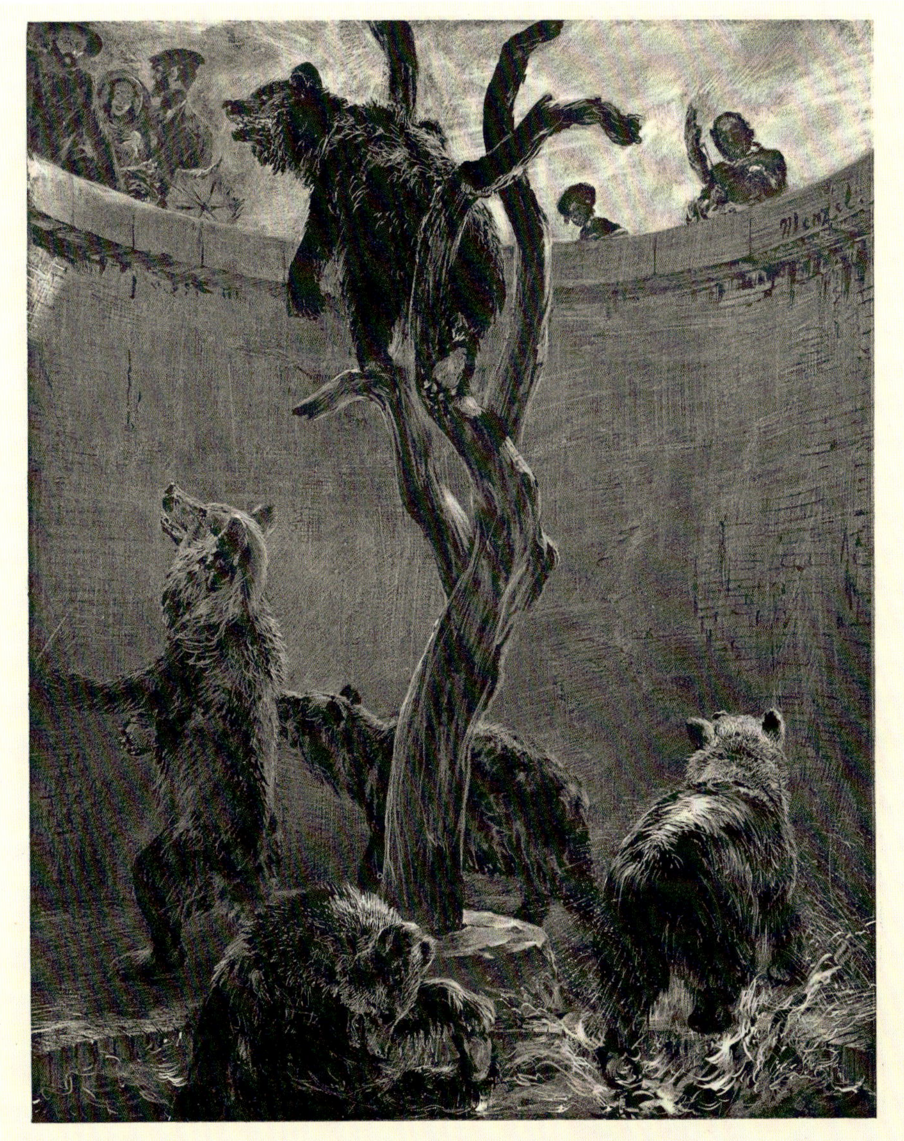
Menzel.

Adolph Menzel's *Bear Pit in the Berlin Zoo,* 1851 (fig. 5), appear to be in a different conversation: Klinger delivering an ironic paraphrase of Menzel's earlier didactic tour de force on the subject of human-animal relations. In 1881 the Berlin Secession lay far in the future; Menzel was fully entering his fame, whereas Klinger was just starting out. Menzel's lithograph depicts a bear castle in the Berlin zoo, a structure that allowed visitors to look at the animals both at ground level and from a platform above.[43] Menzel dramatized the site by cropping the space to establish an unlikely proximity of bears and onlookers, eliminating iron grills on the ground floor, his and our viewpoint, and a high iron railing around the top. At center is a dead tree for the bears to climb; below, a water basin for their diversion. Five bears circle the tree, creating a spiral of increasing attention to their five human counterparts. The bear at the bottom grooms itself while the bear at the top engages a group of two men and one woman. This bear's profile matches that of the man who has turned away, humorously pointing up their difference and indifference and the futility of positing a decorum of relations between man and beast. Humor also contrasts relations between human and pet and pet and beast: shielding herself and her pet from the sun with a parasol, an older bespectacled woman at right holds her lap dog so that it, too, can see the wild animals. We can easily see human illusions about animals and perhaps nature in general as the target of Menzel's humor, but what was his purpose? Arguably he demonstrates it in the boy framed by the treetop. As the one person who observes the bears closely, he is Menzel's model onlooker and perhaps alter ego, gaining perceptual knowledge that he may, or may not, put to use.

Perceptual knowledge, according to Aristotle, by far exceeds the information actively sought in a given situation; however, the distinctions instantly made between what is sought and what is in excess of it do not erase the latter.[44] It stays with us, lingers as a personal or private memory trace, ambience, or echo, to be called up another time, and then perhaps as central and actively sought, not as marginal and accidental.[45] Menzel's bear on the right registers some of this duality. As it leaves the basin, vigorously shaking off water, its casual attention is caught by the boy looking down. What does Klinger, a grown-up version of Menzel's boy, make of all this? The pit's circle becomes a bay on an Asian Pacific coast; the climbing tree intertwines in the most unlikely ornamental twists and turns of branches in full bloom and of no help to the bear, which is stuck where it is. Klinger combines Menzel's grooming bear in the basin with the head of Menzel's standing bear looking straight up at the hooded young woman with sunken parasol. Interpreting this relation, Klinger's bear is a sexually aroused male teased by the object of its lust. The naked fairy lightly swings on bamboo and tickles the bear, her outstretched arms measuring and balancing her pleasure in the teasing and her risk of falling, and falling prey. She, too, is hampered, for Klinger has made her wingless, and the situation we see might bring about a bear hug on the ground. For the time being, bear and fairy are supported and suspended by vegetation twisted into ornament. The print invites the viewer to roam over the emphatically two-dimensional, cropped image, using his or her storehouse of perceptual knowledge, as well as the *Bildungsbürger*'s historical knowledge of pastoral pastimes, rococo chinoiserie, nineteenth-century *japonisme,* and more.[46] The invitation is itself a tease, for we cannot help accepting it. In short, in *Bear and Fairy* and *Bear Pit,* Klinger's seductive and playful fantasy and Menzel's didacticism face each other in a conversation that credits Menzel with unrealized ideas that would later inspire others. But Klinger rejects Menzel's humorous insistence in *Bear Pit* on the strict observation of nature rather than illusory, even ridiculous, empathy with it.[47] Whereas Julius Meyer-Graefe, a champion of modern art, regretted that "Menzel is almost a genius in the skill with which he silences his own genius," Klinger, despite his apparent irreverence in *Bear and Fairy,* pays playful critical homage to Menzel.[48]

If we consider these early prints for their metaphorical (Menzel and Liebermann) or symbolist (Kollwitz and Klinger) practices, and if we bear in mind Klinger's and Liebermann's focus on artistic imagination and yet also on the empirical model in nature or society, we come to understand a largely contradictory aspect in symbolist art in Protestant northern and eastern Germany. Unlike many of their French, Bavarian, and Belgian colleagues, these artists avoided Christian symbolism. They were Aristotelians, as it were, looking for and representing the potentiality in the empirical model in nature. And this combination of perceptual knowledge and imagination explains in part the tremendous importance of Menzel as a model, but also as a model to overcome, for Klinger, Kollwitz, and Liebermann. On the whole, formally Klinger's and Kollwitz' early prints share much more with each other than they do with Liebermann's prints. And Liebermann's etchings share more subject matter with Kollwitz' than with Klinger's. Liebermann moved formally from both as he developed such impressionist printmaking techniques as a seeming sketchiness (see fig. 1) and erasures (see fig. 15). But throughout, Liebermann challenged deeply ingrained notions of "German interiority," "thoroughness," and contemplative immersion in work, and he did so from within his knowledge of this tradition.[49] He accomplished this subversion even as he emphasized his work ethic, which in principle was close to Menzel's motto: "Not a day without drawing."

THRESHOLDS

In representations of interiors, the threshold indicates one of three possible situations, either by itself or in combination with the others: the view from inside to outside, from outside to inside, or from inside to inside.[50] With varying metaphorical weight, such transitions are found in the three artists' renderings of the world inside with its walls, steps, and gates. Max Klinger's *At the Gate,* 1887 (fig. 6), represents a threshold of transgression rich in warnings ignored by the two protagonists. The magnificent wrought-iron gate vainly holds captive motifs of sexual passion—pinnacles, seahorses, dragons, snakes, flower festoons, and primitivistic masks.[51] The lush vegetation beyond the gate mocks such control, the distant tree doubling as a faun's face, reminiscent of Klinger's borrowings from Goya.[52] Surely, here reason sleeps. In his fervor the passionate suitor rushes to kiss the pleasantly surprised woman's hand and loses his hat, a comic detail Klinger first used in his cycle *A Glove.* The woman's tiny step forward, a lingering at the threshold between private and public spaces, suggests an awareness of this fateful moment that the man brushes aside. The threshold is mirrored in the break from light to shadow, and so inserts the moment of arrest into the narrative flow: the image is split vertically in half, so that the couple's encounter happens in the daylight made somewhat sinister by the tree-mask and the man's leap forward below the wall. The dense chestnut tree, the shadowed sidewalk, and the stone marker on the right point to what comes next, the lovers' secret meeting at night on the mansion's lakeside terrace (fig. 7). The passionate embrace of *In the Park* repeats but also flips the dynamic of *At the Gate.* The dramatic motion is now from right to left. As threshold, the balustrade marks the vertical split between light and dark, inside and outside, garden and wilderness, woman and man. Now he crosses the threshold over the curving balustrade, the massive tree behind him following his example. As a tree branch above them rises phallically and the woman's white hand draws her lover in and down, his knee pressing against her, the viewer's imagination is not much challenged to find a way into the bedroom scene that follows in the cycle *A Love.* The fundamental motion "at the Gate" is from inside to outside, and "in the Park" it is from outside to inside.[53]

Klinger's *Shame,* 1885 (fig. 8), compares interestingly with Kollwitz' *At the Church Wall,* 1893 (fig. 9). Both show women at a low point, which means something different for each in her social class. In *Shame* a pregnant upper-class woman walks along a brightly illuminated wall, casting her concealing shadow on it. Another unshakable shadow accompanies her, mimicking her gait, loose clothes, and folded arms. Larger than life, the figure of Public Shame exhibits her to the people above. All the women

6 Max Klinger, *At the Gate,* from *A Love (Eine Liebe),* no. 3, 1887, etching and engraving (proof state iii/vii), 40.9 × 27, Singer 159, National Gallery of Art, Washington, Gift of the Epstein Family Collection 2001.132.18

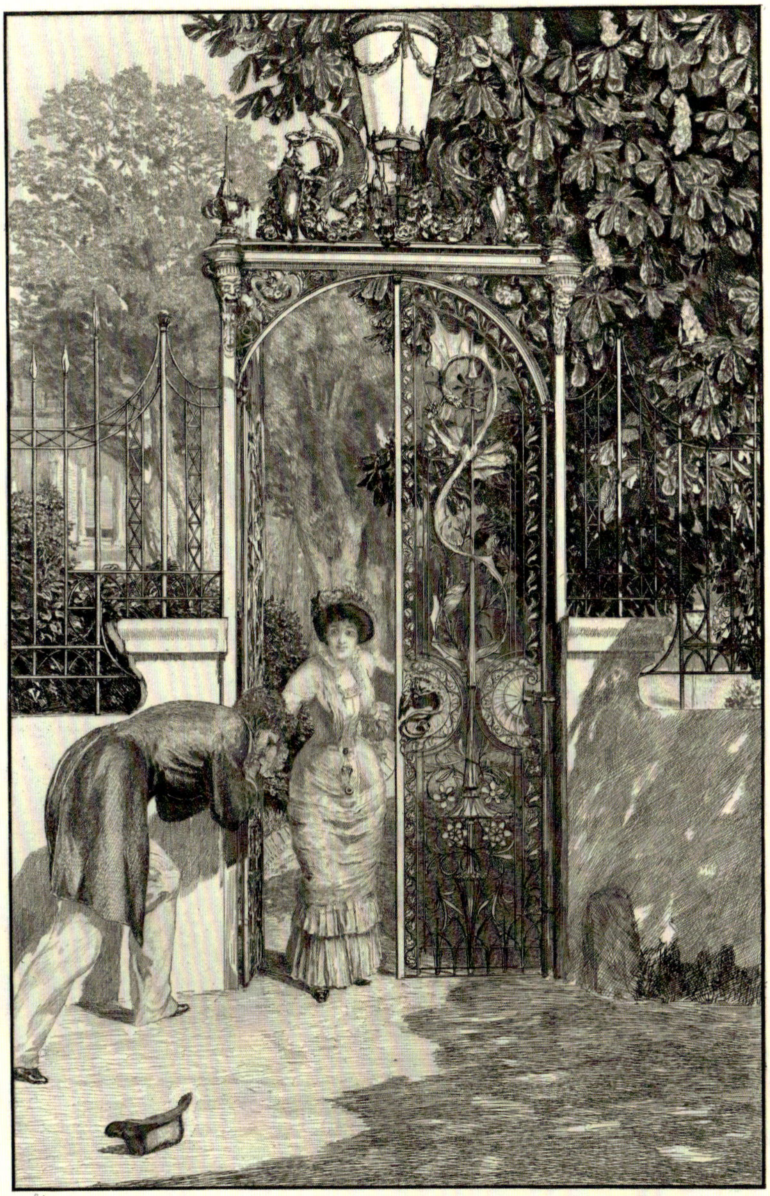

M. Klinger
Berlin 18[illegible]

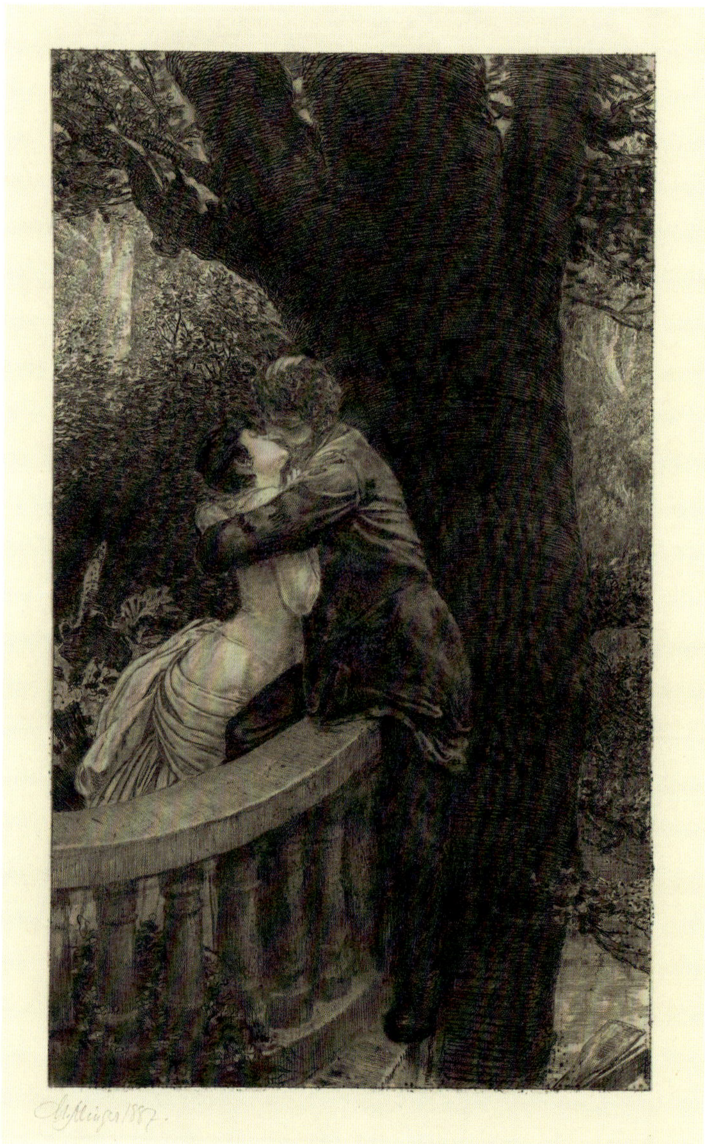

7 Max Klinger, *In the Park,* from *A Love (Eine Liebe),* no. 4, 1887, etching and engraving (state iv / vii), 41.2 × 24.9, Singer 160, National Gallery of Art, Washington, Gift of the Epstein Family Collection, 2001.132.19

8 Max Klinger, *Shame,* from *A Love (Eine Liebe),* no. 9, 1885, etching, engraving, and aquatint (state iv / vii), 41.5 × 26.6, Singer 165, National Gallery of Art, Washington, Gift of the Epstein Family Collection, 2001.132.24

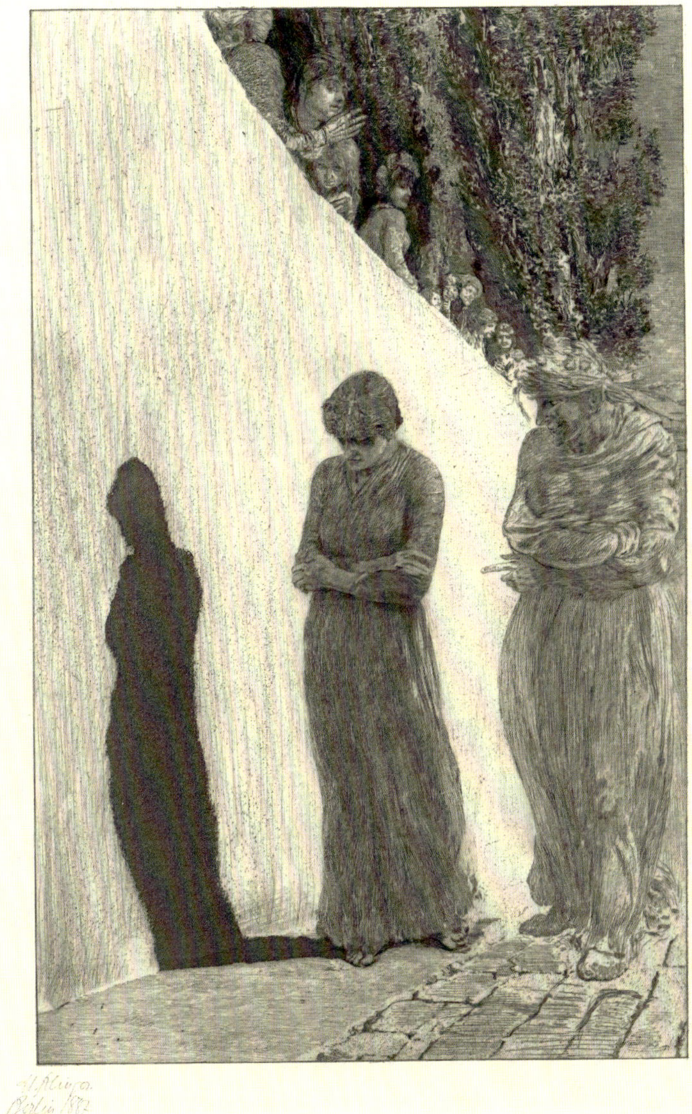

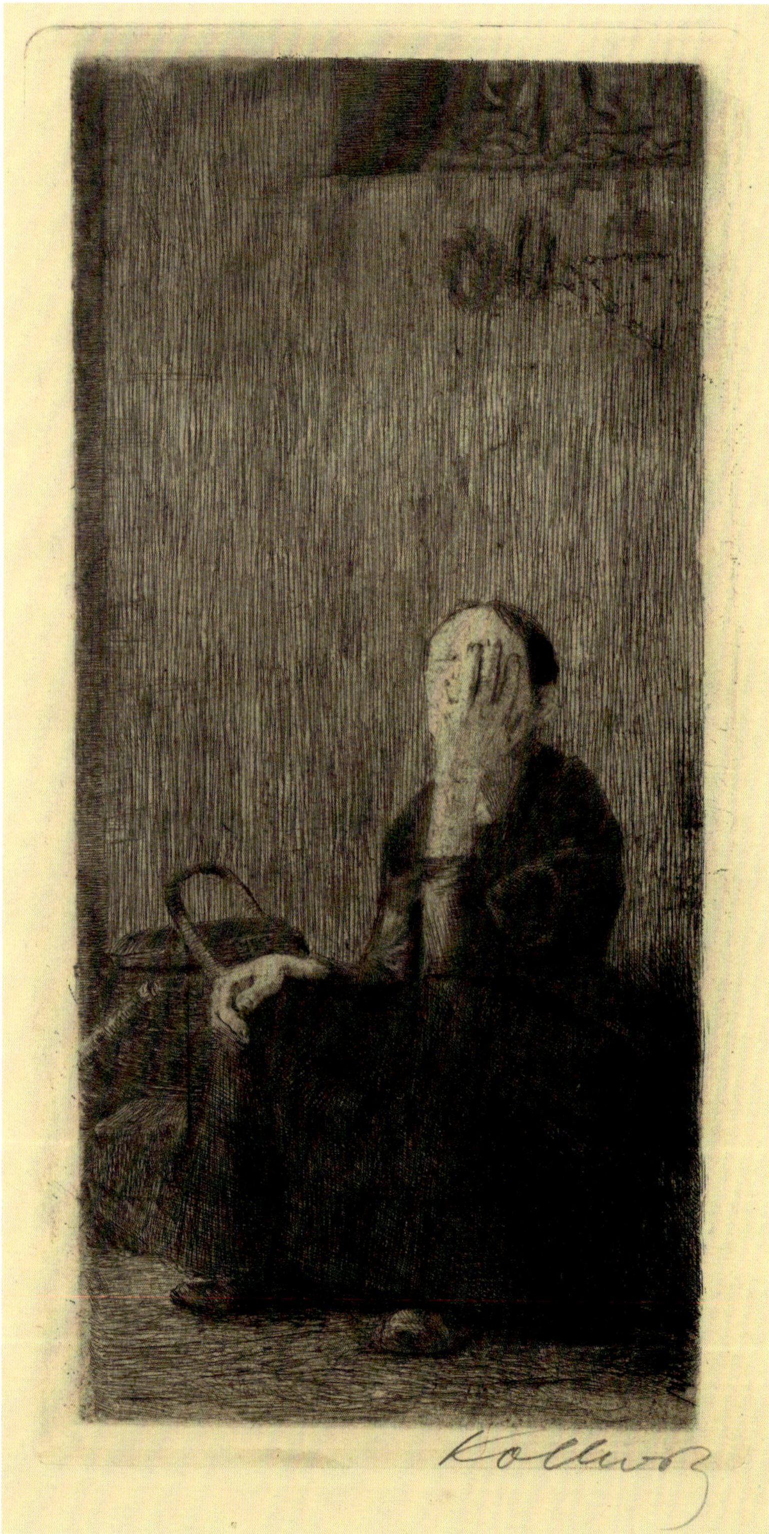
Kollwitz

stare and laugh at her in contempt, warning their children against her bad example. Moral self-righteousness and condemnation correspond here to the composition's "high" and "low," distantly echoing Menzel's *Bear Pit*. The two registers converge in the figure of Shame. So far, this image seems to be all about privacy dragged into the public sphere. But this wall along a river promenade also does something for, not only to, the woman, for unlike her two unshakable shadows, her weightless form seems to be imprinted in it. Indeed, her bowed head and folded arms calmly suggest the futility of self-protection against public humiliation. All alone by now, nine scenes into the story, she appears to accept her fate. Like a low-relief carving in the river's retaining wall, she has become an unlikely monument and in the final scene will die in childbirth.[54]

Whatever one thinks of Klinger's attempt at artistic redemption, it is clearly absent from Kollwitz' *At the Church Wall*. The exhausted worker has been sitting for a while on a raised footer, one large hand on her right knee, the other propping up her head on her left knee. Her eyes are closed. Perhaps resting, perhaps even asleep, she will not get up soon. Her basket looks almost forgotten, though not like something she can afford to forget. In her coarsely patched dark dress she looks poor, on the verge of begging. Does her wall do something for her? No. Its merciless, streaky graininess threatens to scrape her back, and she doesn't even lean against it. Like Klinger's woman, she knows she is utterly alone, but unlike the pregnant figure, she even lacks the support of a wall. Exactly above her, amply carved folds of drapery play around the feet of a human figure in a niche, usually considered to be a carved saint or Madonna, but Kollwitz' suggestive cropping leaves everything to surmise. Just below, vague marks on the wall do nothing to mediate sculpture and woman.[55] In placement and genre the two are "high" and "low" and entirely indifferent to each other. Yet the sculpture is sheltered as the woman is not. This may be Kollwitz' point: this woman does not expect anyone's attention; she keeps to herself, and we, in turn, know nothing about her. Such is her isolated interiority in the bright light of day that interpretations have ranged from identifying her as the fallen Gretchen in Goethe's *Faust* to an anonymous homeless woman.[56] The image seems entirely without narrative until we begin to think about her placement in Marxist terms. *Bau* and *Überbau*, foundation and superstructure, suggest the narrative of revolution that interested Kollwitz in these years.[57] She forces us to shift our attention from the statue to the overlooked woman, thus from bourgeois culture and interiority to social reality. Several of the changes made to the plate from state to state and edition to edition pertain to the woman's face, largely unseen behind her hand, and others to the marks

9 Käthe Kollwitz, *At the Church Wall*, 1893, etching with drypoint, 25.2 × 13, Klipstein 19, National Gallery of Art, Washington, Rosenwald Collection

on the wall below the sculpture. Serving perhaps as a trace of past human engagement with the sculpture, the marks appear to be patches, stains, and illegible graffiti, thus corresponding to the woman's part-covered, part-blank face.[58] In this way Kollwitz implies a mutual cancellation of the views from outside in and inside out, as if to say that this woman exists in neither public nor private sphere.

As a study in thresholds, Liebermann's *Child at the Door,* 1891 (fig. 10), recalls seventeenth-century Dutch genre scenes of women and children at home. But here the furnishings and details of everyday life that play such an important role in a work by Pieter de Hooch (such as *The Bedroom,* 1658–1660, National Gallery of Art) are absent. Presenting a sequence of four or five thresholds, Liebermann offers a view from inside (a room) to inside (another room) to outside (the street) to inside (a garden and house across the street). In the second room, just beyond an inconveniently raised threshold, we see a woman crouching and, with minimal support, encouraging a small child to climb the steps leading outside. Liebermann scales the view on this child's adventure to the child's perspective. The angle is so low that the effort to master the huge steps measures the desire to climb them. In fact, everything above the level of three feet is dissolved into lines and scribbles. Liebermann also contains the woman in a space at a level just below the range of the toddler's perception—hence the strangely raised threshold in the foreground, the wide and empty street; hence also the neighbor about to bend down to encourage the child. For the grown-up viewer all this amounts to another threshold, that of unlearning assumptions about the spaces of everyday life: about the relation of inside and outside, private and public. What we know about them is of no importance to the child; what the child knows about them, we have forgotten. Far from advocating an innocent eye, Liebermann's print is a playfully focused reminder of how one's relations to inside and outside tend to be conceptual rather than perceptual, and therefore normative as well.

10 Max Liebermann, *Child at the Door,* 1891, etching with drypoint, 25.3 × 13.3, Schiefler 17, Fine Arts Museums of San Francisco, Achenbach Foundation for Graphic Arts 1963.30.34010

WITNESS, OBSERVER, VOYEUR

Privacy is also the right *not* to bear witness either against oneself or others.[59] In turn, witness may be replaced by noncommittal observation or even voyeurism. This is the case in Klinger's three plates *A Mother I, II,* and *III* of 1883 (figs. 11–13), which form an expository narrative sequence: domestic abuse, murder and suicide, and court trial.[60] All three images are vertical compositions of sites without a firm or measurable ground, each reiterating the woman's abysmal situation, as the plot moves from narrow tenement balcony to upper-class urban space to courtroom. The situation in *Mother I* recalls

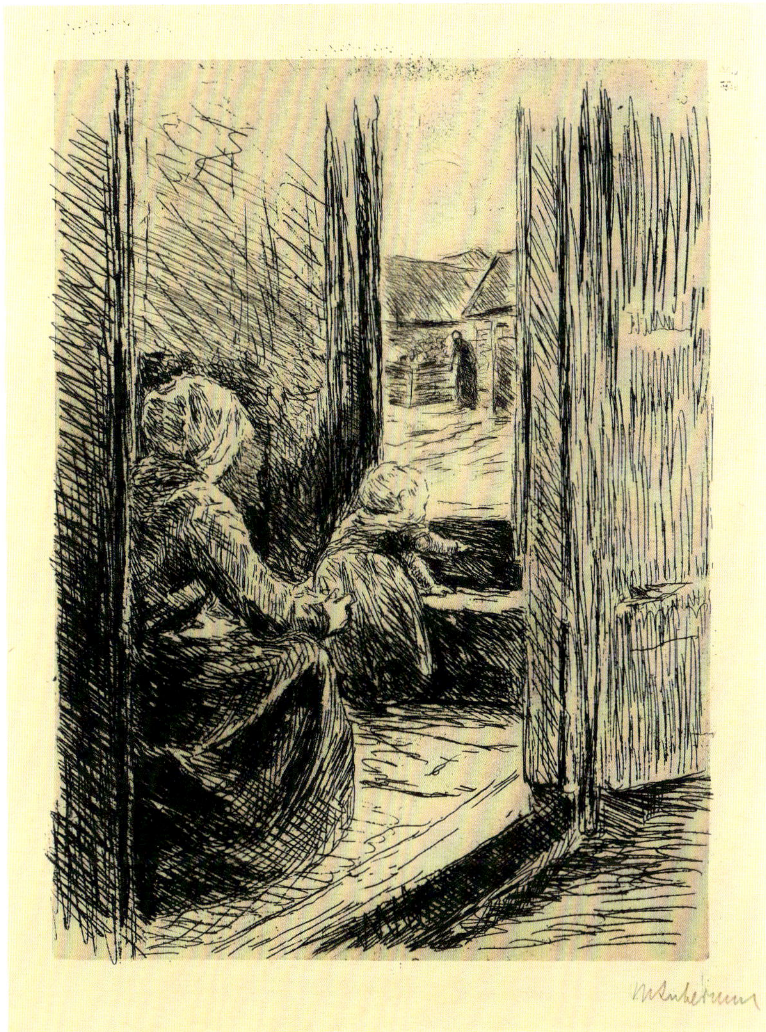

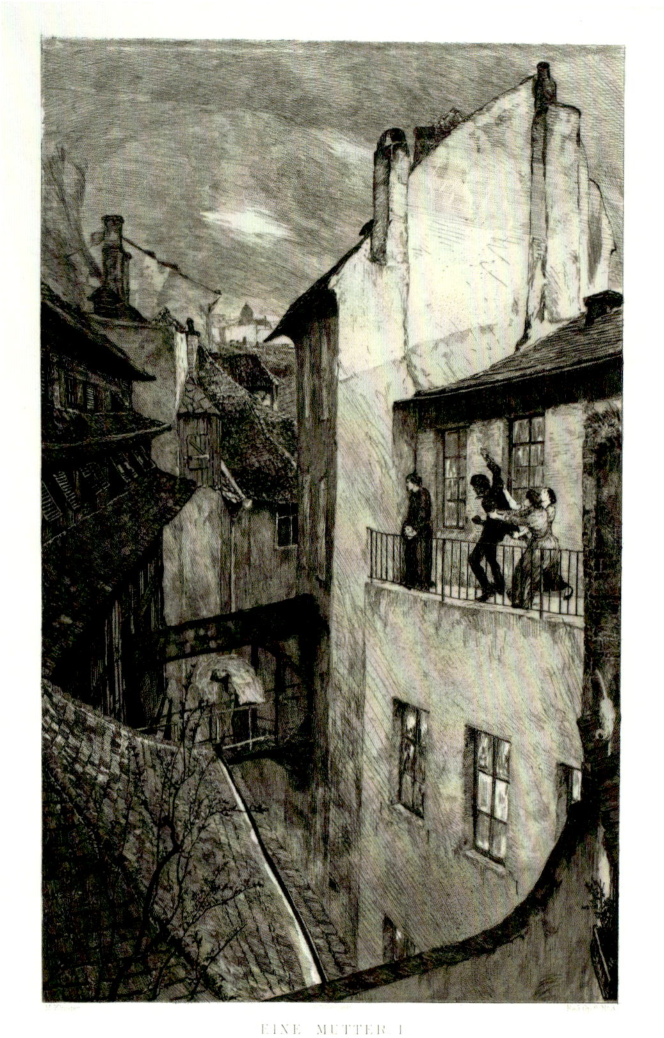

11 Max Klinger, *A Mother I,* from *Dramas (Dramen),* no. 3, 1883, etching and aquatint, 45.3 × 31.8, Singer 149, Princeton University Art Museum, Gift of Carl E. Schorske in honor of Professor Hajo Holborn

12 Max Klinger, *A Mother II,* from *Dramas (Dramen),* no. 4, 1883, etching and aquatint, 45.4 × 31.8, Singer 150, Princeton University Art Museum, Gift of Carl E. Schorske in honor of Professor Hajo Holborn

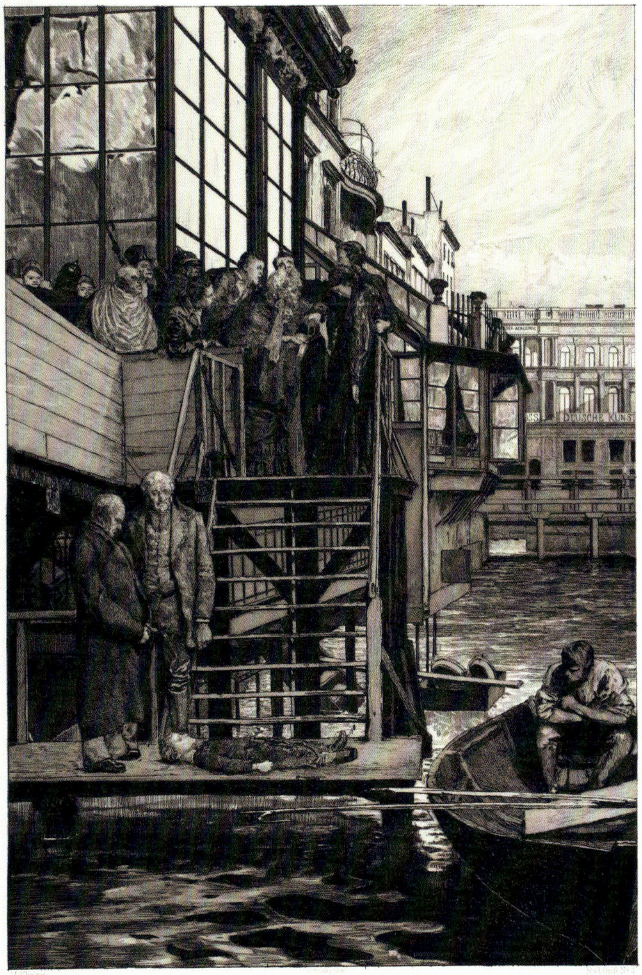

EINE MUTTER II

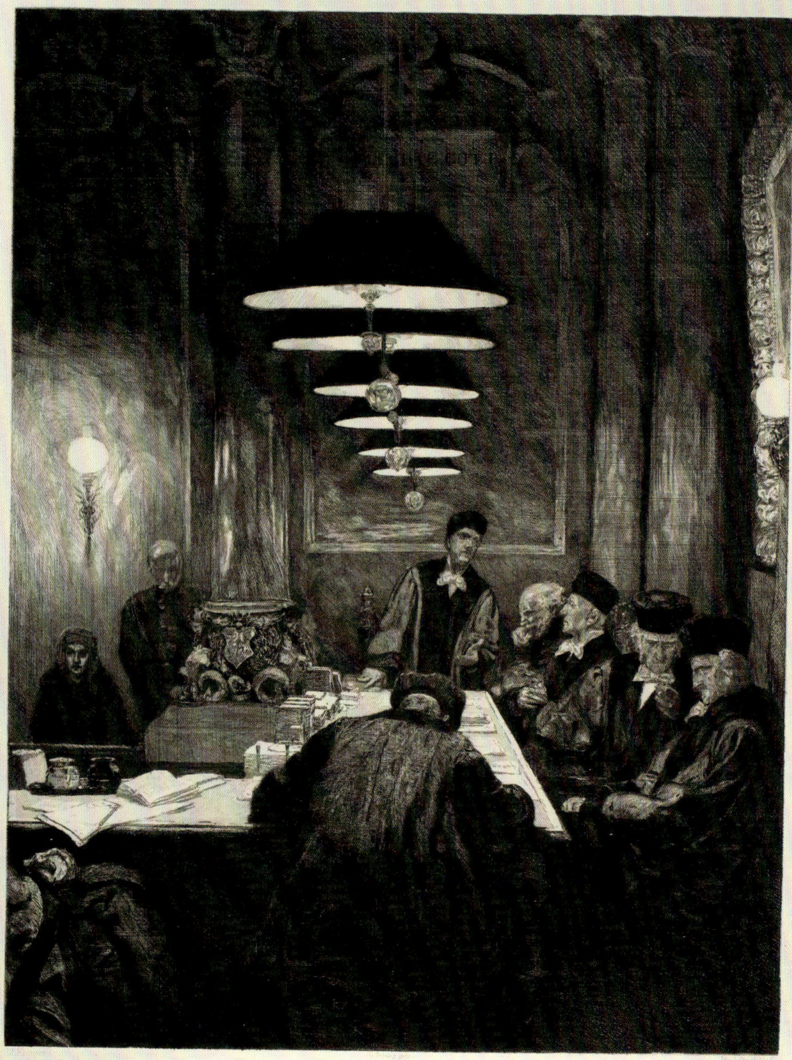

EINE MUTTER III

Zola's novel *L'assommoir* (1877), set in the tenement slums of Paris, as well as Kollwitz' later account about one of her husband's working-class patients: "Frau Pankopf was here. Had an entirely black eye. Her husband had been in a rage."[61] Klinger's series offers no resolution. We find the woman literally cornered in each image. A Berlin newspaper article from the summer of 1881 was Klinger's inspiration: a woman and child attempted double suicide by drowning, which left the son dead and the mother his surviving murderer. Klinger imbues the story with a tragic tone, even as in *A Mother I* the scene of domestic violence on the balcony barely draws attention from the laundress or the cat. Contrasting with the rickety and labyrinthine structures there, the rigorously and intricately griddled site in *A Mother II* suggests the *Schlossfreiheit* on the Spree across from the Imperial Palace, once a residential address but by then housing upper-class shops and cafés.[62] In this vertically oriented, rationally measured space horizontality refers to death, water, accusation, curiosity, and, in the boatman, perhaps the melancholy contemplation of it all, or even outraged brooding over the status quo rather than the woman's guilt. Like a large billboard poster, her unseen face is displaced to the reflection of sad, gazeless features in the large windowpanes to the upper left, while the white, blank stare of the other panes matches the conduct of the crowd barely contained by the police. Only three men pay quiet respect to the boy's corpse.

In 1899 the art historian Max Schmid commented on *A Mother III:* "If only they send her to prison. There she at least has her daily bread and sleep—there she is saved from the perpetual fear of abuse."[63] The courtroom scene borrows heavily from Honoré Daumier's caricatures of lawyers, and the woman is barely visible to the left of the vertical axis of justice. Whatever the prosecutor argues, it will not go to the core of what matters to her. Klinger's sympathetic style of reportage links the always formally and thematically sidelined mother with the figures around the boy's dripping corpse and especially with the man in the boat. The prominent stairs in *A Mother II* and the scale of courtroom lamps refer to the motto that prefaces the series *Dramas:* "But we are fated, / To find no foothold, no rest." The lines are from Friedrich Hölderlin's poem "*Hyperions Schicksalslied*" (Hyperion's song of destiny),[64] which Klinger would illustrate and interpret in 1890 as one of Johannes Brahms' *Fünf ernste Gesänge* (Five serious songs):[65]

13 Max Klinger, *A Mother III*, from *Dramas (Dramen)*, no. 5, 1884, etching, 45.4 × 35.9, Singer 151, Princeton University Art Museum, Gift of Carl E. Schorske in honor of Professor Hajo Holborn

But we are fated
    To find no foothold, no rest,
        And suffering mortals
            Dwindle and fall
                Headlong from one

Hour to the next,
Hurled like water
From ledge to ledge
Downward for years to the
vague abyss.

Humanity's tragically fated blind fall from ledge to ledge, which the gods will or cannot hinder, also pertains to the lives of the rich. *In Flagranti,* 1883 (fig. 14), offers an alternative plot to *In the Park.* A husband has just killed his wife's lover. For the surrealist Giorgio de Chirico *In Flagranti* represented the "romantic sense of modern life" in a cinematic idiom, "where in precisely the same way, characters of tragedy and of modern life become identical in magic moments within scenes of terrifying reality."[66] The print is formally brilliant, although the subject may seem trite today. Klinger did not intend a humorous or cynical contrast within the series between the banal in *In Flagranti* and the tragic in the sequence *A Mother I–III.* He had a keen sense for the tragic and the comic, and he took both too seriously to mix them carelessly. He sometimes linked them dialectically, especially in series including his self-portrait (such as *A Glove* and *A Love*). But he had no doubt that the rich, among whom he counted, could suffer. The series is entirely serious. The splayed legs of the cropped corpse on the terrace's moonlit steps thus recall humanity's fall from cliff to cliff in Hölderlin's poem, as does the murderer above—Klinger's high definition of decorative rustication down the corner of the mansion, each rough-hewn ashlar block resembling a ledge or cliff, one above the other, both connects and isolates the men. Klinger moves the woman out of the men's relentless vertical axis and into the lush vegetation.[67] Socially condemned and divinely fated, in Klinger's concept of the tragic, the lovers' secret meeting prompts the murder just as the balcony scene in *A Mother I* must lead to murder and suicide. In this way Klinger's *Dramas* are suspended ambiguously between Hölderlin's ode and Kollwitz' lapidary: "Always the same old song. Illness, joblessness, drink," and violence.[68]

14 Max Klinger, *In Flagranti,* from *Dramas (Dramen),* no. 1, 1883, etching, 45.5 × 32.1, Singer 147, Princeton University Art Museum, Gift of Carl E. Schorske in honor of Professor Hajo Holborn

A middle-class observer sits alone at one end of a table in Liebermann's *"Kellergarten" in Rosenheim,* 1895 (fig. 15), a relaxed impressionist scene of leisurely modern life. The poesy of mingling conversation, fading in and out of hearing, floats in the air like the sunny erasures in Liebermann's print. He wraps this world of part-focused, part-distracted togetherness in a casual but regular semicircle, anchoring the scene's multiple privacies for the viewer. Only the waitresses cast their eyes and ears widely. The image's subtle dynamic implicates the viewer as just another figure seated

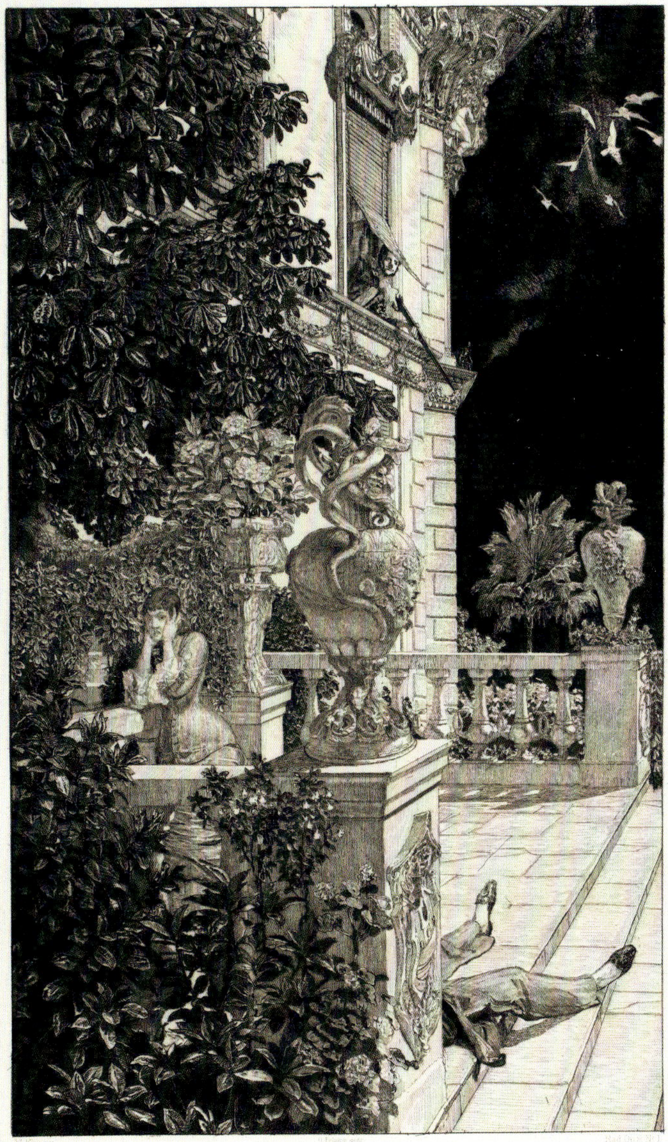

IN FLAGRANTI

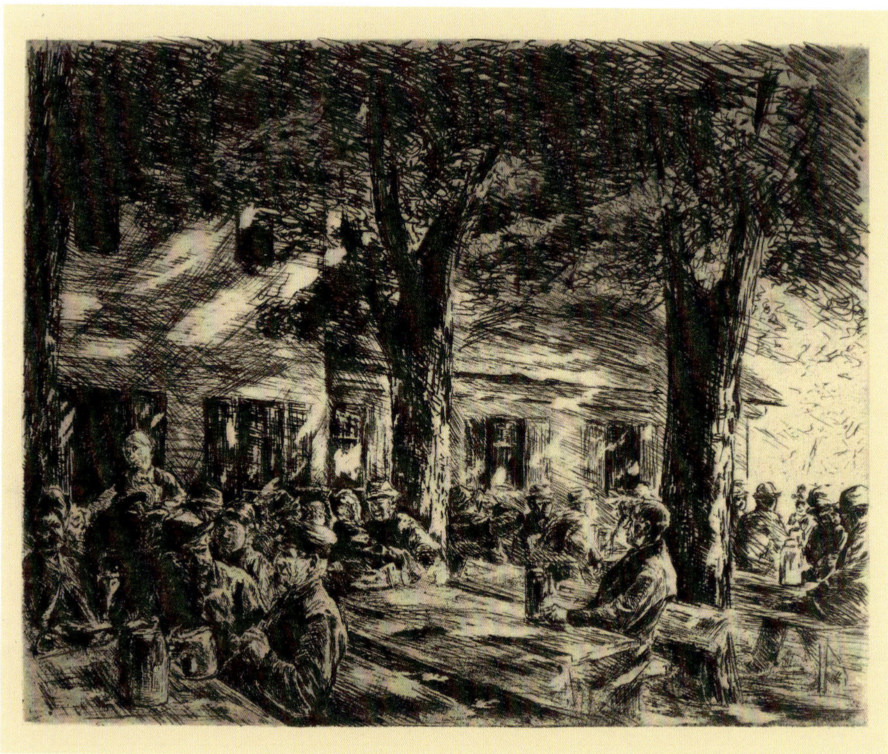

15 Max Liebermann, *"Kellergarten" in Rosenheim,* 1895, etching (state iv / iv), 19 × 23.1, Schiefler 35, National Gallery of Art, Washington, Ailsa Mellon Bruce Fund 1992.47.1

in the beer garden, like the observer whose back is turned toward us in the scene. Kollwitz lived in Munich between 1888 and 1889, studying painting under Ludwig Herterich (1856–1932) and printmaking at the newly formed etching association. There she had ample opportunity to see Munich school paintings of tavern scenes, peasant kitchens, beer gardens, and outdoor cafés teasing out the "psychogram" of simple wooden tables and benches, single or grouped villagers or burghers, and isolated or precariously placed tableware.[69] Their influence is also found in Liebermann's paintings and prints of outdoor cafés and beer gardens of his Munich years, 1878–1884, and translated into an impressionist idiom here in his *"Kellergarten" in Rosenheim.* Our casual inclusion in this scene, however, could not be more different from our unlikely and hidden presence in Kollwitz' *Scene from "Germinal,"* 1893 (fig. 16). Missing in the work by Liebermann is the extreme tension in the placement of mass and weight of pictorial elements that we see in Kollwitz' scene.[70] This composition grew out of Kollwitz' reading of Zola's novel *Germinal* (1885) and her first print series based on the novel, a project that resulted in this single print. Étienne, who leads the miners in their strike, and Chaval, exemplar of the brute bred by conditions in the mines, confront each other over Catherine, this time to fight, and next time, when trapped together in the flooded mine, to kill. The almost endlessly long tavern shows Catherine both as a frightened observer and as the object of the fight standing against the door and yet leaning forward as if to shout, as she does in the novel: "Look out! He's got his knife!"—at last betraying her preference for one man over the other.[71] Like a ball of energy the men roll in the pool of diffused light. Other onlookers, the innkeeper Rasseneur, his wife, and the Russian anarchist Souvarine, are, if anywhere, where we are, unseen. In several years of work, including sketching in taverns, making preparatory drawings, and relentlessly and self-critically editing proofs, Kollwitz paid the utmost attention to the setting, with its sparse, partly overturned furnishings, and to the placement of the figures to achieve an image of explosive tension. The horizontal format, the low ceiling, and the figures' poses—Catherine bent forward and the men fighting below the low bench that spans the back wall—suggest the corridors of the mines. This single image thus captures much more about the world in Zola's novel than a single moment of personal rivalry. There as here the men's struggle allegorizes and yet privatizes the political cause of struggle for justice and against exploitation.

Kollwitz abandoned the projected *Germinal* series in favor of *A Weavers' Rebellion,* inspired by a performance she saw of Gerhart Hauptmann's play *Die Weber* (The weavers) in February 1893. Yet Zola's scenes of the miners' three or four leaders conspiring to organize a strike and sabotage the mines

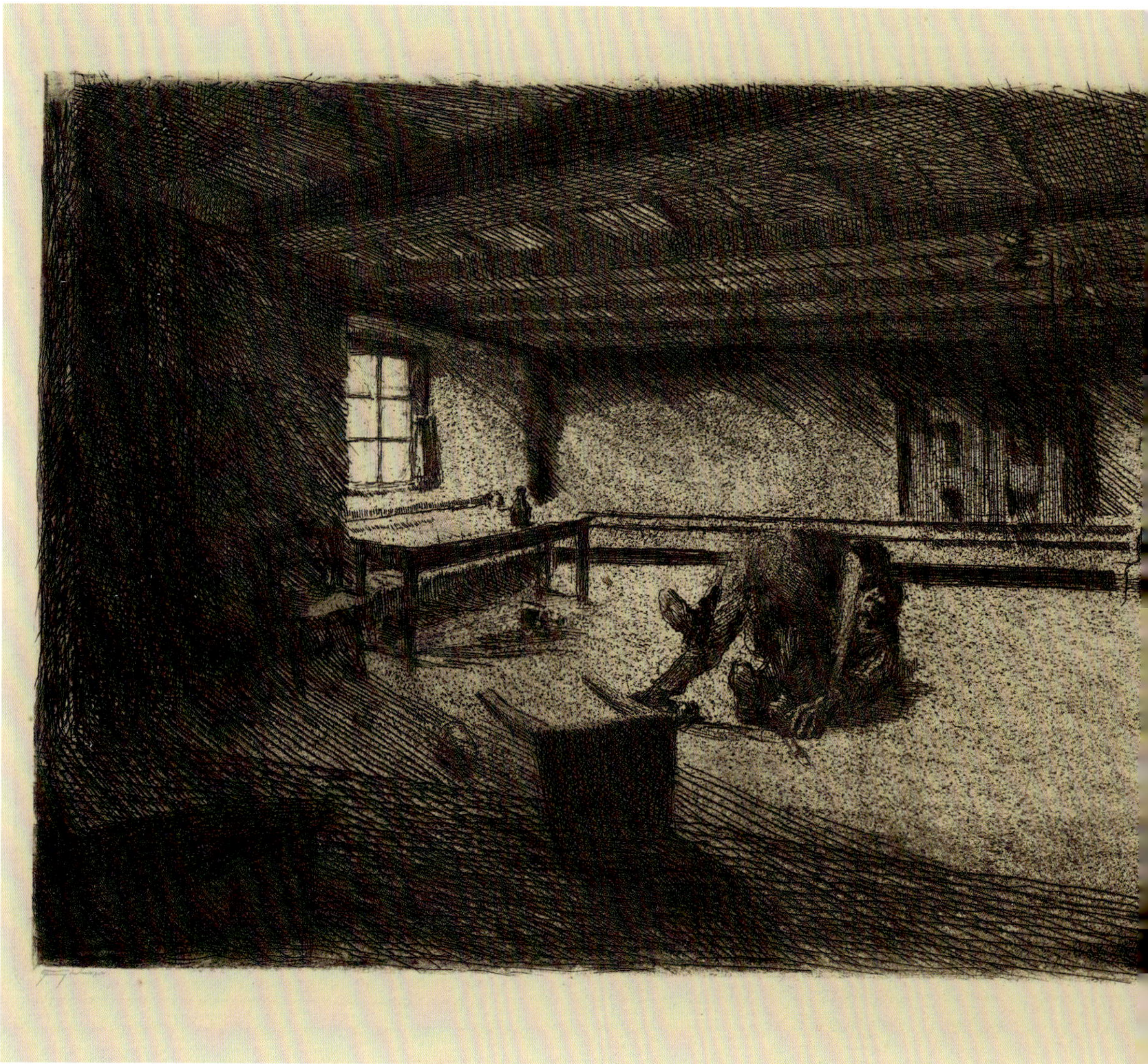

16 Käthe Kollwitz, *Scene from "Germinal,"* 1893, etching with drypoint, 22.5 × 53, Klipstein 21, National Gallery of Art, Washington, Rosenwald Collection

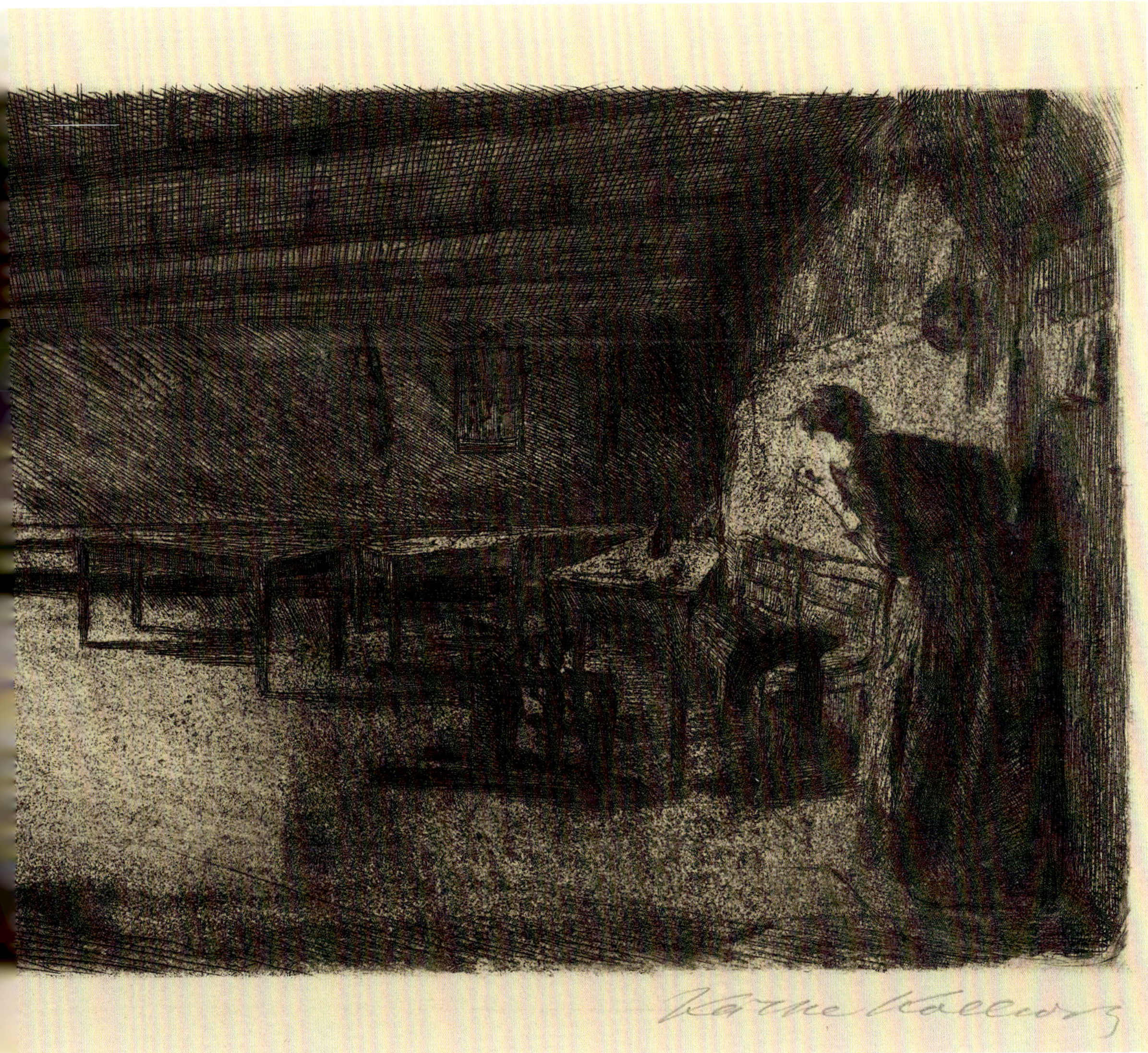

reverberate with several prints Kollwitz made between 1888, when *Germinal* appeared in German, and 1895.[72] In these, as in *Scene from "Germinal,"* Kollwitz deepens the common use of "milieu as portrait" or even as "psychogram" in nineteenth-century genre imagery by presenting a force field of tremendous energies.[73] The margins of several proofs for these and related scenes now at the Dresden Kupferstichkabinett are filled with Kollwitz' self-criticisms, which focus on the dual goal of technical perfection and expressive intensity.[74]

If in her early work it is the entire image that emphatically and powerfully speaks its thematic, later she would often choose the monumentalized human figure as her primary form of expression. Kollwitz' well-known etching *Woman with a Dead Child,* 1903 (fig. 17), contracts the most fundamental human relation in her oeuvre, that of mother to son, in such a way that the fight between men in *Scene from "Germinal"* becomes a mother's violent grief over her son's death. The world inside her is truly that of their joined bodies. There is no other world in this print, and the fated distance separating mother and son in Klinger's *A Mother II* is unthinkable. As Kollwitz' friend Beate Bonus-Jeep later recalled, seeing *Woman with Dead Child* so shocked her that she had to leave the exhibition gallery to collect herself. As in Freud's definition of the uncanny as something come to light that should have remained hidden, "pure passion itself, the force, sleeping contained in the mother animal, is yielding itself to the eye here, is fixed by Käthe Kollwitz as by someone free to reach under the ultimate layers."[75] For Bonus-Jeep, who recognized Kollwitz' son Peter as the model for the corpse, the image forewarned of his death in World War I. In 1903, however, the image was autobiographical in a different sense, for Kollwitz also used herself as a model: "I drew myself in the mirror holding him in my arm. This was very exhausting, and I could not but groan. A little child's voice said consolingly: 'Be quiet, Mother, it will be very beautiful.'"[76] Strange to say, it is, but we would rather not know of this situation. One wonders how she could bear the confluence in it of anticipatory witnessing, detached observation, and also voyeurism. Here Kollwitz' "free reach under the ultimate layers" perhaps exploited what Jürgen Habermas has called the kernel of truthful intimacy and of voluntary, loving, and free relations within the private sphere otherwise fraught by ambition, class or status, economic imbalance, unequal gender roles, and authority of adults over minors.[77]

Liebermann transfers the imagined or real violation of trust in the private sphere to the level of biblical narrative, striking nevertheless very close to home. His two versions of *Samson and Delilah,* 1906, show two naked studio models on the floor, without any comfortably historicizing props or costume, barely backed by a multiple-use curtain. In the second version (fig. 18) he edits

17 Käthe Kollwitz, *Woman with a Dead Child,* 1903, etching and softground etching with drypoint, proof impression worked up with graphite, charcoal, and gold wash, 41.7 × 47.2, Klipstein 72, National Gallery of Art, Washington, Gift of Philip and Lynn Straus, in Honor of the 50th Anniversary of the National Gallery of Art

18 Max Liebermann, *Samson and Delilah,* 1906, etching, 21.5 × 28, Schiefler 55, Smith College Museum of Art, Northampton, Mass., annonymous gift SC1050:45

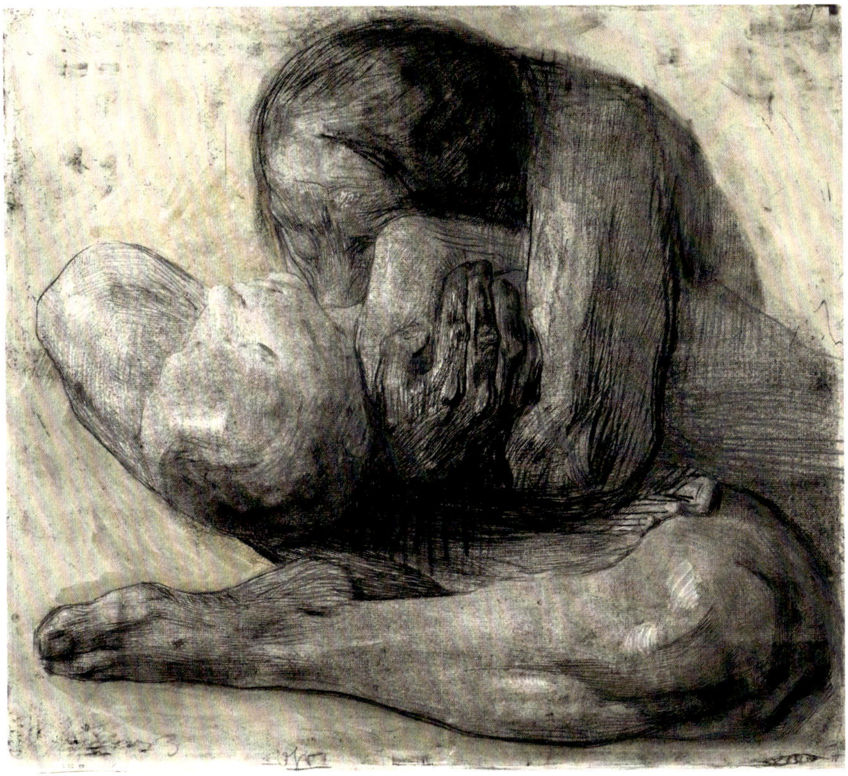

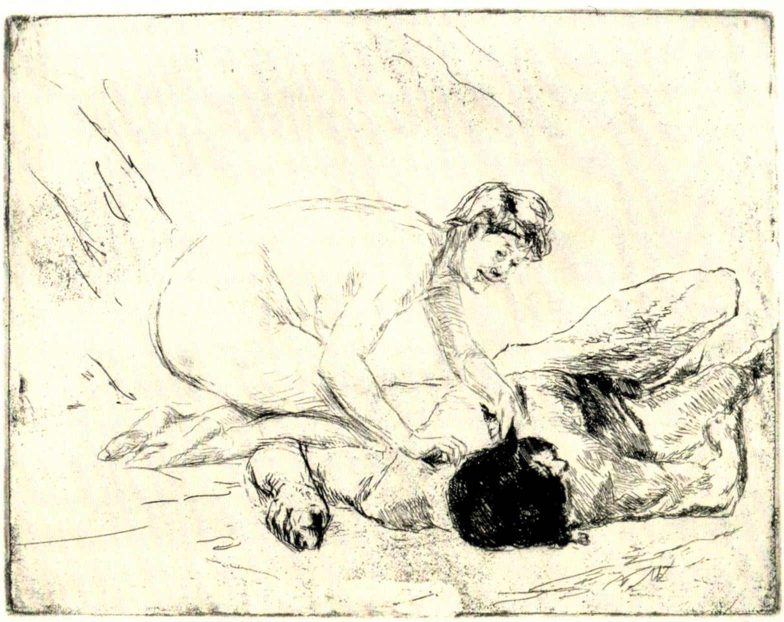

out the gleeful expression of Delilah's face, while like an amateur hairdresser using nail scissors she carefully cuts a thin strand of hair from her sleeping lover's head. The kneeling Delilah is presented in a more faintly outlined silhouette, whereas Samson is a volumetrically drawn, sprawling, unprotected male nude. Delilah's smiling face now looks almost maternal.[78] Other than the artist's presence, there is no sign of impending intrusion. Nothing indicates what we know about Samson's fate from this moment on. As Max Friedländer wrote in regard to the art of omission and suggestion Liebermann had developed by 1900: "The fear of emptiness is overcome. For the pure white of the paper is not empty, but rather is a site for the re-creative imagination."[79] To achieve this strange mutual suspense of subject and barely indicated setting and yet also guide the viewer's re-creative imagination, Liebermann takes away any iconographic context but gives the work an unmistakable title.

Something comparable happens in Kollwitz' *Raped* from the series *Peasants' War,* 1906 (fig. 19). Like the corpse in Klinger's *In Flagranti,* the rape victim's splayed legs leave no doubt about what has just happened. Just as she used Liebermann's *The Weaver,* not with the emphatic intention to criticize him thereby (though this happens, of course), here Kollwitz appropriated and radicalized for her purposes the potential she saw for dramatic peripety in Klinger's *In Flagranti,* in which discovery and catastrophe coincide.[80] From such uses we may conclude that Kollwitz took an analytical and technical approach to the work of others, an approach that includes rigorous use, or appropriation, of form, composition, and configuration, and then also frequent reuse to some extent apart from the given subject. In the end this dispassionate way of working resulted in her own emotionally charged work. Probably the most extreme example of this is her posing of herself with her son as a corpse for *Woman with a Dead Child.* The focus on Kollwitz as a compassionate proto-expressionist has overlooked this aspect of her work. Put differently, her work process is in some ways the private and occasionally darker side of Kollwitz' early prints; empathetic socialism is their public side.

In *Raped,* Kollwitz thematically links the private with the public, making violation of the private the turning point for the public's disruption by civil war. In what is at once a very detailed and anonymous rendering, the woman's head is thrown back in anguish and almost bored into the earth beneath and the vegetation around her. Sudden, extreme violence is manifest in the moonlit, devastated kitchen garden near the farmhouse. Broken sunflowers and trampled cabbages tell of the peasant woman's resistance despite having her arms bound behind her back. But it is clear that she is dead as, almost unseen among the leaves, the bowed head of a small child

19 Käthe Kollwitz, *Raped,* from *Peasants' War (Bauernkrieg),* no. 2, 1906, etching and softground etching, 30.6 × 52.9, Klipstein 97, Käthe Kollwitz Museum, Berlin KKMB 51

20 Max Liebermann, *Bleaching,* 1891, etching, 14.8 × 19.8, Schiefler 25, Fine Arts Museums of San Francisco, Achenbach Foundation for Graphic Arts 1963.30.35010

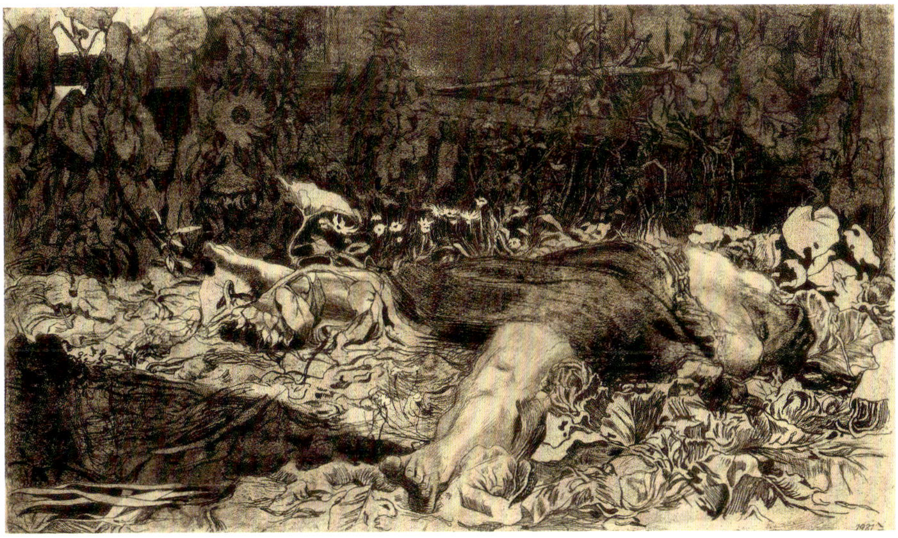

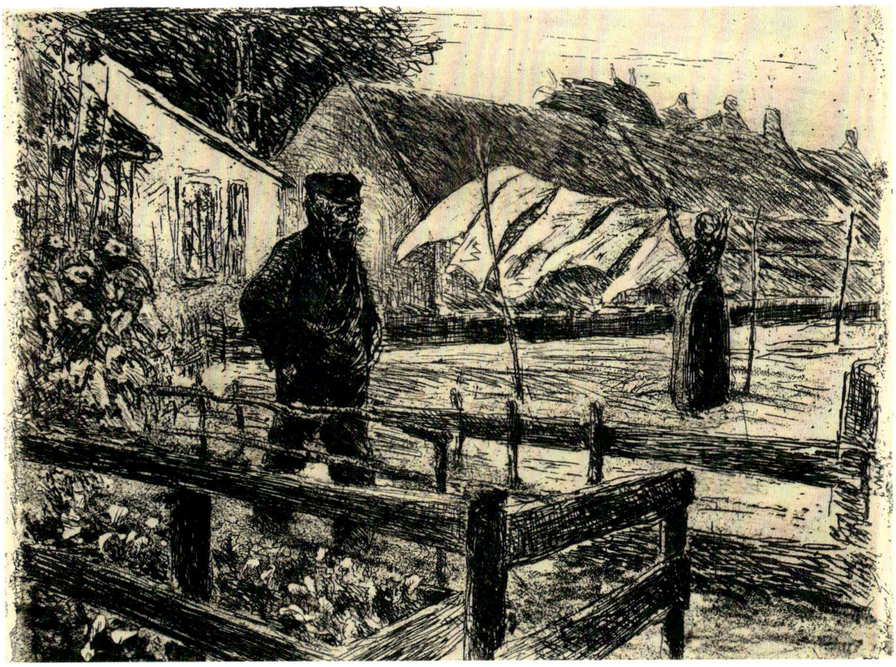

leans in sadness over the fence and the sunflower lowers its broken head like a mourner. If *Woman with a Dead Child* fused the two, *Raped* shows a child and dead mother separated. Kollwitz read Klinger's *Painting and Drawing* in 1892 and was impressed by his series *A Love;* here she turns his metaphorically loaded vegetation (see figs. 6 and 7) and his confidence in the expressive ability of an image to her utmost advantage.[81] At the same time, not unlike Liebermann in his *Child at the Door* or her own *At the Church Wall,* she forces a particular perspective. The woman's left foot marks vectors at a very low angle to imply the viewer perhaps as voyeur, but certainly as witness. As the triangular shadow, like the rapist's afterimage, enters the frame from its left edge, on the opposite side, quite near the woman's head, the devastated vegetation dissolves into line and negative forms, leaving the image almost unfinished, as if to suggest loss. Thus Kollwitz amalgamates sudden violence and boundless anguish but also prompts her narration. Nothing at this farm will be as it was before, and from here the *Peasants' War* takes its course.[82]

CLOSENESS AND DISTANCE

The expressive potential of conspicuously empty space or unfinished form is crucial to such prints as Liebermann's *Child at the Door* and *Samson and Delilah.* Liebermann's *Bleaching,* 1891 (fig. 20), replaces the dynamic between presence and absence with that of closeness and distance. Two fences separate us from the man leaving his house, hands in pockets, collar turned up, and a pipe in his mouth. Three fences separate us from the woman hanging up sheets to dry and bleach on rickety scaffolding.[83] The blowing wind requires her to work with her back turned to us. Neither man nor woman seems to notice the other, whereas we see their inverse relation to inside and outside. The fences narrowly determine the man's path and freely frame the woman's bleaching meadow. Though turned and bound to the row of village houses she faces between her sheets, she seems to be in a faraway place performing magic within her mundane task. The man has three choices once he has reached the short distance to the end of the two properties. In what has been called Liebermann's typical "swelling" space, unfolding from a vanishing point to the left, the figure could instantly walk in our direction and largely block our view of the distant silhouetted woman, leaving us with her near-abstract sheets.[84] Liebermann makes this dynamic unavoidable, only to dissolve it near the print's right-hand edge, where the fence post becomes just so much scribble on paper.

The powerful impact of Kollwitz' *Poster for the German Homeworkers Exhibition,* 1906 (fig. 21), lies in the image's simultaneous closeness and distance, reminiscent of that seen in *Woman at the Churchwall.* At first sight the

21 Käthe Kollwitz, *Poster for the German Homeworkers Exhibition,* 1905, lithograph (proof without text), 69.2 × 48.5, Klipstein 93, Käthe Kollwitz Museum, Berlin KKMB 47

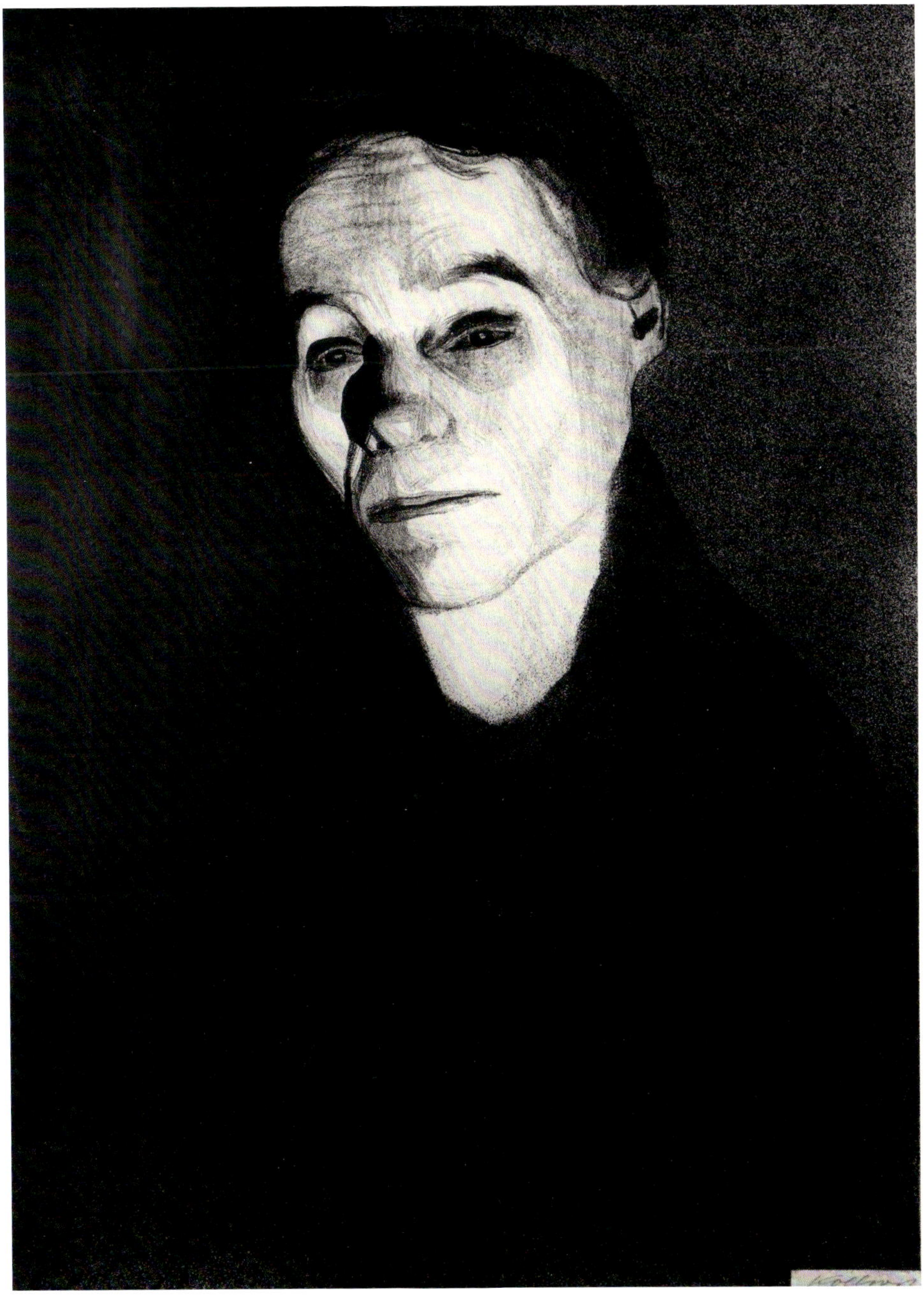

poster monumentalizes the exhausting life of homeworking women.[85] Yet, as Kollwitz observed, the women themselves saw each other differently: "The standard which I find female workers use for each other is always the same: She can work or she cannot work. The worker's world is entirely separate from the world of the bourgeoisie. Completely different values dominate in it."[86] Thus, the fact that "she can work" would not be noticed by the bourgeoisie as a positive value. Instead, the woman's masklike face seemed a direct accusation leveled against bourgeois society and Wilhelmine empire alike. Indeed, Empress Augusta rejected this image, ordering that all the posters be taken down before she visited the exhibition. In some sense Kollwitz' *Homeworker* also resembles the billboard-size reflected face in Klinger's much earlier *A Mother II* (see fig. 12), a face that no person within the image sees, yet a portrait that the viewer must complete. In Kollwitz' *Homeworker,* the woman's hard life is graphically clear in the hard outline of her illuminated face against the dark background to the left, whereas to the right her face has a slightly undulating contour framed by loose strands of hair and her collar seen against a soft tonal ground. This contrast between the left and right contours of her face suggests more than mere resignation and instead conveys the woman's sadness and prolonged vulnerability. Moreover, once we see this, and we see it best in versions of the print without text, we better understand Kollwitz' claim about her early work—namely, that it was primarily not pity that prompted her focus on the working class but the beauty she saw in it.[87] We might also consider her striking observation about working-class mothers compelled to care for so many children—namely, that they emptied their lives of sensual beauty and life energy.[88] Made in the context of her effort to help such women, this judgment cannot be taken as either arrogant or ignorant but, rather, as cognizant of the women's own "completely different values." In this way the woman's face is shockingly close, and yet the print makes her fate distant.

As we have seen, Klinger often omitted and overdecorated in one and the same plate, as if to insist on the complete representability of an interiorized and reflected world or of an inner, psychological state (see, for example, fig. 6). This insistence set him apart from both Kollwitz and Liebermann. For example, Kollwitz' *Death* from *A Weavers' Rebellion,* 1897 (fig. 22), shows personified Death among a small family in their attic. The woman leaning against the wall is about to die and looks at no one. The husband looks on, his powerless hands folded behind his back. Only the wide-eyed child stares at Death's hand about to touch his mother and senses his merciless smile right next to his face.[89] In the tradition of Holbein's *Images of Death* of 1525 / 1538 or Rethel's *Another Dance of Death,* Kollwitz' *Death* sets up a triangular relation: like the child, we see Death present, whereas whatever the others know, they know in isolation and silence. Their premonition and experience are so close they cannot find relief in articulation. Explicitly, and then redundantly, the allegorical figure of Death is there solely for us. In Liebermann's work, closeness and distance have no such determined relationship. For example, his portrait *Wilhelm von Bode's Daughter,* 1895 (fig. 23), shows a girl perhaps at her homework. Something has just startled her, be it an internal or external distraction from her work or a sudden insight into her task. This registers on her wide-eyed face and in her pose, noticed only by the artist-observer. The moment is entirely real, not a dream. Characteristically, Liebermann makes no claim to articulating the content of her thought, vision, or feelings. Here, the world inside exists perceptively but also inaccessibly. The viewer is left to imagine, or remember, such a moment.

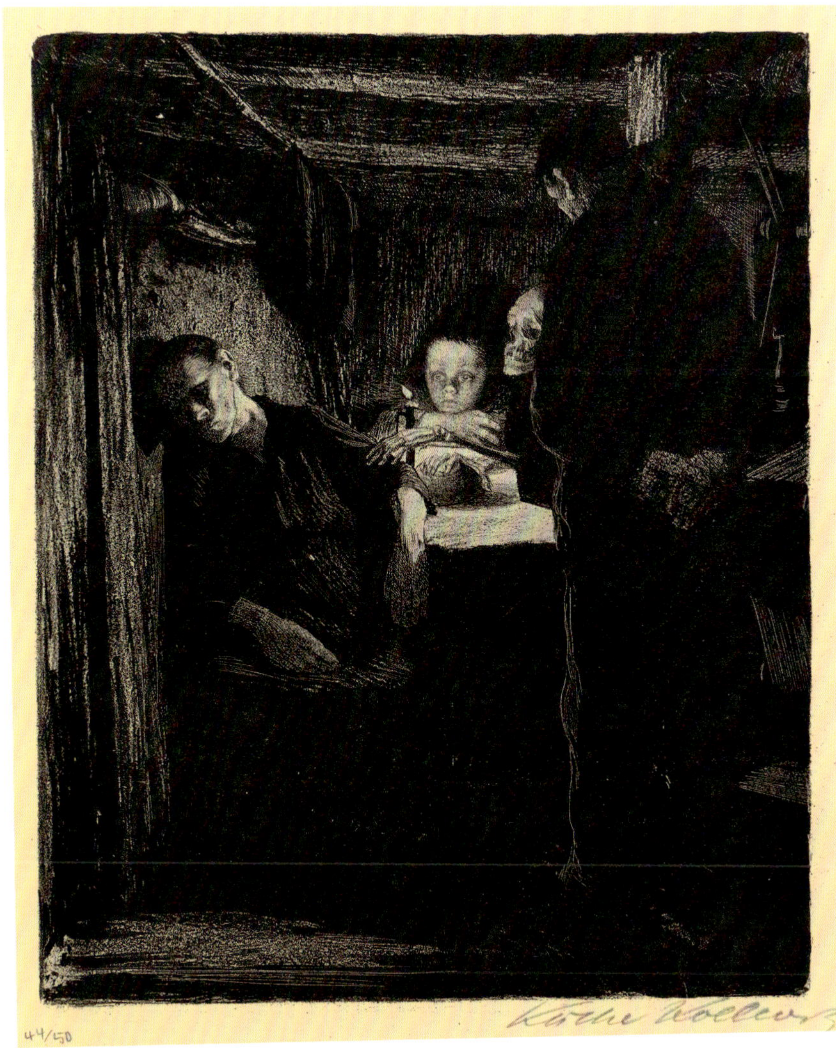

22 Käthe Kollwitz, *Death,* from *A Weavers' Rebellion (Weberaufstand),* 1897, lithograph (state ii / iic), 22.4 × 18.5, Klipstein 35, National Gallery of Art, Washington, Rosenwald Collection 1943.3.5305

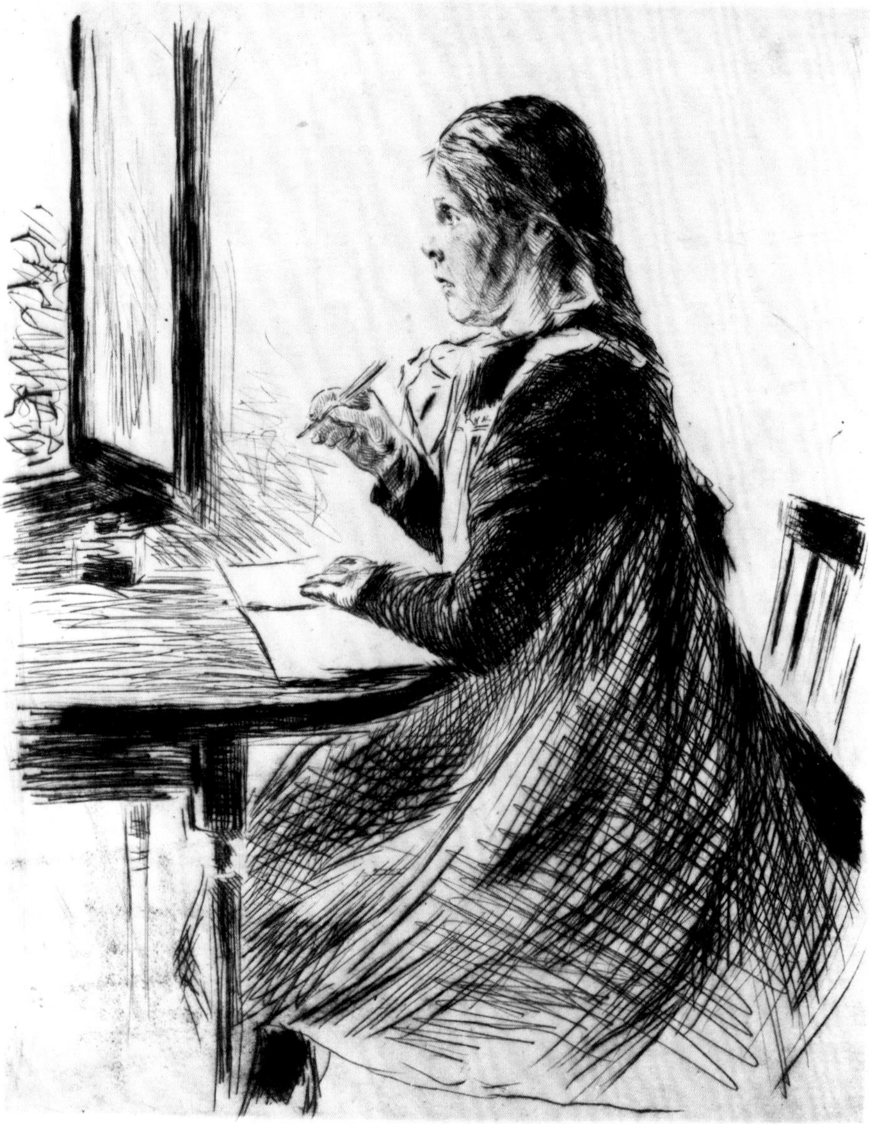

23 Max Liebermann, *Wilhelm von Bode's Daughter,* 1895, etching, 19.8 × 16.3, Schiefler 34, Kupferstichkabinett, Staatliche Museen zu Berlin

It is perhaps a moment related to the practice of *Griffelkunst*. For Klinger, Liebermann, and Kollwitz, the term *Griffelkunst* must have recalled, as it would for several later generations of Germans, the primary meaning of *Griffel* in the context of elementary school education. Learning to write and read meant learning to control and manipulate white chalk or a stylus called a *Griffel* on a wood-framed piece of black slate. No traces would remain of the countless efforts and exercises wiped away as soon as they were completed. Once deemed satisfactory, these efforts in white on black were succeeded by less ephemeral efforts in pencil or ink on white paper. It is thus tempting to think of Klinger's term *Griffelkunst* as referring not only to an art in which the "positive," the print, mirrors the "negative," the plate, the two of them moving in tandem through proof after proof, but also to a process in which the "negative" has the quality of committing the artist's effort to acquire and interiorize graphic literacy to oblivion, an effort barely intimated from Kollwitz' marginal notes to herself on some proofs. Still, certain developments are visible within the prints examined here, which date from up to two decades in each artist's oeuvre. Kollwitz increasingly moved away from subjects anchored in literary models and entered ever more directly into her own experiences and those of people whose life or plight mattered to her personally and politically. As she did so, she often monumentalized the figures in her images. Liebermann increasingly explored and refined the representational versatility and openness of printmaking, his development resulting in prints that are neither preliminary nor reproductive variants of his paintings; instead they are keenly perceptive, yet rather sensitive and sparely interpretive approaches to similar subjects. Klinger, who did so much for the German etching revival and was an extremely prolific printmaker until the mid-1890s, eventually could or would not break the model of the print cycle, which enclosed its world within itself. Instead, inspired by the example of Auguste Rodin, he began to apply to sculpture, the art he did not define in his *Painting and Drawing,* his insights about *Griffelkunst*.

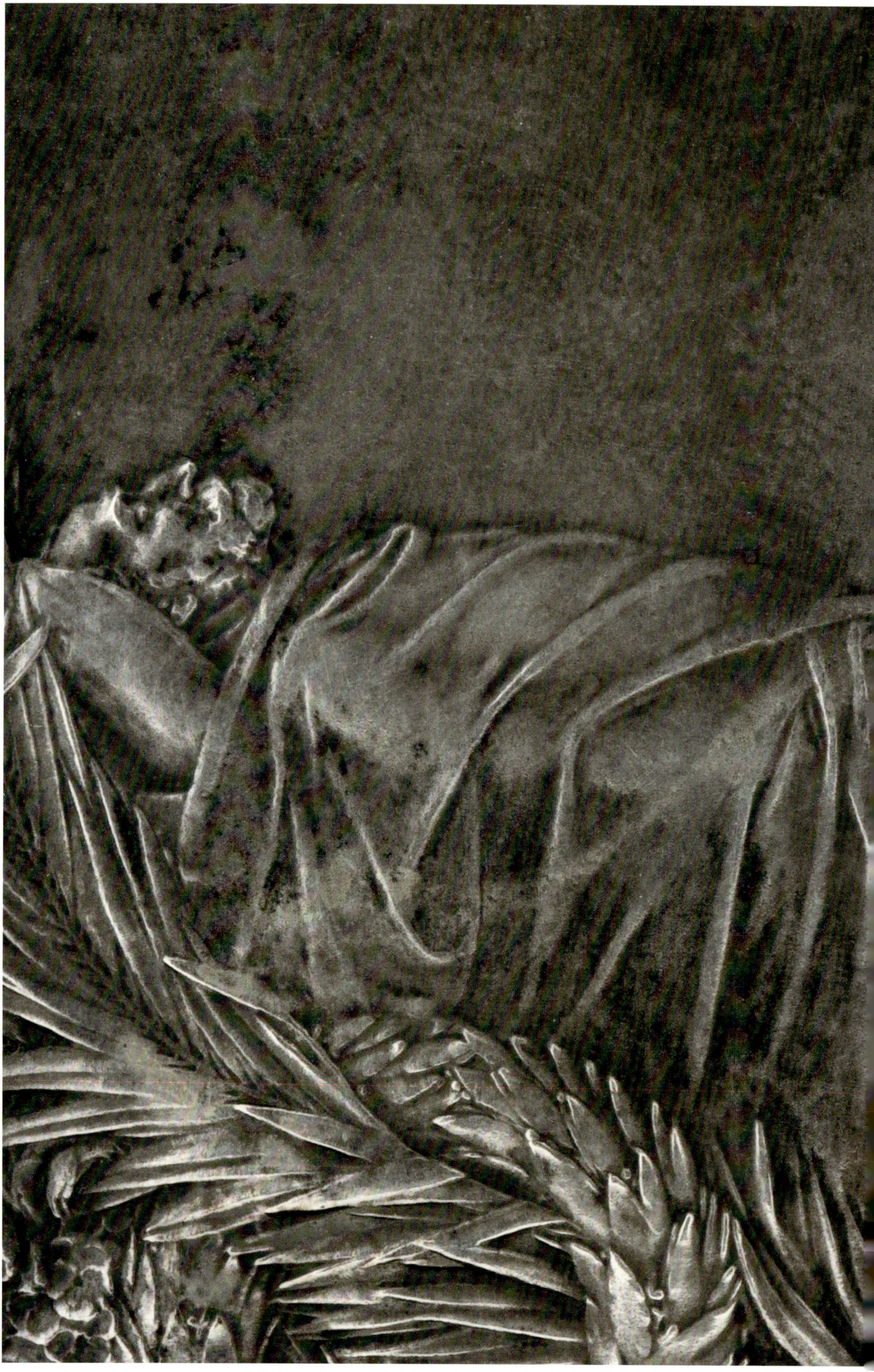

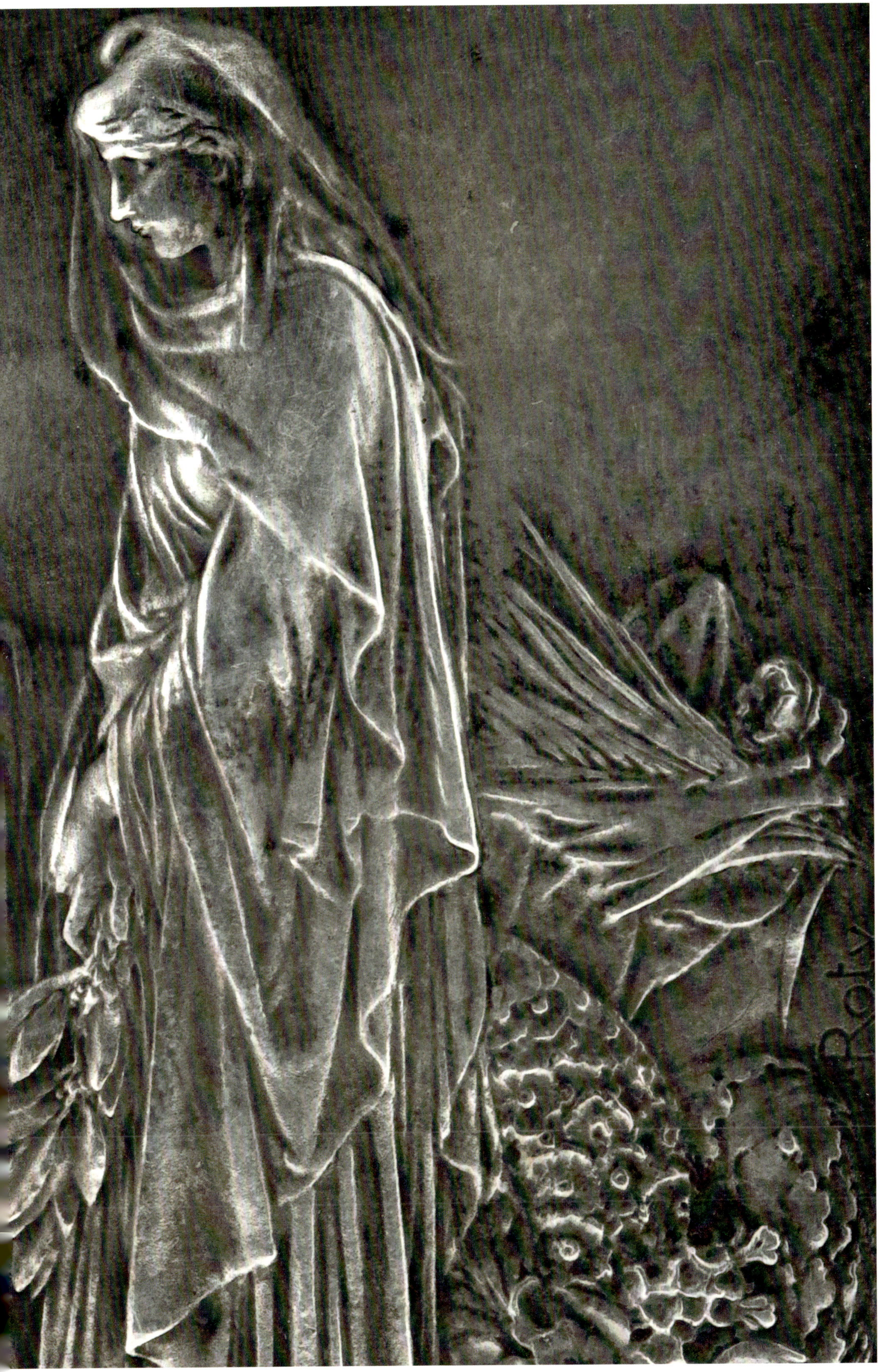
Roty

SCULPTURE AND PRIVACY

Nicholas Penny

THE STATUETTE AND ITS MEANINGS

In the increasingly secular world of the nineteenth century, archaic—usually medieval—conventions were adopted in order to elevate the sacred to a higher plane and to drain it of any sensual or sensuous contaminants. Then, in the last decades of the century, artists began to borrow, for profane purposes, the incense and mystery of religious art in order to disguise, or transform, the erotic with iconic conventions and sacerdotal solemnity. Much of the art that is generally described as symbolist has this character, and its central subject is the priestess or goddess. The worship the goddess receives or the priestess directs is never that of an official religion but belongs, rather, to a private realm.

A notable example of this tendency is the statuette of a woman by Louis-Ernest Barrias (fig. 1). Her ample robes suggest the garb of priestess or mourner, and the exposure of her breasts seems like a ceremonial revelation, which may be intended to make the voluptuous seem respectable—and certainly makes it more exciting. The bronze illustrated here is relatively quiet in its patination (in other examples the gilded and silvered bronze drapery is contrasted with ivory flesh) but includes a malachite brooch of scarab form suggestive of the mysteries of ancient Egypt.[1] Such a bronze would have been displayed in a private space. It requires an "inner sanctum," for its mysteries would be diminished, if not lost, in public circumstances.

The first version of this sculpture, adorned with rather less drapery, however, was a life-size marble figure entitled *Mysterious and Veiled Nature Uncovering Herself before Science,* which was exhibited at the Paris Salon of 1893 and was acquired by (perhaps intended for) the École de Médecine in Bordeaux.

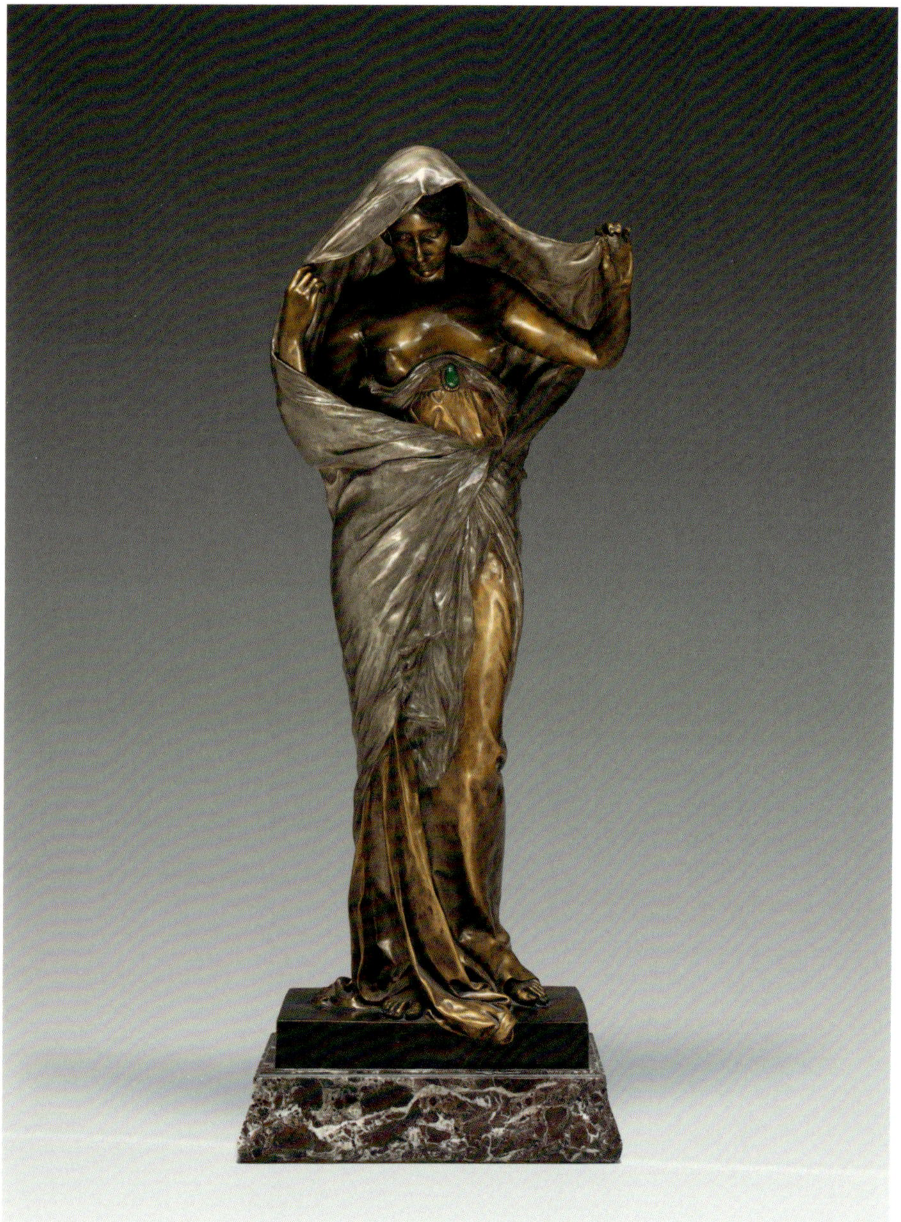

Another large marble was commissioned for the École de Médecine in Paris in 1902.[2] We are not obliged to consider the exhibition piece as the original—all large sculpture at that date began life as a small model—or the official title as definitive; but even if we were to do so, even if we were able to believe that the sculptor intended to create an allegory that would inspire medical students with an exalted sense of their vocation, other ideas may have crept in. It was in 1899 that Barrias first exhibited a large version of the figure that was made of colored marbles, onyx alabaster, and semiprecious stones—marvels of nature and products of the colonies, but also exotic substances with ancient and magical associations.[3] The polychrome bronze statuettes such as the one in the National Gallery of Art were cast soon thereafter, apparently with great success.

Allegory often served, in the late nineteenth century, as a disguise or an excuse for symbolism. The white-marble mourning figure, half-draped, which is wrapped around, or has collapsed below, a granite pedestal supporting a bronze bearded public man may be officially designated as Hygène or Philanthropy or the city of Bordeaux, but it may still impress us rather as the embodiment of Grief or Destiny, or even as something disembodied—a spirit, or at least a spiritual idea—something abstract, but not as an easily defined personification. The facts about the Barrias may shock us at first. It is like discovering that a poem by Stéphane Mallarmé began life as an Ode to the Inventor of the Electric Light. But the sculpture of this period is full of such paradoxes. The centenary of the Banque de France in 1900, for example, was marked by a medallion showing an androgynous heroine clothed in fantasy armor (see fig. 10). What seems clear is that there is a relation between scale and meaning. A certain poetry flourishes in a private setting and on a small scale—which is not, of course, to suggest that all sculpture of domestic size possesses such poetry.

1 Louis-Ernest Barrias, *Nature Unveiling Herself before Science,* model 1895/1899, cast c. 1900, bronze with silvering and malachite, height without base 57.2, National Gallery of Art, Washington, Gift of Frank Anderson Trapp

In nineteenth-century Paris the huge industry of ornamental bronze casting complemented the unrivaled state support for the training and support of sculptors, so that a marble carving awarded a prize in a public exhibition would be bought for a national institution but would then also be made available for sale as a small bronze. In Britain there were fewer public commissions and official incentives, and there was no tradition of bronze casting to rival Paris. The major commissions available to British sculptors were marble church monuments and bust portraiture, with occasional gallery sculptures. Smaller works such as the library statuettes of bronzed terra-cotta and plaster by John Michael Rysbrack in the mid-eighteenth century or the poetic models made for silversmiths by John Flaxman in the early nineteenth were exceptional. This does not mean that no small bronzes were to be found in British houses. The reduced reproductions of antique statues that were supplied by Roman foundries in the late eighteenth century, in a size adapted to the chimneypiece, were probably designed chiefly for British travelers, and in the mid-nineteenth century there was a large British market for the many ponderous clock cases, allegorical nudes, and groups of battling crusaders (or jaguars) being made in Paris.

The Hungarian émigré Edgar Boehm was probably the first sculptor in Britain whose success as a portrait sculptor was supplemented by the popularity of the skillfully modeled and meticulously chased bronze statuettes cast after his models. Some of these were also portraits, but of racehorses.[4] Although Boehm's pupil Alfred Gilbert was determined to make his reputation by other means, he must have learned much from his master about the medium of bronze. When he traveled to Italy he was surely deeply impressed by Vincenzo Gemito, a genius with a passion for exploring the possibilities of bronze sculpture and in particular of lost-wax casting, whose hero was Benvenuto Cellini.[5] Gilbert became the first major British sculptor to work chiefly in bronze and the first whose fame derived from the bronze statuettes he made for private collectors. Gilbert's *Perseus, Icarus,* and *Comedy and Tragedy* (fig. 2) have themes inspired by ancient Greece, but they recall the sculpture of fifteenth-century Italy and were originally conceived as bronzes to be cast by the lost-wax technique.

Before considering Gilbert's sculpture further it is valuable to identify the types of sculpture that had, by 1890, begun to bore and repel people of taste in London and New York. Edith Wharton's novel *The House of Mirth,* published in 1905 but set in a slightly earlier period, describes with precision some of the features of Mrs. Peniston's residence on Fifth Avenue that made it intolerable to any person of sensibility: the *Dying Gladiator* (presumably a reduced copy in marble or bronze) in the window of the drawing room, the vases on the chimneypiece flanking an "ormolu clock surmounted by a helmeted Minerva," the "steel engravings of an anecdotic character," the black walnut furniture, the "magenta 'flock' wall-paper."[6] The *Minerva* and the *Gladiator* would certainly have been sand-cast bronzes.

2 Sir Alfred Gilbert, *Comedy and Tragedy: "Sic Vita,"* model 1891–1892, cast probably 1902/1905, bronze, with attached marble base 34.6 × 15.6 × 13.7, National Gallery of Art, Washington, Pepita Milmore Memorial Fund

Most European foundries in the first two-thirds of the nineteenth century employed the technique of sand-casting. This technique had previously been used mostly for the production of ornaments attached to furniture (*bronzes d'ameublement*). It is not known who pioneered the application of the technique to complex figurative sculpture. In the leading Parisian foundries the final pieces were assembled out of numerous parts with great ingenuity and then skillfully tooled and patinated by a succession of specialists. Neither the methods of assembly nor the degree of afterwork were unprecedented,

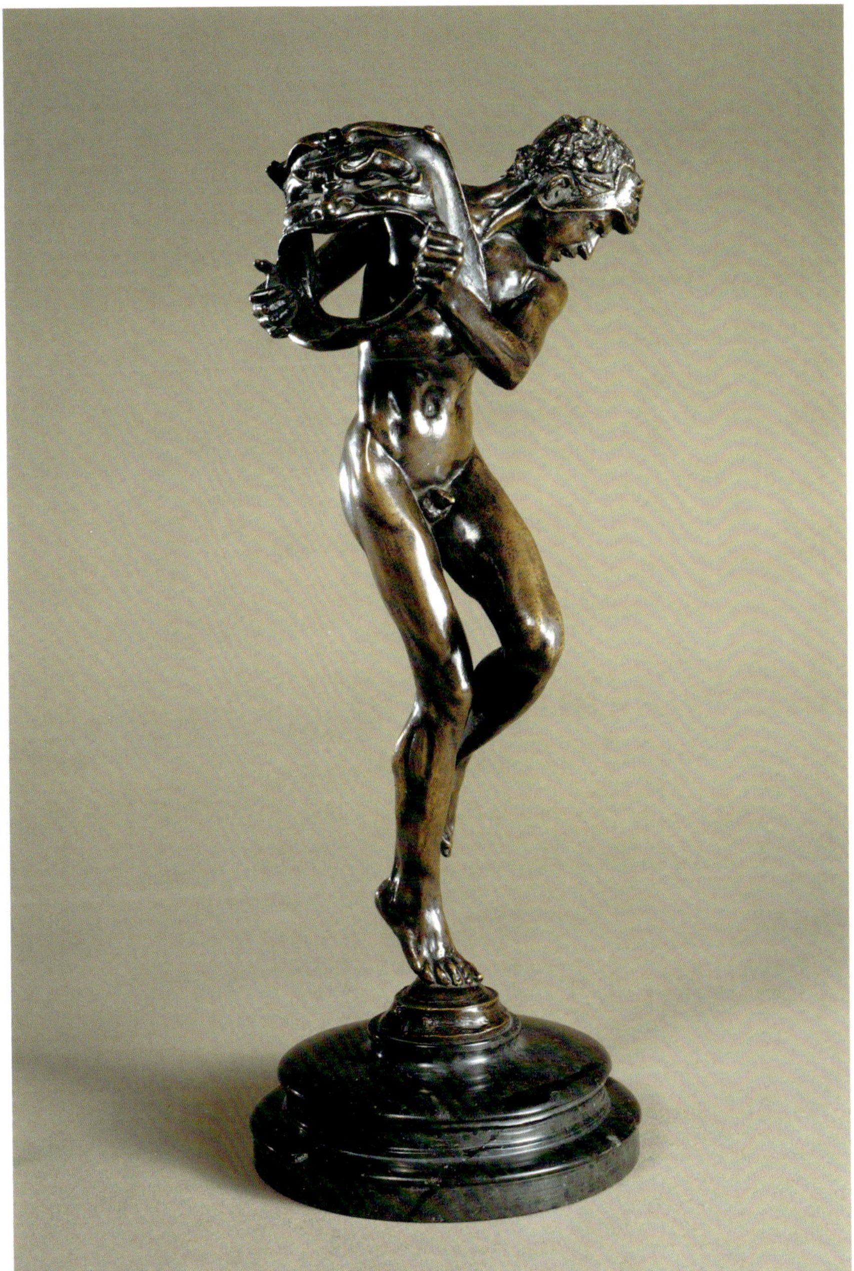

but the extent of the division of labor and the size of the editions probably were. Moreover, the models employed were frequently made with the help of a mechanical reducing machine patented by Achille Collas.[7] Such sculpture was generally reproductive and often reproduced a famous work of far larger size. It also came to be considered as industrial in character, and the very precision of the workmanship was thought to be mechanical, which explains why in Wharton's description it is classed with steel engraving, another reproductive medium that owed something to modern technology. The reaction against this sort of bronze sculpture was associated with an enthusiasm for lost-wax casting, just as the revival of etching accompanied an aversion to steel engravings.

The revival of lost-wax casting has been documented in France (the Gonon family, which was closely associated with the great *animalier* sculptor Antoine-Louis Barye in the first half of the nineteenth century, played a key role) and in Belgium (where the Compagnie des Bronzes in Brussels was especially admired for its lost-wax casts).[8] Boehm's introduction of lost-wax casting into Britain dates from 1883.[9] In Italy it seems unlikely that the technique was ever abandoned. Nevertheless, a new excitement about its possibilities was felt especially strongly from the late 1870s and in Naples. There Gilbert would have seen the bronze sculptures by Gemito with their uncanny reproduction of urchins' hair, fish scales, rough textiles, and elderly creased skin. Several Neapolitan foundries were also interested in reproducing antique statues for foreign visitors. The most popular subjects were the *Dancing Faun* and *Narcissus,* neither of which are large works in the original.[10] These were the bronzes of the private gardens and pools of antiquity (Narcissus was supposed to be contemplating his reflection), cast in the same way as the originals. Such works were acceptable to those who despised the cold monumentality of the *Minerva* clock or the stale rhetoric of the *Dying Gladiator.*

Many inaccurate claims were made for lost-wax casts. Thus, in *The Decoration of Houses,* published in 1897 by Ogden Codman and Edith Wharton, we are told that "the distinction, the personal quality, of a beautiful object is certainly enhanced when it is known to be alone of its kind—as is the case with the old bronzes made *à cire perdue.*"[11] But the truth is that most "old bronzes"—those by Giambologna that were cast and chased by Antonio Susini, for instance—were cast by an indirect method, from an "intermodel" of wax, made in a piece mold, not directly from a unique wax model. Nor was it only—or even usually—the "master's chisel" that gave the bronze its "final touches," as Codman and Wharton assert, and as might be supposed from the reader of Cellini's autobiography. Nevertheless, the lost-wax cast was rightly valued for the precision with which it could reproduce a model without extensive afterwork—in other words, for its autograph or "personal" quality, which would of course be most easily appreciated in a work of modest scale. Moreover, lost-wax casting by the direct method (the method employed by Donatello, for example) was revived by both Gemito and Gilbert, although only for a limited number of works.[12]

With the interest in the special effects of lost-wax casting came a revival of interest in "nature casts." Little is known about the makers of these, except that there is a tradition that they were made in Japan in the late nineteenth century. We do know that they were made in Rome by Giovanni Nisini, a founder whose showroom was at 63, via del Babuino. His trade card (fig. 3) tells us that his foundry won gold medals at the Antwerp exhibition in 1894 and the Exposition Universelle of 1900 in Paris. The Paris medal is actually embossed, front and back, on the card, where the snakes and lizards and crabs keep company with low-relief vases and medals and with a cast of Giambologna's *Bathing Venus* and of the Naples *Narcissus,* who is here converted into a snake charmer.[13] The minute surface pattern of the lizard's epidermis, broken only by tiny creases, is beyond the power of even the most accomplished chaser to imitate, and when this creature, proverbial for its fleetness, is frozen by fire into motionless metal, it seems a work of magic rather than of art. It is known that such "nature casts" were made in Renaissance Italy, perhaps especially in early sixteenth-century Padua—but it is possible that many of the Renaissance crabs and frogs in collections today were made by Nisini and his competitors.[14] The goldsmiths of the late sixteenth century, such as Wenzel Jamnitzer, were also known to have cast insects from life, and the new technology of electroplating that contrived to plate flies with silver was seen as a modern equivalent to these feats.[15] Gilbert, who saw himself as a goldsmith-sculptor, seems to have devised his *Comedy and Tragedy* as a figure sculpture that would incorporate precisely such a metal insect.

In its original bronze version, a statuette of a size similar to that of the *Narcissus* of Pompeii, the reason why the boy has raised his leg and turns his face, grimacing with pain, away from the comic mask he carries is apparent, for the bee that stings him is attached to his leg. (The insect is included in only a few versions.) The sculptor was also attracted by the precarious pose—something impossible in a sculpture carved in stone. This must have owed something to Cellini's statuette of *Mercury* made for a niche in the base of the *Perseus* in Florence.[16] But Gilbert also wanted his sculpture to be seen in the round, indeed wanted its meaning to unfold only when it was rotated, so that we see first the mask and then the face through the mask and then the expression on the face and then the reason for the expression. The idea

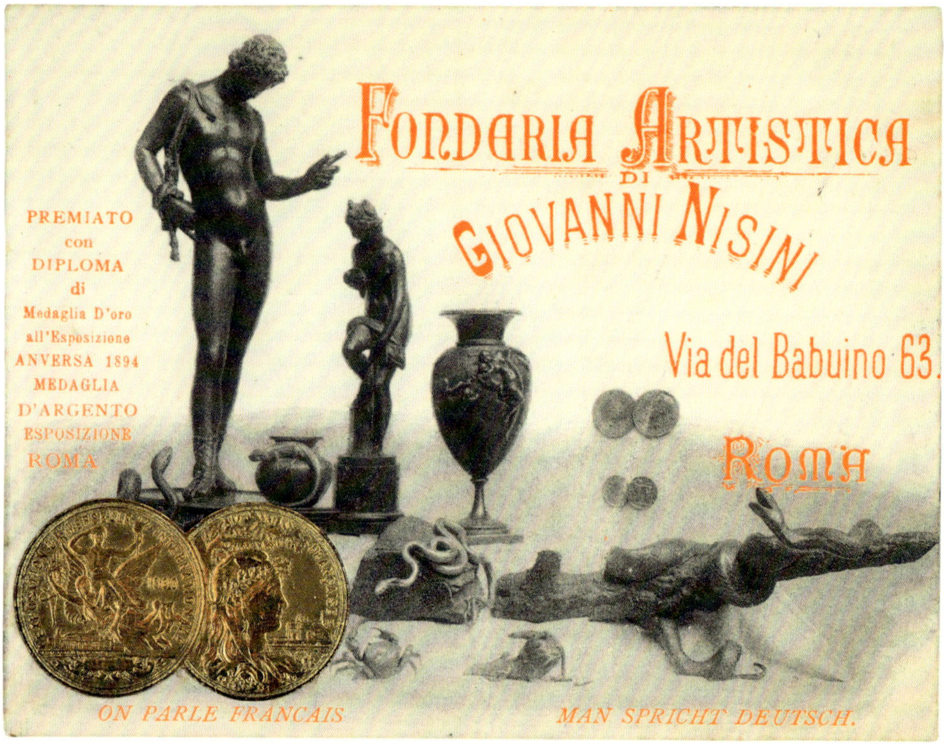

3 Trade card for the Art Foundry of Giovanni Nisini, Rome, c. 1900, 9.5 × 12.4, Private Collection

must have owed something to a curious antique marble of a boy with a mask in the Capitoline Museum in Rome.[17]

According to Gilbert's autobiographical musings, the title *Comedy and Tragedy* came from the popular one-act play by his namesake, W. S. Gilbert. The sculptor claimed that he wanted to find a symbol for the tension between his social success and artistic celebrity on the one hand, and his domestic misery (a sick wife and heavy debts) on the other, between the world's applause and the painful service of art.[18] This claim, written ten years after the work was exhibited, by which time Gilbert's self-dramatizing had reached nearly demented extremes, has been perhaps accorded too much respect in the literature, given that a prop boy in the Greek theater would never have enjoyed any applause, and the suffering of the artist is ill-represented by an accident to which any other mortal is liable. Furthermore, it is clear that the first idea for the wounded twisted figure did not involve a mask.[19] The figure seems, rather, to embody, or at least to hint at, several meanings. The performance of comedy (itself represented by a mask with a somewhat painful grimace) may conceal suffering in real life, the service of art can be arduous, beauty itself (which stings) can be stung. The appeal of the lean, agile urchins who posed for Gemito is fused with elements found in playful boudoir porcelain statuettes of mischievous cupids and masked lovers to create a blend of the allegorical and the realistic that is disturbing and suggestive. Such a paradoxical and open-ended sculpture would hardly be appropriate on a monumental scale. This figure and the Eros who flies over Piccadilly were Gilbert's last major sculptures of the nude. He turned his attention to figures heavily draped or clad in spiky armor and, doubtless influenced by Barrias, explored the contrast of patinated metal with flesh of ivory or marble.

THE HAND OF THE BELOVED AND THE FINGERPRINTS OF GENIUS

During the eighteenth century European sculptors increasingly employed the services of specialist plaster-cast makers, or *formatori* (they were often Italian in origin). The formatori removed the need to fire small clay sketches and models, as well as larger studies of heads, in order to preserve them; more important, large clay models could be cast when completed and did not require the constant application of damp cloth to prevent premature drying and crumbling. The formatori also supplied the sculptors with casts of parts of famous antique statues, life masks and death masks of the subjects of their portraits, and hands and feet cast from living models. In the nineteenth century plaster casts of such fragments began to circulate outside the artist's studio. A demand arose for casts of the hands of eminent writers and artists and other celebrities, a parallel to the collecting of autographs. By midcentury the hands of women and children, especially deceased children, were also being cast and then carved in marble (usually anonymously) by Italian *praticiens*.[20]

The cast of the linked hands of Robert Browning and his wife, Elizabeth Barrett Browning (fig. 4), must be understood in this context, although it is somewhat unusual because it combines the idea of a secular relic of genius with a testimony to, and exemplar of, deep domestic sentiment. Also unusual, if not unprecedented, is the fact that the hands are cast in bronze and signed (on the stump of Robert's wrist, by the American sculptor Harriet Hosmer), because the documentary value, the authenticity as relic, was surely diminished by the assertion of artistic mediation. However, the sculpture also commemorates Hosmer's intimacy with the couple. Since it is unlikely that the hands were molded as a unit, she must have planned carefully to ensure that the separate hands could be happily united. She also did the molding herself. Indeed Elizabeth Barrett Browning's consent was said to have been conditional on this: "I will not sit for the *formatore*." No anonymous and possibly uncouth mechanic was to play a part in this most personal business. When the hands were cast in bronze "many years later," Hosmer was proud of the lack of "finish" because she did not want any specialist metal chaser to diminish the "characteristics of texture"—that is, the inimitable impress of the mortal flesh of these immortal poets, eternally united.[21]

Such objects may seem especially characteristic of the High Victorian era—of the world of "anecdotic steel engravings" and magenta "flock" wallpaper. However, Auguste Rodin in 1908 arranged for the carvers in his employ to make a marble relief (fig. 5) of his plaster cast of the hand of Sally Hicks Croswell, deceased daughter of his American admirer Elizabeth Merrill, by her first husband. "Every day I bend over this little hand," Merrill wrote to Rodin, "and I still cannot imagine that it is only marble."[22] In the spiritualist séances so popular at this date, the dead often revisited the world briefly in the form of a disembodied hand. In this case the rough matrix of the stone slab stands for the world of shadows from which the dead may emerge only partially. Similar sculpture was already a feature of the cemetery (that most private of public spaces), and we may wonder where such an object was placed in Merrill's home. This relief is something of an embarrassment to Rodin's admirers, but it cannot be dismissed as an aberration in taste or a marginal commercial enterprise. The theme of partial emergence from matter is central to Rodin's art, and the idea of the hand rising from the tomb was one that he took up in a late uncommissioned sculpture.[23]

Still more disturbing is a plaster cast of Rodin's own hand (fig. 6). Léonce Bénédite appears to have directed Paul Cruet, one of Rodin's

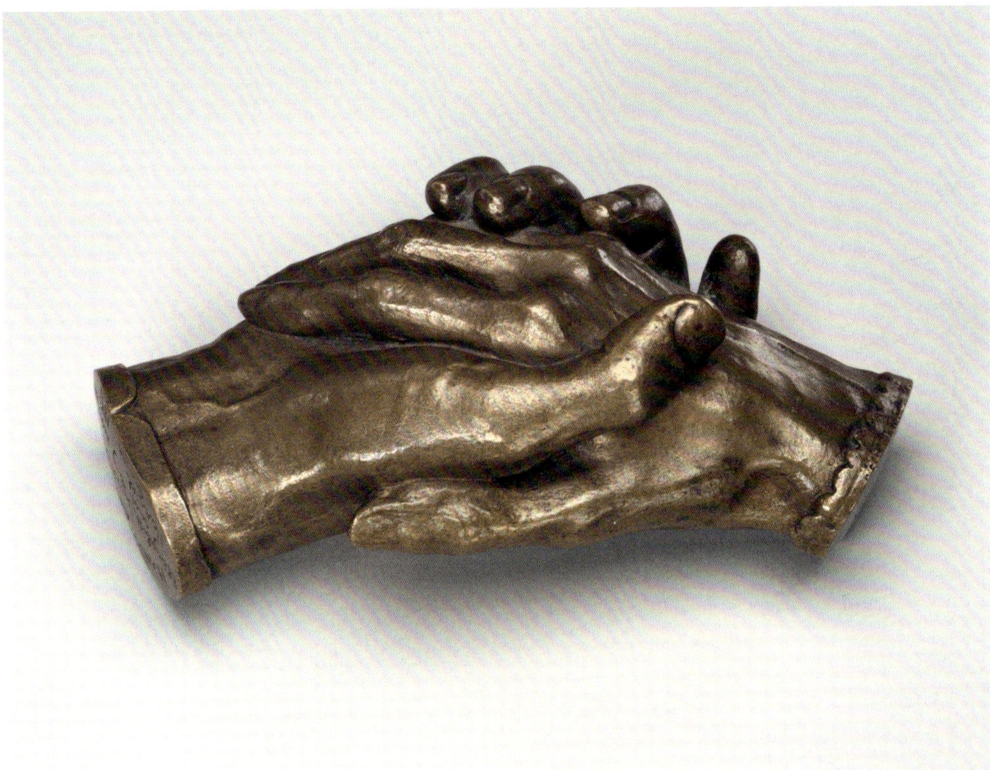

4 Harriet Goodhue Hosmer, *Clasped Hands of Robert Browning and Elizabeth Barrett Browning,* model 1853, bronze, 8.3 × 21 × 10.8, National Gallery of Art, Washington, Gift in honor of Margaret and Raymond Horowitz

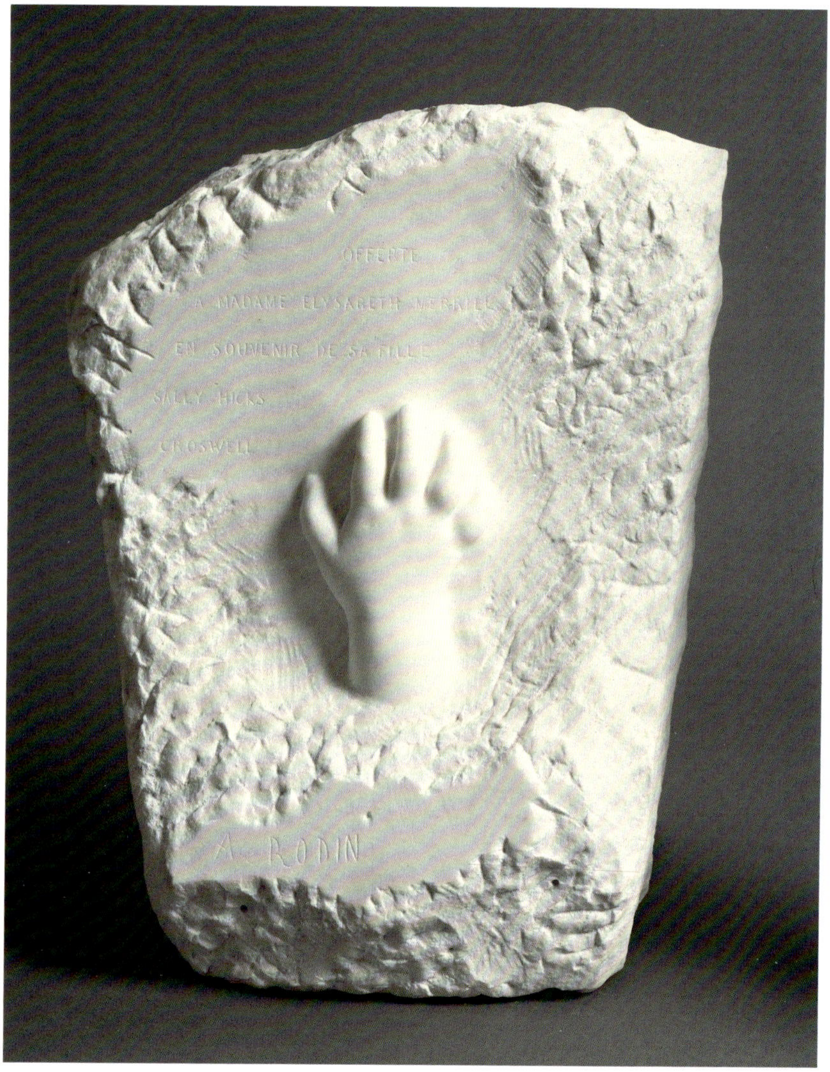

5 Auguste Rodin, *Memorial Relief (Hand of a Child),* 1908, marble, 40.8 × 32.7 × 14.9, National Gallery of Art, Washington, Gift of Elizabeth Merrill Furness 1982.6.1

6 Auguste Rodin, *Hand of Rodin with a Female Figure,* 1917, plaster, greatest extension 22.9, National Gallery of Art, Washington, Gift of Mrs. John W. Simpson 1942.5.22

7 Auguste Rodin, *Right Hand,* possibly 1880, plaster, greatest extension 10.2, National Gallery of Art, Washington, Gift of Mrs. John W. Simpson 1942.5.26

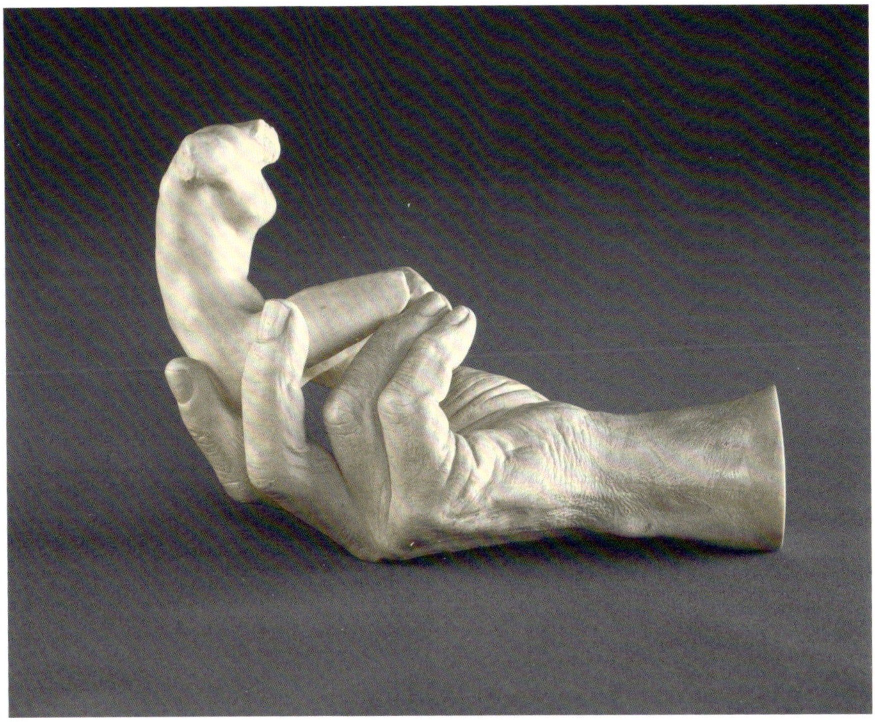

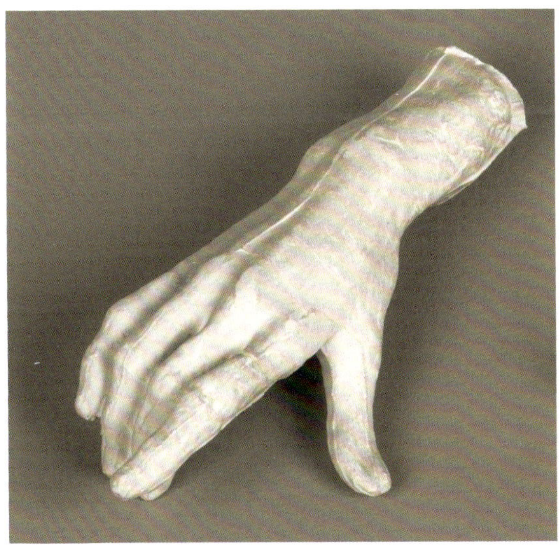

formatori, to make a cast of the sculptor's hand a few weeks before he died—presumably with Rodin's consent—and Bénédite then combined the cast of Rodin's hand with the cast of a model of a female torso made by the artist. In his capacity as first curator of the Musée Rodin, Bénédite was able to present this kitsch souvenir to supporters of the museum and related commemorative enterprises (Mrs. John W. Simpson, who bequeathed this work to the National Gallery of Art, paid for the restoration of Rodin's house at Meudon).[24] It should not be considered as a work by Rodin, but it does reflect a view of the sculptor's godlike status, which he had done little to discourage, and was a by-product of the way his studio worked, combining casts and making new compositions out of fragments.

Early on Rodin had advocated incompleteness; later, he exploited the pathos of the fragmentary; and in the *Burghers of Calais,* he found a strangely powerful if somewhat disjointed eloquence in figures assembled out of drapery and expressive heads, hands, and feet. In making his huge, complex, seething relief of the *Gates of Hell,* he "came to recognize that dismembering could be as fertile an activity as molding and joining in creating sculpture."[25] In the highly publicized and successful exhibition of 1889 that he shared with Claude Monet at the Galerie Georges Petit in Paris, he exhibited torsos and heads; at about the same date he is said to have started making gifts of hands (also, occasionally, of feet and legs) to his patrons and admirers. The so-called *Hand of a Pianist* or *Right Hand* (fig. 7), made out of nine sections of a piece mold, is one—perhaps the finest—of a group of such hands, probably presented to Simpson in the early twentieth century but modeled by the artist at the height of his powers in the 1880s.[26]

The great sculptors of the previous generation in France, Jean-Baptiste Carpeaux and Albert-Ernest Carrier-Belleuse (Rodin's first master) were dedicated to the commercial exploitation of their inventions, their "ateliers" serving as factories for the reproduction of their inventions in marble, terracotta, and plaster and for the finishing and patination of bronzes subcontracted to foundries. It does not seem to have occurred to either of these artists to reproduce preliminary, fragmentary, or merely rough sketch models. Nor were either Jean-Alexandre-Joseph Falguière or Aimé-Jules Dalou, Rodin's contemporaries and rivals, interested in emulating Rodin's promotion of work of this nature. The contents of their studios, however, do seem to have attracted the notice of a remarkable entrepreneur.

Adrien-Aurélien Hébrard, born in 1865, was the son of a wealthy newspaper editor and senator. He had a keen interest in modern science, especially chemistry, as well as in modern sculpture. The bronze foundry he opened in 1902 quickly secured publicity for the precision of its lost-wax casts and for the special quality of the alloys and patinas employed (the alloys included the mixture of silver and copper—*shibuichi*—used by Japanese foundries, and it was claimed that the patinas were produced by simulating the volcanic gases held to be responsible for the distinctive colors of the bronzes discovered at Pompeii).[27] Hébrard's first foundry trials date from before 1900, as we may infer from his proud statement that they had obtained "the approval of the great artist Falguière," who died in that year.[28] A model by Falguière of the bandaged head of a wounded—perhaps dead—young man (fig. 8) seems to have been one of Hébrard's earliest casting experiments. Falguière and Hébrard may have selected it together as a suitable piece for casting because of its size and character, for it was hardly likely to be in great demand.

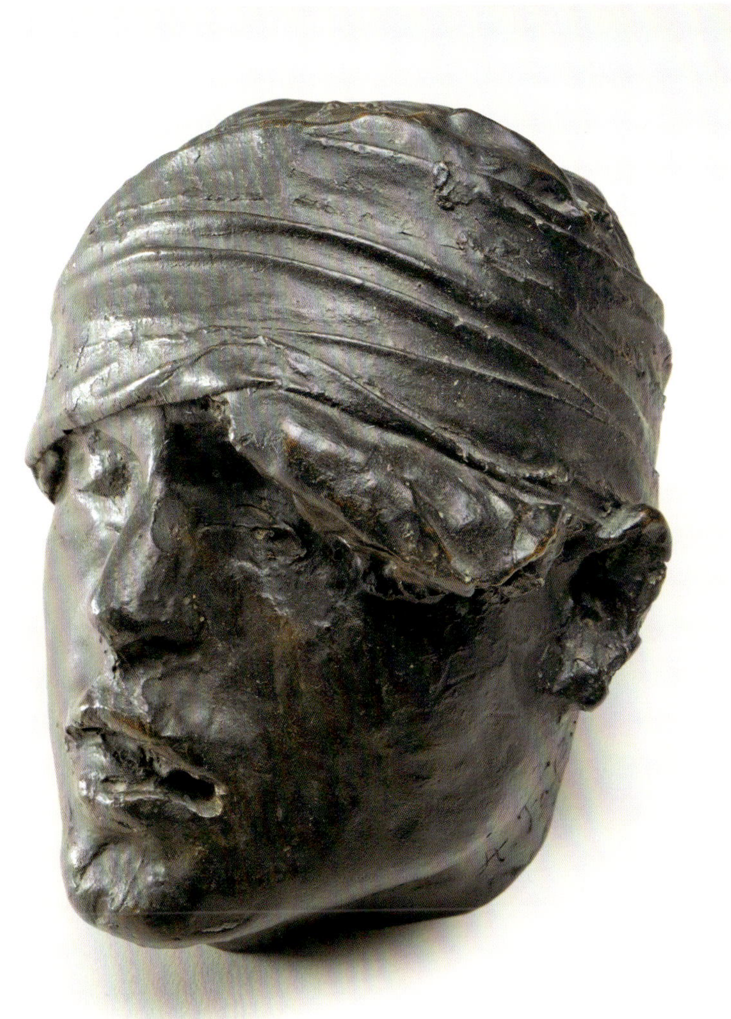

8 Jean-Alexandre-Joseph Falguière, *Study of a Wounded Soldier's Head*, model c. 1880–1890, bronze, cast by Hébrard foundry c. 1900, height 15, Private Collection

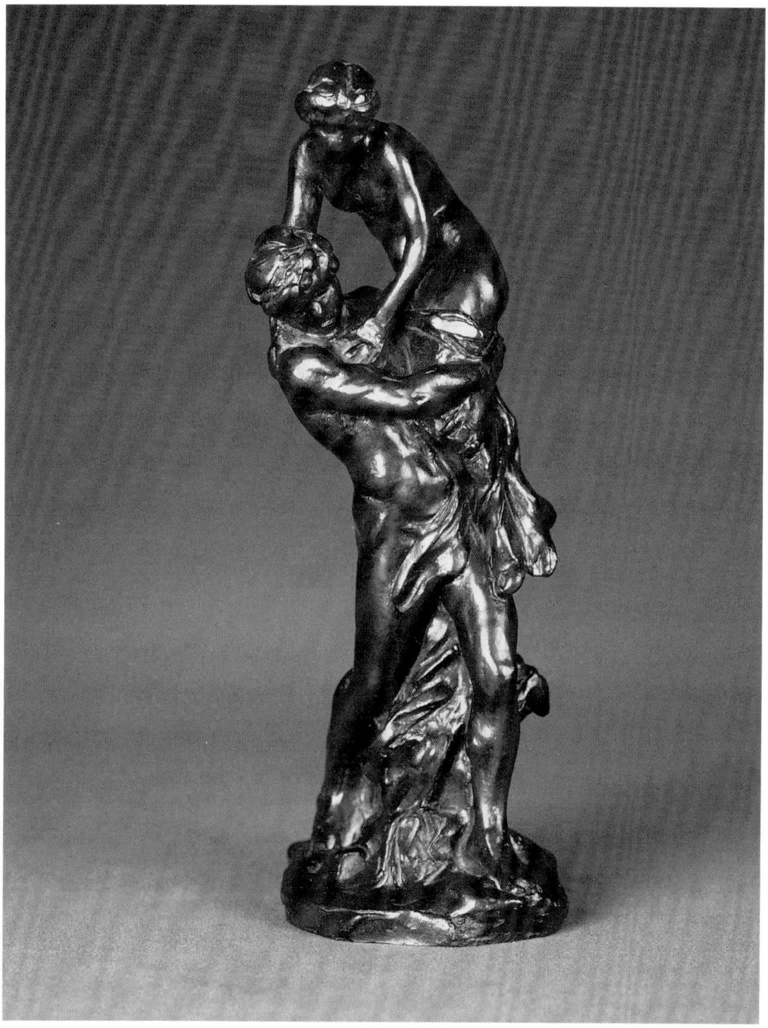

Some of the roughness of this work seems to derive from damage to the clay model (or the plaster cast from the clay) sustained in the artist's studio, but it is rough also because it was a sketch. The idea may have originated in Falguière's experiences during the siege of Paris in 1870, but it may also have been a by-product of his work on a monument to commemorate the French Revolution—a commission that preoccupied him during the last decade of his life—as one model for the monument (exhibited in 1876) includes a severed head with bandaged eyes and open mouth.[29] Perhaps the clay model was inspired by a cast from life. Certainly the bandage appears to reproduce the texture of an actual textile.

Dalou died in the year Hébrard's foundry opened, and Hébrard wasted no time in approaching the sculptor's heirs with the idea of casting in bronze the sketch models left in his studio—works of a kind that had generally been valued only by other artists and a few exceptional connoisseurs. He obtained the right to do so by contracting to make payments to the orphanage (administered by the city of Paris) in which the sculptor's disabled daughter was confined. A couple of sketches that Dalou had given to his lawyer and executor, Charles Auzoux, were added to the list of works to be cast, and one of these was an exceptionally beautiful small group now known as *The Espousal* (fig. 9). Some casts of this piece are likely to date from 1907, when Hébrard signed the contract with Auzoux, but the model must date from 1890 or soon after, when Dalou began work on an important commission for the duc de Gramont and his wife (née Marguerite de Rothschild).[30]

9 Aimé-Jules Dalou, *The Espousal (The Passage of the Rhine)*, model 1890/1892, cast c. 1907, bronze, 26.5 × 11.5 × 12.5, National Gallery of Art, Washington, Gift of Patricia Bauman and John L. Bryant, Jr., in Honor of Douglas Lewis and in Honor of the 50th Anniversary of the National Gallery of Art 1990.68.2

The ambitious marble group (now untraced) was erected in the new Parisian *hôtel* that had been built for the couple (demolished after World War I), part of a fountain set between the sweeping lines of a double staircase.[31] It was thus designed to be seen from in front, from both sides at different heights, and from above and behind. When exhibited in 1892 at the Société Nationale des Beaux-Arts, the group was entitled *Les Espousailles*, the newlyweds; but the sculpture was also entitled *The Crossing of the Rhine*, and because more than a decade had passed since the duke brought his bride to France from Frankfurt, the group was clearly more than a commemoration of their union. The sculpture must have been intended as an allegorical celebration of peaceful relations with Germany as well as an allusion to the crossing of the Rhine by French soldiers led by the duc de Gramont during the reign of Louis XIV.[32]

Dalou's champions, well aware of his interest in the sculpture of the seventeenth century, have been more comfortable with his adaptation of baroque themes and style to modern democratic and republican commissions than with the work he undertook for Queen Victoria or for this French nobleman and his Rothschild wife in which his exceptional sympathy with the sculpture of the seventeenth century is most apparent. Even the dynastic and political character of the Gramont fountain allegory is of a kind that would not have surprised Charles Lebrun. In style the group recalls Gian Lorenzo Bernini's great early gallery sculptures—notably, his *Aeneas and Anchises* and his *Pluto and Persephone* in the Borghese Gallery—although Dalou is likely to have absorbed Bernini at second hand, through the sculpture made for the gardens of Louis XIV that he studied so carefully.[33]

In creating his small clay sketch, Dalou probably used a simple modeling tool to make a few divisions for the fingers and to hint at a bunch of reeds, but most of the work was done with his hands, and his fingerprints on the model are retained in the bronze casts. Such is its fresh and personal character that we might suppose it was a first idea and an idea of his own, but in fact the spiral composition responds to the unusual domestic location for which the sculpture was commissioned. Moreover, the economy of means is breathtaking: so much of the apprehension and tender trust of the woman is conveyed merely by the tilt of her almost featureless face and the position of her left arm. Considered either as architectural ornament or as narrative group, this cannot be a first idea, and unlike the sketch models of Rodin (or indeed the waxes by Degas), the composition has a satisfying completeness. Indeed, as a composition it is hard to believe that the marble group was more successful.

Baroque terra-cotta sketches, similar in their compositional character and spontaneous handling, which have survived from the seventeenth and eighteenth centuries, began to come into fashion with collectors at this very date.[34] The idea that connoisseurs and fellow artists could appreciate such works was obviously not new—it is indeed the precondition for their survival. But there was much wider acceptance of such sculpture in the late nineteenth century because of the success of Rodin and the slightly later initiatives of Hébrard.

Hébrard went on to secure from the heirs of Degas the wax models from the artist's studio, which were then repaired and cast for his foundry by Albino Palazzolo in limited editions (Hébrard was a pioneer in promoting the strict numbering of casts) from 1921. After half a century of sales the "master bronzes" were acquired by Norton Simon. Then it was revealed that the original waxes had survived, and these were sold to Paul Mellon, who bequeathed most of them to the National Gallery of Art.[35] It is possible to argue that Degas had thought of some of these waxes as finished works of art, and their poor condition at the time of his death can be explained by his often imprudent technical experiments and the general neglect of his studio. He certainly toyed with the idea of having some of his sculpture cast in bronze, but it is quite certain that he never intended these models to be reproduced in the way that they were. It is also true, however, that a significant portion of his paintings—as also those by many other great modern masters—were left in his studio without clear indication as to whether he considered them as complete in any sense or even worthy of display. Artists have reasons for preserving not only the roughest ideas but also false starts and interesting failures. Rightly or wrongly, if an artist is believed to be a genius, every scrap by his or her hand is liable to be venerated as a relic.

In the case of sculpture, our hands can trace the impression of the sculptor's fingertips—an intoxicating sensation even when the imprint is not in the clay but in a bronze cast from a wax model that was in turn cast from a plaster model that was cast from the clay. Most of these sculptures cannot be given an appropriate base. Their intimacy also implies an informality in the manner of their display. They lie, as it were, in wait.

EVANESCENCE AND LOW RELIEF

The late nineteenth century witnessed the rediscovery of exceptionally low relief sculpture, sculpture quite unsuited to any form of public display not only because it was generally small in scale but also because it required unusual lighting to be appreciated at all. This coincided with an interest in Florentine fifteenth-century sculpture, especially the work of Desiderio da Settignano, then gradually being disengaged from the oeuvre of Donatello. The armor-clad female profile by Louis-Oscar Roty on the medallion struck to celebrate the centennial of the Banque de France in 1900 (fig. 10) includes an accomplished imitation of the fantasy armor known from inventions by Verrocchio and Leonardo da Vinci.[36] The combination of plate mail and maidenhood was familiar to the French from the great icon of Joan of Arc, but here perhaps France herself, or the bank, is represented by this image of spotless purity and impregnable probity, cast—or at least electrolytically plated—in silver. The lines of the impassive face are continued in the more animated forms of curled metal, curved plumes, and pointed leaves and contrasted with the flutter of a light ribbon and the tangle of loose hair over the shoulders. Turn it a little, and the entire image fades into light—or dark—as if to emphasize that this is only an idea or abstraction or, indeed, a dream of the past.

A relief made in 1897 by George Dupré during his stay at the Académie Française in Rome (fig. 11), inscribed with the word "Meditation," shows a woman in profile whose veil suggests the seer or priestess or widow withdrawn from the business of the world. The subject of her thoughts or at least the objects that have provoked them—the ruins of ancient Rome—are seen in the distance and are found on the verso (devoted to the abandoned, ivy-

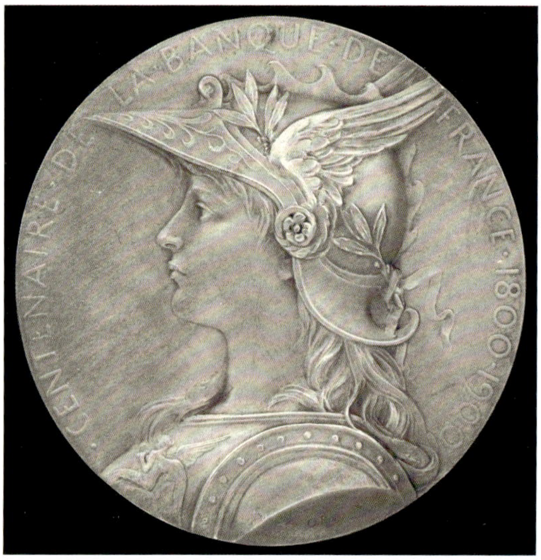

10 Louis-Oscar Roty, *Centennial of the Bank of France, 1800–1900,* 1900, silver, diameter 7, National Gallery of Art, Washington, Gift of David and Constance Yates 2004.49.1.a

clad Coliseum).[37] In this case the legibility of the very low relief is enhanced by the subtle, partial wiping of the chemical patination of the bronze, which thus becomes lighter in the salient folds of the veil and the columns in the distance and, of course, in the raised letters. Clarity of meaning, so often associated with allegory, is replaced by imagery and an idea that is deliberately crepuscular and even spectral.

Similar qualities can be found in Roty's masterpiece: a relief (figs. 12, 13) made to commemorate a public event—the funeral of a great statesman who had been assassinated in office—that also turned the event into a highly personal experience. On one side of the plaque the body of the president, Sadi Carnot, is carried to the Panthéon. No profile and no face are visible, only the foreshortened pallbearers (all veiled, all female) advancing toward their destination. On the reverse the president lies on his bier contemplated by his bereft motherland, La Patrie Veuve—a rigid horizontal corpse, a veiled erect matron, both in profile. On the obverse, receding lines of linear perspective are avoided, so the three separate elements of Roty's design—bier, temple, text—float in discrete zones. Like the long intervals in a funeral oration, the empty spaces are exceptionally eloquent. Furthermore, the emphasis changes as we move the relief in the light: one moment we read the text and admire a two-dimensional design; the next, the surface dissolves into space.

Sometimes it is not the fading of forms in the distance but the emergence of the figure from the ground, or from the material of which it is composed, that is striking in the low-relief sculpture of this period, and this may remind us of one aspect of the appeal of sketch models. Alexandre Charpentier's plaquette with a personification of Painting (fig. 14) is the opposite of Roty's profile on the medal of the Banque de France.[38] Line is avoided, as is clarity of contour. The further side of the body is only indistinctly defined. In addition to the melting profile and disappearing palette there are the softly rounded forms of hair and muscle that fit together like the swelling letters of the artist's monogram.

Many new developments in European and North American sculpture at the close of the nineteenth century may be associated with the idea of privacy. Bronze statuettes, especially those of a symbolist character, often presuppose private communion with the beholder. The appeal of the incomplete sketch and of the body fragment is also intimate. Medals obviously had always demanded scrutiny, often with the aid of a glass, commonly in private circumstances, but what is distinctive about the miniature sculpture at this date is how meditation on the intangible and elusive becomes the true subject, or at least an important part, of the work of art. And meditation is itself a private act.

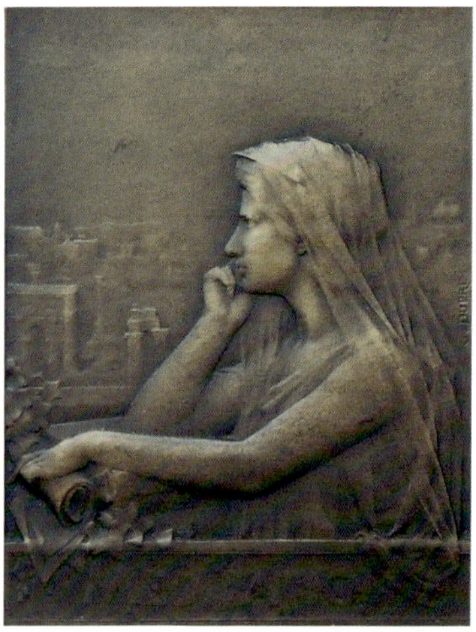

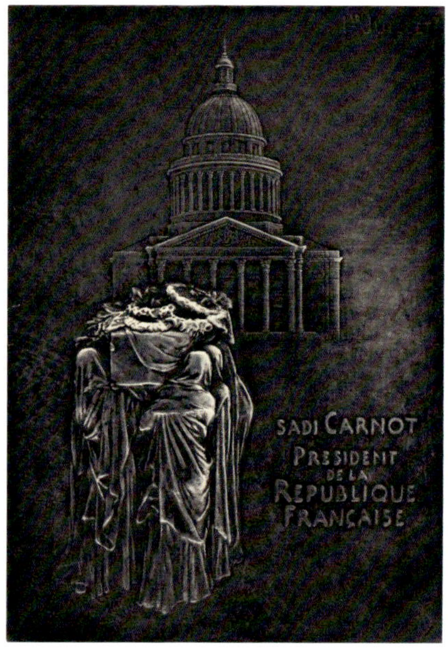

11 Georges Dupré, *Meditation,* 1902, bronze, 6.2 x 5, struck medal reduced from the cast version (26 x 20.5) completed in 1897, Private Collection

12 Louis-Oscar Roty, *The Body of President Sadi Carnot Borne to the Panthéon* (obverse), 1894, silvered bronze, 7.8 x 5.7, National Gallery of Art, Washington, Anonymous Gift

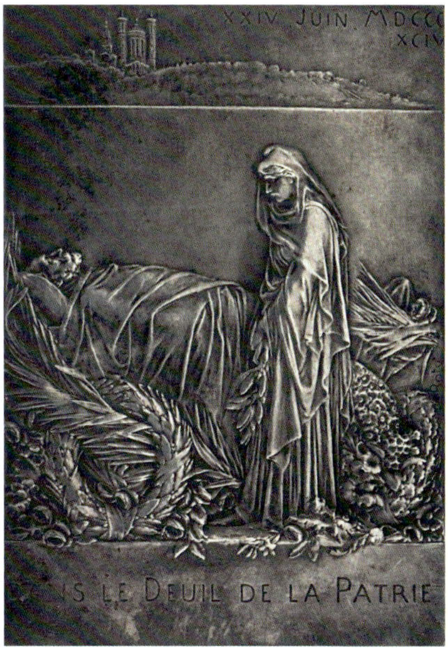

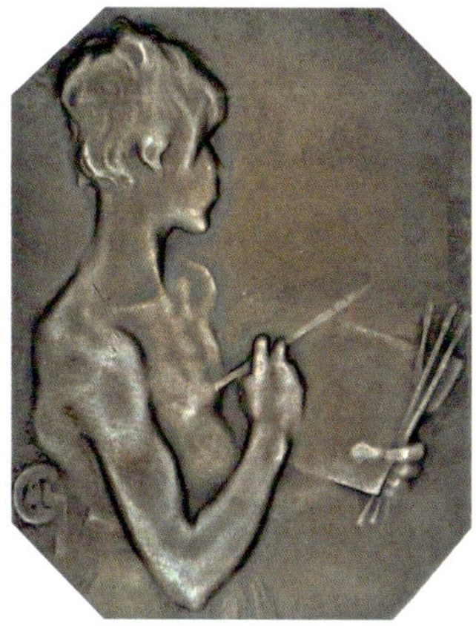

13 Louis-Oscar Roty, *France Mourning the President of the Republic* (reverse of fig. 12), 1894, bronze, 7.8 × 5.7, National Gallery of Art, Washington, Anonymous Gift

14 Alexandre-Louis-Marie Charpentier, *Allegory of Painting*, 1897, silver, 5.3 × 4.1, National Gallery of Art, Washington, Gift of Mark and Lynne Hammerschlag

A DARKER SIDE OF LIGHT: PRINTS, PRIVACY, AND POSSESSION

EPIGRAPH: "Emanation spontanée, immédiate du génie de l'artiste, l'estampe requiert d'être accueillie, goûtée un peu à la manière d'une confidence, dans l'intimité du calme avec la dévotion du silence." Quoted in Frits Lugt, *Marques des collections* (Amsterdam, 1921; reprint, San Francisco, 1975), 417, no. 2229.

1 This is reported by Charles Blanc, *L'Oeuvre complet de Rembrandt*, 2 vols. (Paris, 1859–1861), 1:98 (cited in Lugt 1921, 88–90, no. 485).

2 Charles Blanc, "Le Cabinet de M. Thiers," *Gazette des Beaux-Arts*, 1st ser., 12 (1862): 304–305: "Il y a, parmi les trésors de l'art et de la curiosité, des richesses qu'il faut avoir toujours sous les yeux pour entretenir le feu sacré dans son âme,... Mais il est des choses qu'il importe de ne pas voir à toute heure, du matin au soir, parce qu'on finirait par se blaser sur le plaisir qu'elles font. Une collection de dessins et d'estampes est mieux placée, par example, dans des portefeuilles que sous verre."

3 "Avec ses ressources, en apparence si bornées, elle a su fournir à Rembrandt les lumières tremblotantes, les pénombres mystérieuses et les noirs profonds dont il avait besoin pour ses philosophes et ses alchimistes cherchant le microcosme; pour ses synagogues d'architecture salomonique, ses Christ ressuscitant des morts, ses paysages traversés d'ombres et de rayons, et toutes les fantasmagories de son imagination songeuse, puissante et bizarre." Théophile Gautier, "Un Mot sur l'eau-forte," preface to the Société des Aquafortistes portfolio of 1863, reprinted in Janine Bailly-Herzberg, *L'Eau-forte de peintre au dix-neuvième siècle: La Société des Aquafortistes, 1862–1867*, 2 vols. (Paris, 1972), 1:266. See also Alison McQueen, *The Rise of the Cult of Rembrandt: Reinventing an Old Master in Nineteenth-Century France* (Amsterdam, 2003), chaps. 4, 5.

4 On the change in late nineteenth-century social thought, see H. Stuart Hughes, *Consciousness and Society: The Reorientation of European Social Thought, 1890–1930* (New York, 1958), chaps. 1, 2. For more recent analyses of the interconnections between society with the visual arts, see Peter Gay, *Pleasure Wars: The Bourgeois Experience—Victoria to Freud* (New York, 1998); and Richard Thomson, *The Troubled Republic: Visual Culture and Social Debate in France, 1889–1900* (New Haven, 2004).

5 See Martha Ward, "From Art Criticism to Art News: Journalistic Reviewing in Late Nineteenth-Century France," in *Art Criticism and Its Institutions*, ed. Michael R. Orwicz (Manchester, 1994), 162–182, on the professional identities of those who wrote art criticism. On the etching revival in France in general, see Bailly-Herzberg 1972; and Douglas Druick and Peter Zegers, "Degas and the Printed Image, 1856–1914," in *Edgar Degas: The Painter as Printmaker*, comp. Sue Welsh Reed and Barbara Stern Shapiro [exh. cat., Museum of Fine Arts, Boston] (Boston, 1984), xx–xxiv. For England, see Emma Chambers, *An Indolent and Blundering Art? The Etching Revival and the Redefinition of Etching in England, 1838–1892* (Aldershot, Vt., [1999]). For Belgium, see Stephen H. Goddard, "Print Culture in Nineteenth-Century Belgium," in *Les XX and the Belgian Avant-Garde: Prints, Drawings and Books, ca. 1890* [exh. cat., Spencer Museum of Art] (Lawrence, Kans., 1992), 75–97; for the United States, see Gladys Engel Lang and Kurt Lang, *Etched in Memory: The Building and Survival of Artistic Reputation* (Urbana, Ill., 2001).

6 See Stephen Bann, *Parallel Lines: Printmakers, Painters, and Photographers in Nineteenth-Century France* (New Haven, 2001), for the history of reproductive engraving, its production, and its reception. See Pierre Georgel, "The Society of Etchers in the 1860's," *Burlington Magazine* (May–August 1975): 551–552, on the long-term significance of the revival.

7 *Le Boulevard* (September 14, 1862); Charles Baudelaire, *Oeuvres complètes*, ed. Claude Pichois (with Jean Ziegler), 2 vols. (Paris, 1975–1976), 2:1145–1151; Charles Baudelaire, *Art in Paris, 1845–1862*, trans. and ed. Jonathan Mayne (London, 1965), 217–222; Michele Hannoosh, "Etching and Modern Art: Baudelaire's '*Peintres et aquafortistes*,'" *French Studies* 43 (1989): 47–60.

8 Baudelaire 1965, 221; Baudelaire 1975–1976, 2:1149.

9 The fundamental study of the Société des Aquafortistes remains Bailly-Herzberg 1972. A full record of the critical response to each of Cadart's annual portfolios is given

in vol. 2. Among the critics who wrote the prefaces for the society are Théophile Gautier, Philippe Burty, Thoré-Bürger, Jules-Antoine Castagnary, Eugene Montrosier, and Jules Janin.

10 "L'eau forte, telle que nous l'entendons, est un pur dessin ... mais c'est un dessin à plusieurs exemplaires, et, chose bizarre, dans le monde des *curieux*, où toute valeur augmente en raison de la rareté, une planche de laquelle on peut tirer un assez grand nombre d'épreuves est souvent plus estimée qu'un dessin unique. Il est certain que le plus beau lavis de Rembrandt n'a jamais été payé au même prix qu'une épreuve de *La Pièce de cent florins* ou du *Bourgmestre Six*." Charles Blanc, "De la gravure à l'eau-forte," *Gazette des Beaux-Arts*, 1st ser., 9 (1861): 194.

11 Hamerton 1864, 72.

12 Baudelaire 1965, 222. The idea of unmediated expression can be found in many variations from the 1860s on: Philippe Burty, "L'oeuvre de M. Francis Seymour Haden," *Gazette des Beaux-Arts*, 1st ser., 17 (1864): 271–287, 356–366; Théophile Gautier, "Un mot sur l'eau-forte," 1863, reprinted in Bailly-Herzberg 1972, 1:266–267; Thoré-Bürger, reprinted in Herzberg 1972, 1:270–271; Charles Blanc, *The Grammar of Painting and Engraving*, trans. Kate N. Doggett (New York, 1874), 268 (French ed., 1867); Hamerton 1864, 69–70; Jules Ladimir, "Les arts chalcographiques à l'exposition," *Revue des Beaux-Arts* 31 (1861): 244, quoted in Pamela Warner, "Jules de Goncourt aquafortiste: La rhétorique visuelle de l'eau-forte," *Cahiers Edmond et Jules de Goncourt* 11 (2004): 97; and Max Klinger, *Malerei und Zeichnung* (Leipzig, 1885), who subsumes etching under the general rubric "Griffelkunst."

13 Baudelaire 1965, 221–222; Baudelaire 1975–1976, 2:1149. This provides an aesthetic explanation for Blanc's puzzlement over the discrepancy in value between Rembrandt's etchings and his drawings.

14 See Walter Benjamin, "The Work of Art in the Age of Mechanical Reproduction," in *Illuminations*, trans. Harry Zohn (New York, 1968), 217–251.

15 See the complimentary review of his work in Maurice Hamel, "Le Salon de 1887," *Gazette des Beaux-Arts*, 2nd ser., 35 (1887): 480–481; and Alfred de Lostalot, "Exposition internationale de peinture et de sculpture (Galerie Georges Petit)" in the same publication, 525–526, where he was shown alongside James McNeill Whistler, Claude Monet, Max Liebermann, and Auguste Rodin.

16 Although see Clayson in this volume and Debora L. Silverman, *Art Nouveau in Fin-de-Siècle France: Politics, Psychology, and Style* (Berkeley, 1989), 224–228.

17 Frantz Jourdain, "Albert Besnard," in *De choses et d'autres* (Paris, 1902), 38, sees Besnard as the embodiment of Huysmans' character Des Esseintes.

18 On the omissions of the salon, see Philippe Burty, "La gravure et la lithographie, à l'exposition de 1861," *Gazette des Beaux-Arts*, 1st ser., 11 (1861): 172–179. In the mid-1880s salon critics were still interested in its reproductive capacity rather than its originality. Fourcaud, "Le Salon de 1884, part iv," *Gazette des Beaux-Arts*, 2nd ser., 30 (1884): 114–116.

19 Elizabeth Anne Prelinger, "The Symbolist Print" (PhD diss., Harvard University, 1987).

20 Nineteenth-century publications on domestic architecture abound, but they are heavily concentrated on the grand-scale mansions and *hôtels*. The prominent spokesman at the time on the social character of the *maison à loyer* in Paris was Charles Daly, *L'Architecture privée aux dix-neuvième siècle urbaine et suburbaine* (Paris, 1874). On the subject of aesthetics and domesticity in the nineteenth century, with additional bibliography, see especially Lisa Tiersten, "The Chic Interior and the Feminine Modern: Home Decorating as High Art in Turn-of-the Century Paris," in *Not at Home: The Suppression of Domesticity in Modern Art and Architecture*, ed. Christopher Reed (New York, 1996), 18–32.

21 Jacob von Falke, *Art in the House: Historical, Critical, and Aesthetical Studies on the Decoration and Furnishing of the Dwelling*, ed. Charles C. Perkins (Boston, 1879), 313, 315. Translated from *Die Kunst im Haus: Geschichtliche und kritisch-ästhetische Studien über die Decoration und Ausstattung der Wohnung* (Vienna, 1871). The book was based on a series of lectures Falke had given to the Austrian Museum for Art and Industry in Vienna, of which he was vice-director.

22 John Corry, *Satirical View of London: Or, a Descriptive Sketch of the English Metropolis with Strictures on Men and Manners*, 4th ed. (London, 1809), 131. See John Brewer, "'The Most Polite Age and the Most Vicious': Attitudes towards Culture as a Commodity, 1600–1800," in *The Consumption of Culture, 1600–1800*, eds. Ann Bermingham and John Brewer (London, 1995), 355.

23 For several advertisements for lithography shops featuring women patrons, see Diana Ewan Wolfe, *Prints about Prints* (New York, [1981]), nos. 26, 27, 31, 42, 44. On the social aspects of exhibitions and middle-class leisure in Victorian England, see Paula Gillet, *Worlds of Art: Painters in Victorian Society* (New Brunswick, N.J., 1990), 237–238.

24 Charles Locke Eastlake, *Hints on Household Taste in Furniture, Upholstery, and Other Details* (London, 1868), chaps. 5, 7; Robert Kerr, *The Gentleman's House; or How to Plan English Residences, from the Parsonage to the Palace* (London, 1865), 116–119.

25 Eastlake 1868, 194–198, approves of wide white margins, unlike Falke, who considers an array of framed prints or watercolors with large mats "a source of disturbance on the wall." Falke 1879, 221.

26 Anaïs Lebrun, comtesse de Bassanville, *L'Art de bien tenir une maison* (Paris, 1878), 70: "sujets sérieux et des cadres sévères." Antechambers she deems unsuitable for any framed objects unless the space is required as overflow for a committed art collector (191). Paintings, but never engravings, are for the salon (87). Thanks to Dominique Pety for this reference.

27 Edith Wharton and Ogden Codman Jr., *The Decoration of Houses* (New York, 1897), 119–120. Gustav Friedrich Waagen, *Treasures of Art in Great Britain*, trans. Lady Eastlake, 3 vols. (London, 1854), 3:120, favorably describes a house in which old master engravings were hung in the drawing rooms and contemporary engravings were relegated to the dining room.

28 Henri Béraldi, *Les Graveurs du XIXe siècle*, 12 vols. (Paris, 1885–1892), 7:179, cited in Pierre-Lin Renié, *Une image sur un mur: Images et décoration intérieure au XIXe siècle* [exh. cat., Musée Goupil] (Bordeaux, 2005), 31–34.

29 Joris-Karl Huysmans, *Against Nature* (1884), trans. Margaret Mauldon (Oxford, 1998), 52, said in reference to Bresdin's *Good Samaritan*.

30 They acquired the house in the 1860s, and Edmond later published a detailed account of the building and its contents: Edmond de Goncourt, *La Maison d'un artiste*, 2 vols. (Paris, 1881; reissued with introductions by Dominique Pety and Christian Galantaris, Dijon, 2003).

31 See Renié 2005, 46–61, for excerpts and interpretations of passages from contemporary novels employing prints as narrative motifs and 48–49 on Flaubert specifically. Fictional and nonfictional references to interior hangings in boudoirs are also collected in Séverine Jouve, *Obsessions et perversions dans la littérature et les demeures à la fin du dix-neuvième siècle* (Paris, 1996), 207–215. For the earlier history of prints as interior decor, including the eighteenth-century woman's diversion of framing prints, and also papering the walls of entire rooms with prints, see Susan Lambert, *The Image Multiplied: Five Centuries of Printed Reproductions of Paintings and Drawings* (London, 1987), 183.

32 Tiersten 1996, 31–32; Roger Henri-Guerrand, "Private Spaces," in *A History of Private Life*, ed. Michelle Perrot, vol. 4 (Cambridge, Mass., 1990), 541–542. On the nineteenth-century interest in collecting printed oddities, *fantaisies diverses* (playing cards, stamps, tobacco wrappers, and so on), see Alphonse Maze-Sencier, *Le Livre des collectionneurs* (Paris, 1885), chap. 5. On the status of women in relation to the spaces and objects around them, see Elizabeth Prelinger, "Tissot as Symbolist and Fetishist? A Surmise," in *Seductive Surfaces: The Art of Tissot*, ed. Katharine Lochnan, Studies in British Art, vol. 6 (New Haven, 1999), 185–211. See also the classic interpretation of the consequences conceiving a public and private self in opposition in Richard Sennett, *The Fall of Public Man* (New York, 1978).

33 Henry Havard, *L'Art dans la maison* (Paris, 1884), 430: "Si le boudoir est, par excellence, le sanctuaire de la maîtresse de maison, le cabinet de travail est le sanctuaire du maître du logis,—mais un sanctuaire considéré à un point de vue plus élevé, pris dans une acception plus haute, avec une signification plus noble, et surtout avec une destination moins futile." Leaving nothing to the owner's imagination, Havard goes on at

length about the proper furnishing and lighting of the study. For photographs of the collector Edmond Goncourt's *cabinet de travail* in 1886, see Michel Beurdeley and Michèle Maubeuge, *Edmond de Goncourt chez lui* (Nancy, [1991]), pls. 12, 13. Later documentation can be found in Atget's *Interiors*, a photographic essay on Parisian apartments done in 1909–1910. See the interiors of Atget's studio, captioned as "Intérieur de Mr R., Artiste Dramatique Rue Vavin." Most of these studies show cluttered apartments much as they would have been a generation earlier. On their reliability as records, see Molly Nesbit, *Atget's Seven Albums* (New Haven, 1992), 120–126.

34 "A portfolio of Prints may be laid on the table and give variety to the amusement of a winter's night, when variety of occupation is most in requisition, and all the circle, as they sit, may participate in the enjoyment." Joseph Maberly, *The Print Collector: An Introduction to the Knowledge Necessary for Forming a Collection of Ancient Prints* (London, 1844), 8–9. See also J. E. Wessely, *Anleitung zur Kenntniss und zum Sammeln der Werke des Kunstdruckes*, 2nd ed. (Leipzig, 1886), 205–206.

35 Advertising new editions of prints had been the practice in the periodical *Mercure de France* since the early eighteenth century. Peter Fuhring is compiling print publishers' stock lists internationally. For the list of publishers to date, see http://bingweb.binghamton.edu/~gmckee/Fuhring/List.html.

36 Chambers [1999] is the most valuable publication on the broader implications of the fine print in nineteenth-century European culture. Further on England, see Martha Tedeschi, "'Where the Picture Cannot Go, the Engravings Penetrate': Prints and the Victorian Art Market," *Museum Studies* 31 (2005): 8–19; Martin Hopkinson, *No Day without a Line: The History of the Royal Society of Painter-Printmakers, 1880–1999* (Oxford, 1999); and Andrea Fredericksen, "The Etching Club of London: A Taste for Painters' Etchings," *Philadelphia Museum of Art Bulletin* 92, no. 388 (2002). The London club initially published volumes or portfolios of etchings accompanied often by bad poetry or sententious literary texts.

On German etching societies, see Jay A. Clarke, "The Construction of Artistic Identity in Turn-of-the-Century Berlin: The Prints of Klinger, Kollwitz, and Liebermann" (PhD diss., Brown University, 1999); and Henrike Junge, *Wohlfeile Kunst: Die Verbreitung von Künstlergraphik seit 1870 und die Griffelkunst-Vereinigung Hamburg-Langenhorn* (Mainz, 1989). By the last quarter of the century, exquisitely produced periodicals that included original prints were being published by subscription in Berlin and Vienna. See the volumes of *Die Graphischen Künste*, 1879–, published by the Gesellschaft für vervielfältigende Kunst in Vienna at twenty-six marks an issue. The Société Internationale des Aquafortistes à Bruxelles was founded on the French model in 1869 and was dissolved already in 1877.

37 Such retailing was probably common to most prosperous cities by the late eighteenth century. See, for example, a sampling of advertisements published in Liverpool in its prime. Martin Hopkinson, "The Print Market in Liverpool in the Late Eighteenth Century," *Print Quarterly* 24 (2007): 107–115. By the mid-nineteenth century in Germany there was a publication strictly devoted to informing collectors of prints coming available on the market: *Intelligenz-Blatt*, a supplement to the *Archiv für die zeichnenden Künste* from 1855 to 1861–1862.

38 Chambers [1999], 176–177.

39 Already in the 1830s, publishers' advertisements for lithographs included images of women visiting shops and leafing through bound volumes and portfolios. A survey of the nearly three thousand names recorded in Frits Lugt's catalogue of collector's marks yields around a dozen nineteenth-century women who took the defining step of marking the works of art they acquired. There are those who collected prints or drawings in the usual sense, mainly Americans, and then an equal number with collections of fans and playing cards or the work of a single related or acquainted artist. See Lugt 1921, nos. 94, 137, 216, 405, 469, 693, 1248, 1368, 1424, 1871, 1879, and 2288. This list excludes women artists who marked their own work.

40 *The Diary of George A. Lucas, 1857–1909: An American Art Agent in Paris*, transcribed by Lilian Randall, 2 vols. (Princeton, 1979), 2:658, entries for November 3, 5, and 14. Lucas was simultaneously accumulating a major print collection of his own while serving as an agent for William Walters, whose fabulous collection now housed in its own museum in Baltimore includes almost every medium except prints.

41 John Evelyn, *Sculptura, or the History and Art of Chalcography* (London, 1662). See in the following century Karl Heinrich von Heinecken, *Idée générale d'une collection complète d'estampes* (Leipzig and Vienna, 1771); and William Gilpin, *An Essay on Prints* (London, 1792).

42 The classic work in English is Philip Gilbert Hamerton, *Etching and Etchers* (London, 1868). See also Maxime Lalanne, *Traité de la gravure à l'eau-forte* (Paris, 1866); Sylvester R. Koehler, *Etching: An Outline of Its Technical Processes and Its History, with Some Remarks on Collections and Collecting* (New York, 1885); and Wessely 1886. See also the several accounts of collector's practices in Antony Griffiths, ed., *Landmarks in Print Collecting* (London, 1996).

43 An exception is the enhanced edition of Joseph Maberly, *The Print Collector: An Introduction to the Knowledge Necessary for Forming a Collection of Ancient Prints . . . with an Account of Contemporary Etching and Etchers by Robert Hoe Jr.* (New York, 1880). This is a reissue of Maberly's handbook published in London in 1844, but with a supplement on contemporary prints by Robert Hoe, book collector and founder of the Grolier Club.

44 The most extensive attention given to conservation and storage is Maberly 1880, chap. 6; see also Wessely 1886, 242–266. Daniel Carlsson Solander (1733–1782), natural scientist and keeper of printed books at the British Museum, invented the standard box for storing prints and documents. On the virtues of boxes, see Maberly 1880, 107–108. Portfolios were commercially available in the second half of the nineteenth century. On exposure to light, see Blanc, "Le Cabinet de M. Thiers," 1st ser., 12 (1862): 307.

45 For a well-informed and entertaining (though undocumented) overview of this history, see Jean Adhémar, "Le Public de l'estampe," *Nouvelles de l'Estampe* 37 (1978): 7–19. For a range of specific collectors, see Griffiths 1996. For the earlier history, see Peter Parshall, "Art and the Theater of Knowledge: The Origins of Print Collecting in Northern Europe," *Harvard University Art Museums Bulletin* 2, no. 3 (1994): 7–36; and Antony Griffiths, "Print Collecting in Rome, Paris, and London in the Early Eighteenth Century," in the same publication, 37–59.

46 The scholarship on this subject is vast, but see James Smith Allen, *In the Public Eye: A History of Reading in Modern France, 1800–1940* (Princeton, 1991), with further bibliography.

47 Adam von Bartsch, *Le Peintre-graveur*, 21 vols. (Vienna, 1803–1821).

48 See Chambers [1999], 63–69, esp. her discussion of the theories of Jean Baudrillard.

49 On the earliest known large collections of prints, see Mark McDonald et al., eds., *The Print Collection of Ferdinand Columbus (1488–1539)* (London, 2004); Peter Parshall, "The Print Collection of Ferdinand, Archduke of Tyrol," *Jahrbuch der Kunsthistorischen Sammlungen in Wien* 78 (1982): 139–184; William Robinson, "'This Passion for Prints': Collecting and Connoisseurship in Northern Europe during the Seventeenth Century," in *Printmaking in the Age of Rembrandt* [exh. cat., Museum of Fine Arts, Boston] (Boston, 1981), xxvii–xlviii; Jan van der Waals, "Met boek en plaat: Het boeken-en atlassenbezit van verzamelaars," in *De Wereld binnen handbereik: Nederlands kunst- en rariteitenverzamelingen, 1585–1735* [exh. cat., Historical Museum] (Amsterdam, 1992), 205–231; and the Atlas van Stolk, a historical image collection established in the nineteenth century in Rotterdam, and I believe still being expanded.

50 See Marjorie Cohn, *A Noble Collection: The Spencer Albums of Old Master Prints* [exh. cat., Fogg Art Museum] (Cambridge, Mass., 1992), 11–55.

51 Jean de La Bruyère, *Les Caractères ou les moeurs de ce siècle* (Paris, 1688), quoted in Robinson 1981, xliii. On the illicit practices of forgers, see F. C. Joullain, *Réflexions sur la peinture et la gravure, accompagnées d'une courte dissertation sur le commerce de la curiosité, et les ventes en général* (Paris, 1786; reprint, Geneva, 1973), 134–154.

52 Wilkie Collins, *The Woman in White* (1859–1860; reprint, Harmondsworth, 1982), 65–70.

53 Hamerton 1868, 30. See also Maberly 1880; Wessely 1886, 229–230; and esp. Charles Blanc, "Lettre à l'auteur sur la curiosité," in Blanc, *Le Trésor de la curiosité, tiré des catalogues de vente, etc.*, 2 vols. (Paris, 1857), 1:i–v, on the distinction between *amateurs* and *curieux d'estampes*.

54 The letter is written to Dürer's close friend Willibald Pirckheimer. Heinz Lüdecke and Susannne Heiland, *Dürer und die Nachwelt* (Berlin, 1955), 24.

55 See Baudelaire 1965, 179; and Michele Hannoosh, "Etching and Modern Art: Baudelaire's *Peintres et aquafortistes*," *French Studies* 43 (1989): 51–53.

56 See Max Klinger, *Malerei und Zeichnung* (Leipzig, 1891), 14, 21, 29. See also Hertel in this volume, pages 87–88, 125.

57 Baudelaire 1965, 221.

58 Degas' technical experiments beginning in the late 1870s constitute an altogether different dimension of the print as a medium of avant-garde modernism, one that had more to do with formal strategies than with content per se. On Degas' engagement with the print, see Douglas Druick and Peter Zegers in Boston 1984, xv–lxxiii.

LOOKING WITHIN THE CELL OF PRIVACY

EPIGRAPH: Christoph Asendorf, *Batteries of Life: On the History of Things and Their Perception in Modernity*, trans. Don Reneau (Berkeley, 1993), 119. I am grateful to Peter Parshall, who stepped out on a limb to invite my contribution and who shaped my thinking and writing decisively and kindly. I also thank Andrew Nogal and the participants in the Modern France Workshop at the University of Chicago, November 2, 2007, who worked over an earlier version of this essay.

1 Sharon Marcus, *Apartment Stories: City and Home in Nineteenth-Century Paris and London* (Berkeley, 1999), 136. I agree with Marcus' persuasive critique of the orthodoxies concerning Second Empire Paris as a preponderantly extroverted city. According to Marcus, "Private life did not emerge only as the nostalgic and belated antidote to an expanded public realm; rather, Haussmannization itself directly promoted the containment of urban spaces" (139). See also Hermann Muthesius, *Das englische Haus: Entwicklung, Bedingungen, Anlage, Aufbau, Einrichtung und Innenraum* (Berlin, 1904–1905).

2 Charles Rice, for example, explains that the interior as a cultural form always bears its "newly illuminated impossibility as a space of retreat and immersion." Rice, *The Emergence of the Interior: Architecture, Modernity, Domesticity* (New York, 2007), 35.

3 Rice 2007, 2.

4 Marcus 1999, 138. On the architecture of the interior, see Monique Eleb with Anne Debarre, *L'invention de l'habitation moderne: Paris, 1880–1914* (Paris, 1995); Monique Eleb-Vidal with Anne Debarre-Blanchard, *Architectures de la vie privée: Maisons et mentalités, XVIIe–XIXe siècles* (Brussels, 1989); and Donald J. Olsen, "Inside the Dwelling," in Olsen, *The City as a Work of Art: London, Paris, Vienna* (New Haven, 1986), 101–131.

5 Marcus 1999, 143.

6 Walter Benjamin, "Paris—Capital of the Nineteenth Century," 1939 exposé, quoted in Rice 2007, 26.

7 Marcus 1999, 148.

8 Indeed Michael Fried (following Edmond Duranty) argues that interiority and its "absorptive worlds or cloisters" defined the thematic or spatial modernity of much nineteenth-century French painting. Fried, *Manet's Modernism, or the Face of Painting in the 1860s* (Chicago, 1996), 259–261. I cannot say, however—having been asked—whether a "development" (as change) occurred between 1850 and 1900.

9 See Peter Parshall's essay in the present catalogue.

10 See Beverly Gordon, "Women's Domestic Body: The Conceptual Conflation of Women and Interiors in the Industrial Age," *Winterthur Portfolio* 31, no. 4 (1996): 281–301.

11 On bibelot-filled interiors, see Rémy G. Saisselin, "Woman, Desire, and the Bibelot," in Saisselin, *The Bourgeois and the Bibelot* (New Brunswick, N.J., 1984), 51–74; and Lisa Tiersten, "The Chic Interior and the Feminine Modern: Home Decorating as High Art in Turn-of-the-Century Paris," in *Not at Home: The Suppression of Domesticity in Modern Art and Architecture*, ed. Christopher Reed (New York, 1996), 18–32. Further on nature, according to Asendorf 1993, 125: "The *interieur* compensates for the loss of the connection to nature caused by industrialization."

12 Leora Auslander, "The Gendering of Consumer Practices in Nineteenth-Century France," in *The Sex of Things: Gender and Consumption in Historical Perspective,* eds. Victoria de Grazia and Ellen Furlough (Berkeley, 1996), 79–112.

13 Marcus 1999, 139.

14 He was a member of the Generation of 1863, as Michael Fried has called the cluster of naturalist, Paris-based innovators. The key members were Whistler, Henri Fantin-Latour, Alphonse Legros, and Edouard Manet—all portrayed in Fantin's *Homage to Delacroix*, 1864. Fried 1996, 185–261. Martha Tedeschi, curator in the department of prints and drawings, The Art Institute of Chicago, and coauthor of the 1998 catalogue raisonné of Whistler lithographs, concurs that "Weary" is Whistler's title (personal communication, December 10, 2007). See the two drawings considered to be studies for the etching: *Weary,* Clark Art Institute (1955.1751), and *Sleeping Woman,* National Gallery of Art, Rosenwald Collection (1948.11.306).

15 A contradiction such as the one I have observed here in representations of women alone does not belong exclusively to the arts of the later nineteenth century (compare eighteenth-century boudoir scenes, for example). The salient point is that Whistler's print attempts to maintain the image of a sitter who is not observed or observable by others—devising a new kind of naturalism.

16 André-Charles Coppier writes: "[La pièce] représente une jeune fille à sa toilette, derrière un paravent de Coromandel, dont on aperçoit deux feuillets déployés" (The work represents a young woman at her toilette; behind is a screen from Coromandel [the southeast coast of India], two wings of which are displayed). Coppier, *Les eaux-fortes de Besnard* (Paris, 1920), 73, no. 96.

17 Loys Delteil, *Le peintre-graveur illustré (XIXe et XXe siècles),* vol. 4: *Anders Zorn* (Paris, 1909), no. 103; Coppier 1920, no. 96, 73. Besnard was Zorn's closest friend in Paris, according to Elizabeth Broun, *The Prints of Anders Zorn* [exh. cat., Spencer Museum of Art] (Lawrence, Kans., 1979), 61, no. 31.

18 Nancy Mowll Mathews and Barbara Stern Shapiro, *Mary Cassatt: The Color Prints* [exh. cat., Williams College Museum of Art] (New York, 1989), 151–156; Michel Melot, *Mary Cassatt, Impressions* [exh. cat., Musée d'Art Américain Giverny] (Giverny, 2005); Kathleen Adler, *Mary Cassatt Prints* [exh. cat., National Gallery of Art] (London, 2006).

19 Another drawing (graphite and black chalk) for *The Coiffure* resides in the collection of the National Gallery of Art, Rosenwald Collection (1948.11.50). It is compositionally very close to the final drypoint and aquatint.

20 For example, *Standing Nude (Dark),* c. 1879, softground etching or aquatint on paper (The Art Institute of Chicago, Ursula and Stanley Johnson Collection), and *Standing Nude with a Towel,* c. 1879, softground etching and aquatint with scratching on paper (Private Collection). They are reproduced in Judith A. Barter, *Mary Cassatt: Modern Woman* [exh. cat., The Art Institute of Chicago] (Chicago, 1988), 122.

21 James Smith Allen, *In the Public Eye: A History of Reading in Modern France, 1800–1940* (Princeton, 1991), 155. Allen continues, "Thus by 1900, French portraits assume that books are private concerns, be they profound or trivial, quite apart from the social relations of ordinary life" (174). He argues that the difference between pre- and post-ancien régime images of solitary readers is the degree of engagement: "The subject is not a passive or idle sitter, but an actively engaged reader, especially after the Old Regime.... As a general rule after 1800... most artists depicted more serious readers" (167, 169). Allen eventually reveals that he is characterizing works of art but not necessarily the social practices that they describe. To wit: "Curiously, reading's self-contained nature in portraiture poses a problem: it appears to contradict the remarkable sociability of French readers evident in other historical sources" (174). The contradiction between Allen's identification of solitude in art and sociability in practice is jarring, to be sure. The prints discussed here certainly betray a preference for the trope of the solitary interior reader in modernity.

22 Loys Delteil, *Le peintre-graveur illustré (XIXe et XXe siècles),* vol. 30: *Albert Besnard par Louis Godefroy* (Paris, 1926), no. 82.

23 Coppier identifies her as Madame Besnard: "Mme Besnard lit, le soir, sous la lampe, les dernières nouvelles des journaux. Son profil se détache en ombre chinoise sur le foyer

lumineux qu'elle masque entièrement" (In the evening by lamplight, Madame Besnard reads the latest news from a newspaper. Her profile stands out in Chinese shadow against the luminous foyer that she blocks out entirely). Coppier 1920, 63, no. 79.

24 Delteil 1926, no. 59.

25 In Barter 1988, no. 42, 263, the print is dated c. 1880. Cat. 41, 263, is the closely connected graphite work on paper, *Drawing for "Interior: On the Sofa,"* The Art Institute of Chicago, Ursula and Stanley Johnson Family Collection, also dated c. 1880 in the Barter catalogue.

26 The contrast to an 1892 print by Besnard is instructive: *Reading (Diamond-Shaped Sheet).* Delteil 1926, no. 103; Coppier 1920, 70, no. 89. In many ways cognate to the Cassatt—it also figures a seated reading woman who looks up from the book on her lap to "dream"—Besnard's model, despite the message telegraphed by the deliberateness of placing her head in her hand (she's thinking!), appears to perform reverie with her theatricalized features rather than actually embodying it.

27 Eugenia Parry Janis, *Degas Monotypes: Essay, Catalogue and Checklist* [exh. cat., Fogg Art Museum] (Cambridge, Mass., 1968), pl. 34, checklist 141. "Degas à Lepic" is inscribed on the plate.

28 See the related discussions of the female bodies in Degas' brothel monotypes in Hollis Clayson, *Painted Love: Prostitution in French Art of the Impressionist Era* (New Haven, 1991), 27–55; and Charles Bernheimer, "Degas' Brothels: Voyeurism and Ideology," *Representations* 20 (Fall 1987): 158–186. But contextual differences are important: in contrast to the scenario under discussion here, it is a substantially different matter when the triumph of exteriority is staged within the theater of venal sex, and the body is on offer to others as part of professional routine and marketplace necessity.

29 For example, see the spectator-oriented, erotically enraptured reverie of the female protagonist in *Lady Reading the Letters of Heloise and Abelard* by Auguste Bernard, called Bernard d'Agesci, c. 1780 (oil on canvas, The Art Institute of Chicago 1994.430).

30 Delteil 1926, no. 15.

31 Coppier 1920, no. 12, 4 and 17–18.

32 Mary Cassatt's *Five O'Clock Tea,* 1880 (oil on canvas, Museum of Fine Arts, Boston) centers on the contrast between a hat- and glove-wearing, visiting tea drinker and a hatless and gloveless hostess. In the color print *Afternoon Tea Party,* 1890–1891, the surfaces of the adjacent two pairs of hands are not so easily identified, let alone differentiated. A persuasive case can be made that all four hands are gloveless because they are virtually identical, but the visitor's hands may indeed be a bit darker and hence gloved.

33 Cut from 40 × 76 to 29 × 40 cm. Coppier 1920, 45.

34 Delteil 1926, 67; Coppier 1920, 45, no. 57. Coppier was effusive: "Cette eau-forte magistrale qui ne doit rien à personne, comme conception et comme technique de graveur, marquera une date dans l'évolution de l'eau-forte moderne" (This masterly etching that owes nothing to anyone, in terms of conception and technique, will mark an important date in the evolution of the modern etching).

35 Coppier 1920, 44, finds that she bears an "expression d'angoisse," but I find the face to be more open in its intense rumination and thus less emotional (that is, not conventionally feminized).

36 Delteil 1926, no. 60; Coppier 1920, 43–44, no. 55, and 98. See also *The Dreamer,* 1889? Delteil 1926, no. 88.

37 According to Coppier: "Elle est drapée dans un manteau à collet entr'ouvert sur un corsage à gilet clair" (She is draped in a collared overcoat partially opened over a blouse and pale vest). Coppier 1920, 43–44.

38 It was done in February 1894 in New York at the home of Thomas Wheeler, according to *Zorn (1860–1920): Exposition de son oeuvre gravé* [exh. cat., Bibliothèque Nationale] (Paris, 1952), 29, cat. 37. This production detail sheds little light on its intensities.

39 M. E. Alkman, *Varia* (December 1902), quoted in Delteil 1909, no. 84. "C'est une femme de la famille de Baudelaire et de Edgar Allan Poe—la femme qui éveille le désir le plus chaud, l'horreur la plus mortelle, la haine la plus amère en un mot, la femme-calice du plus doux et du plus dangereux poison."

40 Zorn even gave Deering the use of his studio in Paris in 1893, according to the Northwestern University Library Art Collection Web site (http://www.library.northwestern.edu/art/read_rm_art.html). Douglas K.S. Hyland, "Zorn and His American Patrons," in Hyland and Hans Henrik Brummer, *Zorn: Paintings, Graphics, and Sculpture* [exh. cat., Birmingham Museum of Art] (Birmingham, Ala., 1986), 45. Delteil 1909, no. 78, notes the rarity of the state reproduced and that it came from the Charles Deering collection. Birgitta Sandström, *Anders Zorn, 1860–1920: An Introduction to His Life and Achievements* (Mora, Sweden, 1996), 15–16.

41 Hyland 1986, 24; Jane K. Bledsoe, ed., *Anders Zorn Rediscovered* [exh. cat., University Art Museum, California State University] (Long Beach, Calif., 1984), 21.

42 Hyland 1986, 24.

43 Hyland 1986, 24.

44 See Felix Krämer, *Das unheimliche Heim: Zur Interieurmalerei um 1900* (Cologne, 2007).

45 That the print is set in a music room has not been taken into account. What if the tensions in the etching could be linked to historically specific experiences of listening or of reading in company? I thank Martha Ward for challenging my reading in this way. A satisfactory response would entail the consultation of two recent publications: Garrett Stewart, *The Look of Reading: Book, Painting, Text* (Chicago, 2006); and Martha Ward and Anne Leonard, eds., *Looking and Listening in Nineteenth-Century France* (Chicago, 2007).

46 Delteil 1926, no. 89. Coppier 1920, 58–59, no. 74, describes a tranquil scene and finds the armchair rather unproblematic: "Il n'y a de réel sujet, dans cette pièce puissante, que l'irruption de la lumière d'hiver traversant deux grands rideaux de mousseline et se jouant sur les meubles d'un salon. Une jeune femme lit, le dos tourné à la lumière, tandis qu'un garçonnet se chauffe auprès d'une cheminée luisant dans la pénombre. Un grand fauteuil anglais, de ton assourdi, barre le premier plan et fait valoir par contraste la transparence des mousselines, la luminosité si heureusement rendue, des deux fenêtres closes." (There is no real subject matter in this powerful print other than the irruption of winter light passing through two large mousseline curtains that plays upon the furniture in a living room. A young woman reads, her back turned to the light, while a young boy warms himself in front of a fireplace glowing in the shadows. An English armchair, in a muffled tone, bars the foreground and emphasizes, by contrast, the transparency of the mousseline drapes over the two closed windows, and the felicity of their luminosity.)

47 Sigmund Freud, "The 'Uncanny'" (1919), in *The Standard Edition of the Complete Psychological Works of Sigmund Freud*, ed. James Strachey, vol. 17 (London, 1955), 217–252. On the uncanny in another extraordinary representation of the interior, John Singer Sargent's painting *The Daughters of Edward Darley Boit*, 1882, see Susan Sidlauskas, *Body, Place, and Self in Nineteenth-Century Painting* (Cambridge, 2000), 73–74.

48 Anthony Vidler, *The Architectural Uncanny: Essays in the Modern Unhomely* (Cambridge, Mass., 1992), 4.

49 The visitor's face is even more anxious and pinched in *Drawing of "Interior Scene,"* 1879–1880 (Cleveland Museum of Art), reproduced in Barter 1988, 264, no. 43.

50 Melot 2005, 21. I have elsewhere tried to argue that Cassatt's domestic themes explicitly engage and explore the tensions of Franco-American social encounters: "Maternity as Alibi in Mary Cassatt's Paintings of Women and Children" (unpublished paper, 2001).

51 For discussions of the bonds and the tensions between servants and their employers, including those between women, see Sarah Maza, "Life in the Household," in Maza, *Servants and Masters in Eighteenth-Century France: The Uses of Loyalty* (Princeton, 1983), 157–198; and Bonnie Smith, *Ladies of the Leisure Class: The Bourgeoises of Northern France in the Nineteenth Century* (Princeton, 1981).

52 Two pastels over monotype (both c. 1876–1877) are instructive in this regard. The interaction between the two women in both *Woman Getting Out of the Bath* (Norton Simon Museum, Pasadena) and *Woman Getting Out of the Bath* (Musée d'Orsay, Paris) is much more restrained and the figures are more generalized than in the monotype under discussion here. See Richard Thomson, *Degas: The Nudes* (London, 1988), figs. 82, 83; see also fig. 62. The dark field manner, fireplace, and overall mood of *Woman by a Fireplace* are very close to those in one of

Degas' most ambiguous monotypes: *The Foyer (The Fireplace)*, c. 1880 (Private Collection, France); Eugenia Parry Janis, *Degas Monotypes* [exh. cat., Fogg Art Museum] (Cambridge, Mass., 1968), no. 37. Whether Degas' bathers must be understood as prostitutes or, alternatively, proletarian women accessible to the male gaze, has interested many scholars. For example, Anthea Callen has written about "voyeurism and the narratives of sexual conquest" in such works; see Callen, *The Spectacular Body: Science, Method and Meaning in the Work of Degas* (New Haven, 1995), 71. That the world referenced in *Woman by a Fireplace* may not be unambiguously bourgeois does not detract from the vividness of Degas' imagination of a bathing woman in a private space to some degree threatened by a proximate female servant.

53 Elizabeth Prelinger, "Tissot as Symbolist and Fetishist? A Surmise," in *Seductive Surfaces: The Art of Tissot*, ed. Katharine Lochnan (New Haven, 1999), 187.

54 Prelinger 1999, 207. But Prelinger concludes that "the artist, whose obsession with detail leaves nothing visual to the imagination, has by contrast deliberately left any interpretation open-ended and unfixed." I see less open-endedness.

55 Victoria Rosner, "Studies," in Rosner, *Modernism and the Architecture of Private Life* (New York, 2005), 91–126.

56 Vidler 1992, 17–20.

57 Jay McKean Fisher, *The Prints of Edouard Manet* [exh. cat., International Exhibitions Foundation] (Washington, 1985), 111–116.

58 Fisher 1985, 115. My colleague the architectural historian David Van Zanten has remarked: "The moment I realized that it [my essay] isn't really about space... is Manet having the shutters open inward—shutters NEVER open inward—so that Manet has them do so for some reason of meaning or composition" (personal communication, November 1, 2007).

59 Vidler 1992, 17.

60 An excellent discussion of more decisively moody urban interiors (especially those of the Belgian artist Xavier Mellery) is Sharon L. Hirsh, "City Interiors and Interiority," in Hirsh, *Symbolism and Modern Urban Society* (Cambridge, 2004), 217–256.

THE WORLD INSIDE

EPIGRAPH: Peter Handke, "Unterscheidungen," *Die Innenwelt der Aussenwelt der Innenwelt* (Frankfurt, 1969), 140. Unless noted otherwise, translations from the German are mine.

1 "The right to be let alone" is how in 1928 Supreme Court Justice Louis Brandeis put what he considered a fundamental human right. See Philippa Strum, ed., *Brandeis on Democracy* (Lawrence, Kans., 1995), chap. 8, "The Right to Be Let Alone," 198–207.

2 The three artists are discussed more side by side than together in Frances Carey and Antony Griffiths, *The Print in Germany, 1880–1933: The Age of Expressionism* [exh. cat., The British Museum, London] (New York, 1984). The standard catalogues of their graphic oeuvres are Hans Wolfgang Singer, *Max Klingers Radierungen, Stiche und Steindrucke, Wissenschaftliches Verzeichnis* (Berlin, 1909), hereafter Singer; August Klipstein, *Käthe Kollwitz: Verzeichnis des graphischen Werkes* (Bern, 1955), hereafter Klipstein; and Gustav Schiefler, *Max Liebermann, Sein Graphisches Werk* (Berlin, 1907, 1914, 1923), hereafter Schiefler.

3 The preference of German artists for the print cycle relates to the concept of privacy. See *The German Print Portfolio, 1890–1983: Serials for a Private Sphere* [exh. cat., The David and Alfred Smart Museum of Art, The University of Chicago] (London, 1992); and Gerhard Pommeranz-Liedtke, *Der graphische Zyklus von Max Klinger bis zur Gegenwart: Ein Beitrag zur Entwicklung der deutschen Graphik von 1880 bis 1955* [exh. cat., Akademie der Künste, Berlin] (Berlin, 1956).

4 When we consider the various spaces for viewing such art, Rainer Maria Rilke's description of the Kunstsalon Cassirer, the backbone of the Berlin Secession, comes to mind: "Everything is intended as a backdrop for a good, quiet visit... one leans against the long reading table, bent over an album of Böcklin prints or holding a volume of the Goncourts, one is filled with contentment and unconsciously, almost without gratitude, accepts the pleasure afforded by this comfortable environment." Peter Paret, *The Berlin Secession* (Cambridge, Mass., 1980), 70.

5 Erwin Panofsky, *The Life and Art of Albrecht Dürer* (Princeton, 1971), 3, put the concept of "German interiority" in a nutshell: "German psychology is marked by a curious dichotomy clearly reflected in Luther's doctrine of 'Christian Liberty,' as well as in Kant's distinction between an 'intelligible character' which is free even in a state of material slavery and an 'empirical character' which is predetermined even in a state of material freedom. The Germans, so easily regimented in political and military life, were prone to extreme subjectivity and individualism in religion, in metaphysical thought, and, above all, in art."

6 See Sabine Schulze, ed., *Innenleben: Die Kunst des Interieurs, Vermeer bis Kabakov* [exh. cat., Städelsches Kunstinstitut und Städtische Galerie, Frankfurt] (Ostfildern-Ruit, 1998). The exhibition focused on the concept of bourgeois interiority and on the interior as psychogram and experimental field. This deliberate delimitation of the concept is first addressed in Johann Brändle, *Das Problem der Innerlichkeit: Hamann, Herder, Goethe* (Bern, 1950).

7 The most extreme version of this would be a position many artists and intellectuals in Germany assumed for themselves between 1933 and 1945 as justified and tenable, the so-called inner emigration of one's true, integral self, the withdrawal into silence. Peter-Uwe Hohendahl and Egon Schwarz, eds., *Exil und innere Emigration* (Frankfurt, 1973).

8 See Christiane Hertel, "Dis / Continuities in Dresden's Dances of Death," *Art Bulletin* 82, no. 1 (2000): 83–116.

9 Max Liebermann, *Die Phantasie in der Malerei* (Leipzig, n.d., based on 4th ed., Berlin, 1916), "Vorwort," 6.

10 Liebermann 1916, "Einleitung," 7.

11 Julius Bernhard Rohr's *Einleitung zur Ceremonielwissenschafft der Grossen Herren* (1729), ed. Monika Schlechte (Leipzig, 1990), first laid out the rules for the suspension of rules. Frederick the Great famously mastered the art of private travel. In our day the present king of Jordan made headlines because of his private, "incognito" travels within his country on ascending to the throne.

12 On these instances of rejection or censorship, see Sebastian Müller, "Official Support and Bourgeois Opposition in Wilhelmine Culture," in *The Divided Heritage: Themes and Problems in German Modernism*, ed. Irit Rogoff (Cambridge, 1990), 163–190; Christiane Hertel, "'Mit unserer Metaphysik lässt sich alles machen': Zu Max Klingers Gemälden *Die Kreuzigung Christi* und *Pietà*," *Städel-Jahrbuch*, n.s., 13 (1991): 199–226; Katrin Boskamp, *Studien zum Frühwerk von Max Liebermann mit einem Verzeichnis der Gemälde und Ölstudien von 1866–1889* (Hildesheim, 1994), 75–115; Paret 1980, 21–24; Elizabeth Prelinger, *Käthe Kollwitz*, with essays by Alessandra Comini and Hildegard Bachert [exh. cat., National Gallery of Art] (Washington, 1992), 179; Julius Elias, "Käthe Kollwitz," *Kunst und Künstler* 15 (1917): 540–549, reprinted in *Die Kollwitz-Sammlung des Dresdner Kupferstichkabinettes* [exh. cat., Käthe Kollwitz Museum Köln] (Cologne, 1989), 21–28; and, generally, on the "Lex Heinze," a censorship law proposed and debated in Parliament in 1893, see Ludwig Leiss, *Kunst im Konflikt: Kunst und Künstler im Widerstreit mit der Obrigkeit* (Berlin, 1971).

13 On the difficulty of artistic self-validation in these circumstances, see Irit Rogoff, "The Anxious Artist—Ideological Mobilizations of the Self in German Modernism," in Rogoff 1990, 116–147; also Dieter Gleisberg, "'Ich muss mir stets ein kleines Monument errichten': Max Klinger in seinen Selbstdarstellungen," in *Max Klinger, 1857–1920*, ed. Dieter Gleisberg [exh. cat., Museum der Bildenden Künste Leipzig] (Leipzig, 1992), 13–25.

14 Matthias Eberle, "Max Liebermann zwischen Tradition und Opposition," in *Max Liebermann in seiner Zeit* [exh. cat., Nationalgalerie Berlin] (Berlin, 1979), 11–40; Leipzig 1992, 373–377; Jutta Bohnke, "Biographische Dokumentation," in Cologne 1989, 29–47; Käthe Kollwitz, "Erinnerungen" (1923), in *Käthe Kollwitz, Die Tagebücher, 1908–1943*, ed. Jutta Bohnke-Kollwitz (Berlin, 1989), 717–735. Kollwitz' grandfather Julius Rupp was the founder of the Free Congregation, a Christian denomination akin to Baptists. Membership in this church, along with socialist leanings, prevented her brother Konrad from pursuing an academic career beyond the doctorate. Instead he became a journalist for socialist newspapers. See Alexandra von dem Knesebeck, "Die Bedeutung von Zolas Roman 'Germinal'

für den Zyklus 'Ein Weberaufstand' von Käthe Kollwitz," *Zeitschrift für Kunstgeschichte* 52 (1989): 402–422.

15 Eberle in Berlin 1979, 16.

16 Michael Klant, "'Hommage comique à Liebermann': Eine Studie zum Rezeptionswandel Max Liebermanns im Spiegel der Karikatur," *Kritische Berichte* 13, no. 2 (1985): 5–20, fig. 11.

17 Paret 1980, 182–199. On the prehistory to Vinnen's protest, see Andreas Blühm, "'Ist der Ruf erst ruiniert...': Manet im Blick der Deutschen," in *Jenseits der Grenzen: Französische und deutsche Kunst, Festschrift für Thomas Gaethgens*, 3 vols. (Cologne, 2000), 2:401–413.

18 *Deutsche und Französische Kunst: Eine Auseinandersetzung deutscher Künstler, Galerieleiter, Sammler und Schriftsteller*, 2nd ed. (Munich, 1911), 1–6. The contributions ranged from short notices (Gustav Klimt) to entire essays in defense of cosmopolitanism in art (Franz Marc, Wassily Kandinsky, and the art writer Wilhelm Hausenstein). See Gustav Pauli, *Max Liebermann* (Stuttgart, 1911), xxxix. Peter Paret, "Modernism and the 'Alien Element in German Art,'" in Paret, *German Encounters with Modernism, 1840–1945* (Cambridge, 2001), 60–91.

19 On Liebermann and France, beyond the annual inclusion of French artists in the Berlin Secession's exhibitions, see, for example, Pierre Vaisse, "Max Liebermanns 'Eva' und die impressionistische Ursprünglichkeit?" in Cologne 2000, 2:433–447; and Peter Krieger, "Max Liebermanns Impressionisten-Sammlung und ihre Bedeutung für sein Werk," in Berlin 1979, 60–71. On the Kaiser's "Nordic" vacations and commissions, see Barbara Miller Lane, *National Romanticism and Modern Architecture in Germany and the Scandinavian Countries* (Cambridge, 2000), 73–78.

20 Paul Cassirer, "Vom unwissenden Künstler," in Munich 1911, 159.

21 Paret 1980, 59–91; *Berliner Sezession* [exh. cat., Neuer Berliner Kunstverein] (Berlin, [c. 1980]). See Maria Makela, *The Munich Secession: Art and Artists in Turn-of-the-Century Munich* (Princeton, 1990), 80–132, on connections between the two secessions.

22 Berlin 1979, 105.

23 Bohnke-Kollwitz 1989, "Juli 1920," 477. On her fiftieth birthday in 1917, the Dresden Art Association hosted a Kollwitz exhibition paired with a show of "the young" Klinger. Bohnke-Kollwitz 1989, "16 August 1917," 327. Curt Glaser was among the first to analyze the relationship between Kollwitz' and Klinger's prints. See *Die Graphik der Neuzeit* (Berlin, 1922), 466–467.

24 Werner Schmidt, "Max Lehrs und Käthe Kollwitz: Die Entstehung der Kollwitz-Sammlung des Dresdner Kupferstich-Kabinettes," in Cologne 1979, 10–20.

25 No comparably divisive debate about French influence existed in relation to the art of printmaking. Of course, there were voices, from Charles Baudelaire's essay "Painters and Etchers" onward, of concern about the technical facility especially of etching and the potential dangers of leveling, in the sense of an inflation of artistic value owing to mass production. This concern pertained just as much to the German art of interiority. As Glaser 1922, 466, wrote: "Cycles of etchings poured out in their hundreds [massenhaft] in which the eternal rewarding themes of Woman and Love and Death and the Beyond were treated with much deep meaning and aquatint." Translated in New York 1984, 13. Charles Baudelaire, "Painters and Etchers," in Baudelaire, *Art in Paris, 1845–1862*, trans. and ed. Jonathan Mayne (New York, 1965), 219–220.

26 Wilhelm II gave his infamous "gutter art" speech on the occasion of the dedication ceremony of the Siegesallee in Berlin, on September 18, 1901. See *Kunst in Berlin von 1870 bis heute: Sammlung Berlinische Galerie* (Berlin, 1986), 249, and reprint of the speech, 50.

27 Paret 1980, 93. However, the three artists were rarely discussed together. An early exception is Wolfgang Singer, author of the catalogue raisonné of Klinger's graphic work, who wrote an essay on the drawings of Liebermann and Kollwitz in *Mitteilungen aus den sächsischen Kunstsammlungen* (Dresden, 1912), 83–90.

28 In addition to Klinger's *Bear and Fairy*, see his *Das Menzelfestblatt* of 1884, Singer 268, Leipzig 1992, cat. 172; and Max Schmid, *Max Klinger* (Bielefeld, 1899), 68–71. Max Liebermann, "Adolph von Menzel,"

reprinted in Heidi Ebertshäuser, *Adolph von Menzel: Das graphische Werk,* 2 vols. (Munich, 1976), 2:1357–1375; Peter Paret, "Adolph Menzel from Different Perspectives," in Paret 2001, 34–35.

29 Yet, when approached to exhibit at the Secession, he at first agreed but then withdrew at the last moment. Peter Paret, "Berlin in Menzel's Time," in *Adolph Menzel, 1815–1905: Between Romanticism and Impressionism,* eds. Claude Keisch and Marie Ursula Riemann-Reyher [exh. cat., National Gallery of Art] (Washington, 1996), 72–73.

30 Klinger, *Painting and Drawing,* trans. Fiona Elliott and Christopher Croft, Ikon Gallery (Birmingham, 2005), 7; Klinger, *Malerei und Zeichnung* (Leipzig, n.d.), 3. Klinger's treatise is in many ways based in his artistic practices and has strong connections to eighteenth- and nineteenth-century aesthetics; see Christiane Hertel, *Studien zu Max Klingers graphischem Zyklus "Paraphrase über den Fund eines Handschuhs," 1878–1881* (Frankfurt, 1987), 87–109; Hertel, "Irony, Dream, Kitsch: Max Klinger's *Paraphrase of the Finding of a Glove* and German Modernism," *Art Bulletin* 74, no. 1 (1992): 91–114; and Marsha Morton, "*Malerei und Zeichnung:* The History and Context of Max Klinger's Guide to the Arts," *Zeitschrift für Kunstgeschichte* 58, no. 4 (1995): 542–569.

31 Klinger 2005, 22; Klinger n.d., 26.

32 Klinger 2005, 25; Klinger n.d., 30.

33 Werner Busch, *Die notwendige Arabeske: Wirklichkeitsaneignung und Stilisierung in der deutschen Kunst des 19. Jahrhunderts* (Berlin, 1985), 42–71; Hermann Bauer, *Rocaille: Zur Herkunft und zum Wesen eines Ornament-Motivs* (Berlin, 1962).

34 Klinger 2005, 22; Klinger n.d., 24.

35 Richard Graul, "Max Liebermann," *Die Graphischen Künste* 15 (1892): 51, 54, 56, 57–59. He ranks the expressiveness of Liebermann's etchings far above their technical achievements, considering what is now seen as his impressionist style to be a beginner's sketchiness (57).

36 This also applies to the essay's companion piece, *Max Liebermann Radierungen* (Berlin, 1893). See the extensive correspondence between Liebermann and Graul and also Liebermann's corrections, "Dokumentation: '...dass das Porträt in Hamburg selbst meinen Gegnern imponiert': Max Liebermann schreibt Richard Graul," in *Max Liebermann: Der Realist und die Phantasie* [exh. cat., Hamburger Kunsthalle] (Hamburg, 1997), 228: "innerlich hohl."

37 On the reception of his early paintings, see Boskamp 1994.

38 On the relation between Liebermann's prints, drawings, and paintings, which often treated the same subjects, see Max Friedländer, *Max Liebermanns Graphische Kunst* (Dresden, 1920), 14–21; Sigrid Achenbach, "Die Druckgraphik Max Liebermanns," in Berlin 1979, 48–52; and Günter Busch, *Max Liebermann, Maler, Zeichner, Graphiker* (Frankfurt, 1986), 134–135.

39 Max Liebermann, "Die Phantasie in der Malerei," *Neue Rundschau* (1904), reprinted in Liebermann n.d., 13–15. Liebermann's positions on art tend to be seen as opposite to Klinger's. But Friedländer already took Liebermann's choice of the word *imagination* seriously, emphasizing that rather than presenting a "vermeintlich direkte Naturaufnahme" (a seemingly direct capturing of nature), representation is always of the "durch geistig-seelische Aktion geschaffene Erinnerungsbild, das man die Vision nennen mag" (a memory image created by a mental-psychic activity, which one may call a vision). See Max J. Friedländer, *Von Kunst und Kennerschaft* (Berlin, 1955), 12–13.

40 The work is a good example of Liebermann's early French and Dutch contexts. He made this etching at the invitation of the *Gazette des Beaux-Arts* in 1883 (published there in February) to reproduce his painting *The Weaver,* 1881 / 1882 (Städelsches Kunstinstitut und Städische Galerie, Frankfurt), which he had exhibited at the salon. The painting and the print are comparable to Vincent van Gogh's *The Loom,* 1884 (Kröller-Müller Museum, Otterlo). For decades Liebermann spent his summers in the Netherlands, and a different version of the subject is Liebermann's depiction of a factory, *Weavers in Laren,* 1897 (Sammlung Georg Schäfer, Schweinfurt). One study for it is dedicated to Eugène Fromentin, author of *Les maîtres d'autrefois* (1876) on seventeenth-century Dutch painting. It was especially owing to Jozef Israëls and their

mutual admiration of Rembrandt's etchings that around 1891 Liebermann developed his particular etching style of sketchy and open drawing. See Achenbach in Berlin 1979, esp. 50–51.

41 See the development of *Need* in 1893 and 1894 and then 1897, Cologne 1989, figs. 31–33, 43, cats. 25–27, 41; Klipstein 1955, 22, 23I, 23II, 34IIa.

42 On this criticism, compare Eberle in Berlin 1979 and Boskamp 1994. One might even say that in some ways, Kollwitz' silhouette also reflects forward onto Liebermann's 1917 print of a forsaken corpse hanging from the gallows surrounded by ravens. On the *Rabenstein* (place of execution) thematic, see Wolfgang Kemp, "Walkers in Lonely Places: On the Experience of the Uncanny in Nineteenth-Century German Art," in *The Enduring Instant: Time and the Spectator in the Visual Arts,* ed. A. Roesler-Friedenthal and J. Nathan (Berlin, 2000), 101–125.

43 On the actual site, see Wolfgang Kemp, "'Der Bärenzwinger' von Adolph Menzel," in Kemp, *Der Anteil des Betrachters* (Munich, 1983), 60–62.

44 Jürgen Mittelstrass, "Erkennen und Entdecken oder: Vom wissenschaftlichen Verstand und seinen Mythen" (www.be.schule.de/schulen/humboldt/pdf/vortrag_mittelstrass.pdf). The reference is to Aristotle's *Metaphysics* A.1.980a; see Richard McKeon, ed., *The Basic Works of Aristotle* (New York, 1941), 689.

45 Liebermann connects imagination in art with memory of the phenomenal world; Liebermann n.d., 21, 22. He discusses painting primarily, but occasionally also printmaking and drawing, making no principal distinction between them. Accordingly, he writes in his essay on Menzel, 1369: "Wo Menzel alla prima ganz vor der Natur oder aus dem Gedächtnis nach der Natur malt—beides ist im Grunde dasselbe—schafft er schlechthin Unsterbliches" (Whenever Menzel paints alla prima entirely before nature or from memory after nature—both [practices] are ultimately the same—he creates truly immortal works).

46 Klinger's knowledge of eighteenth-century ornamental prints, including chinoiserie, and his relations to nineteenth-century *japonisme* remain to be examined. Glaser 1922, 445, lapidarily stated: "Japanisches, wie die Zeit es verstand, übt Einfluss." Yet concrete comparative observations on Klinger and *japonisme* are few and far between. See, for example, Memory Jockisch Holloway, "Introduction," in *Max Klinger: Love, Death, and the Beyond* [exh. cat., National Gallery of Victoria] (Sydney, Australia, 1981), 3. On common borrowings of compositional strategies as well as motifs, see Siegfried Wichmann, *Japonisme: The Japanese Influence on Western Art in the Nineteenth and Twentieth Centuries* (New York, 1985).

47 Some of these connections were apparently recognized and invoked by the Berlin Secession member Max Slevogt (1868–1932), who referred to both works in his *Portrait of Suzanne Aimée Cassirer* (1901, Private Collection) at play from a perspective implying the artist's and viewer's standing position (Private Collection, c. 1901–1906). The girl is kneeling on the floor while eating an apple and surrounded by a cardboard "wall," or folding screen, of a harmonica-like, possibly Asian picture book around which a large stuffed lion "paces." Berlin c. 1980, cat. and ill. 356; see also Slevogt's drawings of lions at the Frankfurt zoo, cats. 361 and 362, and Emil Waldmann's monograph published by Bruno Cassirer, *Max Slevogt* (Berlin, 1923), on this phase in his oeuvre, 58–76.

48 Julius Meier-Graefe, "Menzel and His Circle," in Meier-Graefe, *Modern Art,* 2 vols. (London, 1908), 2:108. Menzel scholarship has come to accept his extreme need to explore but also to protect his privacy. See Françoise Forster-Hahn, "Authenticity into Ambivalence: The Evolution of Menzel's Drawings," *Master Drawings* 16, no. 3 (1978): 255–282; and Michael Fried, *Menzel's Realism: Art and Embodiment in Nineteenth-Century Berlin* (New Haven, 2002), chap. 7, "The 'Private' Pictures and Some Others," 75–107.

49 For Liebermann's emphasis on his work ethic, see Eberle in Berlin 1979, 12; Busch 1986, 20; and Boskamp 1994, 31–64.

50 Wolfgang Kemp, "Beziehungsspiele: Versuch einer Gattungspoetik des Interieurs," in Ostfildern-Ruit 1998, 17–29.

51 On this series, see London 1992, 37–44, and on its artistic reception in modern art, Hans-Werner Schmidt and Hubertus Gassner, eds., *Eine Liebe: Max Klinger und*

die Folgen [exh. cat., Museum der bildenden Künste Leipzig] (Bielefeld, 2007). Klinger edited out the primitive mask on the stone marker seen in the preparatory drawing (1882, Niedersächsisches Landesmuseum, Hannover, Landesgalerie), Leipzig 1992, cat. 12. On Klinger's primitivism, see Marsha Morton, "The Ethnographic Vision of Max Klinger," in *Die Schau des Fremden: Ausstellungskonzepte zwischen Kunst, Kommerz und Wissenschaft, Transatlantische Studien,* ed. Cordula Grewe, Deutsches Historisches Institut, Washington, vol. 26 (Stuttgart, 2006), 253–278.

52 For example, Klinger's *Dreams* (1885, *A Life,* no. 3, Singer 129).

53 For Klinger's work process here of compressing, intensifying, editing, and cropping the composition between 1883 and 1887, see Karl-Heinz Mehnert, "Studien und Metamorphosen," in Leipzig 1992, 160–167.

54 The ample literature on Klinger's sympathetic representation of woman's plight hesitates to include this image among them, seeing instead a "reserved criticism" of society's condemnation of this woman. See a summary of the critical reception in Leipzig 1992, 304–305, and cat. 103 (drawing over print, Singer 165I, Leipzig), in which Klinger added the dark shadow on the wall.

55 That this clearly is the purpose of these marks is evident in Kollwitz' charcoal drawing for the print, *Sitzende Frau mit Hand vor dem Gesicht,* c. 1893 (Kestner-Museum, Hannover). See Otto Nagel, *The Drawings of Käthe Kollwitz,* with Sibylle Schallenberg-Nagel and Hans Kollwitz, ed. Werner Timm (New York, 1972), pl. 12 and cat. 93. About 1893, Kollwitz also made a pen-and-ink drawing of a woman kneeling before an image of Mary (Nagel 1972, 90, 91). Moreover, in one drawing both women appear, one above the other (Nagel 1972, 94). However, *Knieende vor einem Marienbild* was never developed into a print.

56 Max Lehrs draws a connection to Goethe's *Faust* in his essay, "Käthe Kollwitz," *Die Graphischen Künste* 26 (1903): 55–67, reprinted in Cologne 1979, 199. Alessandra Comini concludes homelessness in "Kollwitz in Context: The Formative Years," in Washington 1992, 98.

57 See Kneesebeck, "Die Bedeutung," on the relations of art, politics, and family life in Kollwitz' early oeuvre. In 1922, Max Lehrs warned against seeing in Kollwitz "lediglich eine politische Parteigängerin und Kämpferin für den Sozialismus" (solely a political partisan and fighter for socialism), albeit in order to defend the great artist in the woman artist. See Max Lehrs, "Käthe Kollwitz," *Berliner Tageblatt und Handels-Zeitung* (December 5, 1922), 2. The debate about Kollwitz' art, politics, and feminism has continued ever since.

58 Compare, for example, the following: patches or stains (Kupferstichkabinett Dresden, 1893, Klipstein 1955, 19 III), graffiti (Käthe-Kollwitz-Museum, Berlin, after 1931, Klipstein 1955, 19 vIb), and a richly suggestive combination of both at the expense of definition in the woman's now seemingly bleached and blank face (National Gallery of Art).

59 On the roots of modern liberalism, see Judith A. Swanson, *The Public and the Private in Aristotle's Political Philosophy* (Ithaca, 1992), 4–5.

60 Bernd Growe, "'Beobachten, aber nichts mitthun': Materialien zum Opus 'Dramen,'" in *Max Klinger* [exh. cat., Kunsthalle Bielefeld] (Bielefeld, 1976), 15–28; *Max Klinger, Die graphischen Zyklen* [exh. cat., Villa Stuck München] (Munich, 1979), 30–35.

61 See the five excerpts specifically regarding working-class living and work environment—the boarding house, the tenement, the laundry shop—from Zola's *L'assommoir,* in Barbara Miller Lane, ed., *Housing and Dwelling: Perspectives on Modern Domestic Architecture* (London, 2007), 133–143 and figs. 19–22. Käthe Kollwitz, September 19, 1908, in Bohnke-Kollwitz 1989, 41. She continues: "I increasingly understand the typical misfortune of working-class families. As soon as the man drinks or is sick and out of work, always the same phenomena. Either he drags down his family like a dead stone and lets himself be fed—cursed by all family members—or he kills himself." Kollwitz moved Klinger's balcony scene indoors in her charcoal drawing *Drunkard,* c. 1908–1909, on loan to Käthe-Kollwitz-Museum, Berlin (Nagel 1972, cat. 474).

62 See www.berliner-verkehrsseiten.de/schloss; with reference to Dietmar and Ingmar Arnhold, *Schlossfreiheit: Vor den Toren des Stadtschlosses* (Berlin, 1998).

63 Schmid, *Max Klinger*, 47.

64 Friedrich Hölderlin, *Poems and Fragments*, trans. Michael Hamburger (London, 1966), 78–79. Friedrich Hölderlin, *Einhundert Gedichte*, ed. D. E. Sattler (Frankfurt, 1989), "Hyperions Schicksalslied," 41–42: "Doch uns ist gegeben, / Auf keiner Stätte zu ruhn, / Es schwinden, es fallen / Die leidenden Menschen / Blindlings von einer / Stunde zur andern, / Wie Wasser von Klippe / Zu Klippe geworfen, / Jahr lang ins Ungewisse hinab."

65 Annegret Friedrich, "Zum Prometheusbild in Max Klingers Brahmsphantasie," in *Brahms-Phantasien: Johannes Brahms—Bildwelt, Musik, Leben* (Kunsthalle Kiel, 1983), 11–15; Eberhard Roters, "Evocation—die Sublimierung des Elementaren," in Leipzig 1992, 26–37; Karl-Heinz Mehnert, "Max Klinger und Johannes Brahms: Begegnungen und Briefe," in Leipzig 1992, 56–64.

66 Giorgio de Chirico, "Max Klinger," 1920, reprinted in Stella Wega Mathieu, ed., *Max Klinger, Leben und Werk* (Frankfurt, 1976), 178, 179. Early critics, such as Jules Laforgue, emphasized and deplored the series' "naturalism" and overlooked its romantic motto, tragic dimension, and magic elements. Laforgue, cited in Claude Keisch, "Max Klinger, Spaziergang ins Unbewusste?" in Cologne 2000, 2:349, nn. 8–13.

67 Compare Klinger's lead pencil drawing solely of the two men in exactly their spatial relation and placement in the print, yet on an otherwise blank sheet (Staatliche Kunstsammlungen, Dresden, Kupferstich-Kabinett, inv. CA. 52).

68 Bohnke-Kollwitz 1989, "30 August 1909," 49.

69 See Eberhard Ruhmer, *Der Leibl-Kreis und die reine Malerei* (Rosenheim, 1984), for works by Wilhelm Leibl, Max Sperl, Fritz Schider, and others. Comparable to Kollwitz' use of the motif, a painting by Adolf Echtler (1843–1914), who had spent the years 1877–1886 in Paris, *Woman by the Fireplace*, c. 1883 (Bayerische Staatsgemäldesammlungen, Munich), shows an enigmatic, long, empty, illuminated table extending out of a cropped window alcove halfway through the horizontally formatted painting. Reproduced in Makela 1990, 36; see also Ernst Zimmermann, "Alois Erdhelt und Adolf Echtler: Münchner Maler der Gründerzeit," *Weltkunst* 50 (1980): 1024–1026.

70 The most detailed accounts of the series are Martin Frisch, ed., *Käthe Kollwitz, Zeichnung, Grafik, Plastik, Bestandskatalog des Käthe Kollwitz Museums Berlin*, catalogue by Annette Seeler (Leipzig, 1999), 15–16, 74–91, cats. 14–24; Kneesebeck, "Die Bedeutung"; and Washington 1992, 20–32.

71 Émile Zola, *Germinal*, trans. L. W. Tancock (Baltimore, 1954), 385.

72 Cologne 1989, figs. 13, 17, 19, 20, 27–30; cats. 22, 23, 24, 106, 82, 13, 19, 20; pages 181–182; Klipstein 1955, 21, 23, 21 III, 74 I, 12 Ib, 17 I, 17 II. Prelinger, in Washington 1992, 18, recounts the "birth" of *Scene from "Germinal"* in Munich as a private moment, but one also witnessed by friends, who as an evening exercise set themselves the task of representing the subject: "fight."

73 On the *interieur* as "psychogram," see Sabine Schulze, "Innenleben: Die Kunst des Interieurs," in Ostfildern-Ruit 1998, 9; and Donat de Chapeaurouge, "Das Milieu als Portrait," *Wallraf-Richartz-Jahrbuch* 22 (1960): 137–158.

74 For example, Cologne 1989, fig. 29, cat. 19, Klipstein 1955, 17.

75 Sigmund Freud, "The Uncanny," in *The Standard Edition of the Complete Psychological Works of Sigmund Freud*, ed. James Strachey, vol. 17 (London, 1955), 225; Beate Bonus-Jeep, *Sechzig Jahre Freundschaft mit Käthe Kollwitz* (Boppard, 1948), 103, quoted in Frisch 1999, 124.

76 Letter to Arthur Bonus, c. 1924–1925, quoted in Bonus-Jeep in Frisch 1999, 122. Although it is not known which drawings were made in this way, one cannot help considering the drawings for her print in light of the passage. See Nagel 1972, 239–251.

77 Jürgen Habermas, *The Structural Transformation of the Public Sphere: An Inquiry into a Category of Bourgeois Society*, trans. Thomas Burger (Cambridge, Mass., 1989), 45–47.

78 Liebermann was undoubtedly aware of Rembrandt's depictions of the subject and therefore of such a conceivably dual relationship between Delilah and Samson in his oeuvre. I thank Rima Girnius for drawing my attention to this modification.

79 Friedländer 1920, 20, 21.

80 Examples include her gradual formal tightening of the dead weavers in drawings (Nagel 1972, 131–134) for the etching *End* (*A Weavers' Rebellion,* 1897, no. 6, Klipstein 1955, 37), and the woodcut *Widow II* (*The War,* 1922–1923, no. 5, Klipstein 1955, 181).

81 Hans H. Hofstätter, *Jugendstil Buchkunst* (Baden-Baden, 1973), 154, goes so far as to include this print, "wo die Natur den Leichnam überwuchert und die Erde ihn symbolhaft zurücknimmt" (where nature overgrows the corpse and earth symbolically takes it back). On Jugendstil and nature, see Paul Greenhalgh, "The Cult of Nature," in *Art Nouveau, 1890–1914,* ed. Greenhalgh [exh. cat., Victoria and Albert Museum] (New York, 2000), 54–71. Compare Kollwitz' drawing for this plate (Private Collection), in which a small boy leans over the fence, looking at his mother; in the print, the child's head has become almost like the surrounding plants. Frisch 1999, 329, fig. 2.

82 Kollwitz risks the accusation of using the peasant woman and her rape allegorically, just as Helma Sanders-Brahms does in her film *Deutschland, Bleiche Mutter* (1980). See Ellen E. Seiter, "Women's History, Women's Melodrama: Deutschland, Bleiche Mutter," *German Quarterly* 59 (1986): 569–581.

83 Perhaps Liebermann was familiar with Winslow Homer's use of fences to graph the psychogram of male-female or child-adult relations. See Kenneth Haltman, "Anti-pastoralism in Early Winslow Homer," *Art Bulletin* 80 (1998): 93–112. The psychological tension of fencing in and out is much more pronounced in this print than in the painting of the same subject, *Die Bleiche* (1884, Private Collection), in Busch 1986, 180, which does not engage the beholder directly but mainly creates a distance between the beholder and an "objective" representation of village life.

84 Rudolf Kuhn, "Die Farbenfolge in Bildkompositionen des jungen Liebermann," *Alte und Moderne Kunst* 27 (1982): 2.

85 See Comini in Washington 1992, 106–109; and Frisch 1999, 382.

86 Bohnke-Kollwitz 1989, "30 August 1909," 49.

87 See Frisch 1999, cat. 178, Klipstein 1955, 93.II. Kollwitz, "Rückblick auf die frühere Zeit" (1941), in Bohnke-Kollwitz 1989, 741.

88 Bohnke-Kollwitz 1989, "30 August 1909," 49.

89 Compare Kollwitz' ink drawing *Hans Kollwitz with Candle,* 1895 (on loan to Käthe Kollwitz Museum, Cologne, Nagel 1972, 115), which shows her son, Hans, pensively staring into a candle's flame about to consume itself. See Cologne 1989, 25.

SCULPTURE AND PRIVACY

1 The Susse foundry cast this model in five sizes with and without ivory parts. Élisabeth Lebon, *Dictionnaire des fondeurs de bronze d'art, France, 1890–1950* (Perth, 2003), 47, illustrates the relevant page of their 1910 catalogue and refers (242) to the notable success of these reductions. See also the entry by Marie Busco and Peter Fusco for an ivory, gilded, and silvered version in *The Romantics to Rodin: French Nineteenth-Century Sculpture from North American Collections* [exh. cat., Los Angeles County Museum of Art] (Los Angeles, 1980), 118–119, no. 10. Their note lists some other Susse casts in public collections (121, n. 15). There is also one in the Walters Art Museum, Baltimore.

2 For the version in Bordeaux, see *Revue de l'Art Ancien et Moderne* 1 (1908): 333. For the sculpture generally, see the entry by Busco and Fusco in Los Angeles 1980, and for Barrias in general, G. Lafenestre, *L'Oeuvre de Barrias* (Paris, 1908).

3 Now Musée d'Orsay, Paris, R.F. 1409, commissioned 1895 for the staircase of the Conservatoire Nationale des Arts et Métiers. It is cosigned by "J. Cantini, Marseilles," the marble workers and importers who conceived of it as a means to advertise Algerian stones. See Antoinette Le

Normand-Romain and Jean-Luc Olivié, "La polychromie," in *La sculpture française au XIXe siècle* [exh. cat., Grand Palais] (Paris, 1986), 150–151.

4 Mark Stocker, *Royalist and Realist: The Life and Work of Sir Joseph Edgar Boehm* (New York, 1988), includes a catalogue of all Boehm's sculpture.

5 This connection between Gilbert and Gemito seems not to have been previously noted, but not only is Gemito's head of a wrinkled old man (see the example in *Sculpture from the David Daniels Collection* [exh. cat., Minneapolis Institute of Art] [Minneapolis, 1979], no. 62), remarkably similar to that by Gilbert dated 1884, which is now in the National Gallery of Victoria, Melbourne, but we also know that the latter was made from a model on Capri and cast by a Neapolitan foundry with which Gemito was associated. Both works are experiments in extreme veracity, employing lost-wax casting by the direct method. For the Gilbert, see Richard Dorment, *Alfred Gilbert* [exh. cat., Royal Academy] (London, 1986), 108–109, no. 14.

6 Edith Wharton, *The House of Mirth* (New York, 1905), 175, 176.

7 For the industrial scale of sand-casting, see Catherine Chevillot, "Édition et fonte au sable," in Paris 1986, 80–94. Collas' invention was adopted by the great foundry of Barbedienne (92).

8 Lebon 2003, 168–171.

9 Stocker 1988, 308. John Saville Lumley's "Bronze Casting in Belgium," *Architect* 33 (1884): 130–133, 140–141, advertises the achievements of the Compagnie de Bronzes. See also Richard Dorment, *Alfred Gilbert* (New Haven, 1985), 58. Gemito, like Gilbert, was closely associated both with the foundries in Naples and in Brussels.

10 Francis Haskell and Nicholas Penny, *Taste and the Antique* (New Haven, 1981), 208–209, no. 35, 271–272, no. 64.

11 Edith Wharton and Ogden Codman Jr., *The Decoration of Houses* (New York, 1897), chap. 16, quotation on 191.

12 For Gilbert's experiments (notably his *Icarus*), see Duncan James, "Alfred Gilbert and His Use of Nineteenth-Century Founding Technologies," in London 1986, 21–26.

13 My attention was drawn to his trade card by Lisa Unger Baskin, whose husband, Leonard Baskin, wrote very interestingly about nature casts and whose sculpture was influenced by them.

14 For a review of this subject, see Norberto Gramaccini, "Das Genaue Abbild der Natur," in *Natur und Antike in der Renaissance* [exh. cat., Liebieghaus] (Frankfurt, 1985–1986], 198–225, and 534–545, entries for nos. 258–282.

15 For Jamnitzer, see Ernst Kris, "Der Stil 'Rustique': Die Verwendung des Naturabgusses bei Wenzel Jamnitzer und Bernard Palissy," *Jahrbuch der Kunsthistorischen Sammlungen in Wien*, n.s., 1 (1926): 137–208. At the section of the Exposition Universelle of 1889 in Paris the firm of L. Magniny exhibited flowers and insects electroplated to serve as ornament. Because Gilbert was a pioneer in the use of the new metal of aluminum for sculpture, he is likely to have been as interested in technical innovations as he was in reviving ancient techniques.

16 This connection was made by Alison Luchs in her entry for the Gilbert in Ruth Butler and Suzanne Glover Lindsay, *European Sculpture of the Nineteenth Century* (Oxford, 2000), 269. For the *Mercury,* see John Pope-Hennessy, *Cellini* (New York, 1985), pl. 112. For the Gilbert in general, see Butler, Lindsay, et al. 2000, 266–271, and Dorment 1985, 131–134.

17 H. Stuart Jones, ed., *A Catalogue of the Ancient Sculptures Preserved in the Municipal Collections of Rome: The Sculptures of the Museo Capitolino* (Oxford, 1912; reprint, Rome, 1969), 317, no. 8 (pl. 79 in separate volume of illustrations). The sculpture, believed to be of early imperial date, is 125 cm high. Gilbert was not the only sculptor influenced by this work. See the marble sculpture of a youth hiding behind the mask of a bearded satyr by Eduard Müller (1828–1895) on the staircase of the Accademia di San Luca in Rome.

18 Joseph Hatton, "The Life and Work of Alfred Gilbert R.A., M.V.O., LL.D.," *Easter Art Annual* (1903): 11–12.

19 Dorment 1985, 131–134; London 1986, 116–118. It has often been proposed that Gilbert may also have been influenced by Leighton's statuette *Needless Alarms,* and that Gilbert was very familiar with this work can be deduced from the fact that a

cast of it lies on his workbench in a famous photograph of him in his studio (reproduced in Dorment 1985, opposite the title page and on the back of the jacket).

20 I know of no attempt to trace in detail the fashion for sculptured hands of this type, but valuable observations are found in the section "Main Mémoire" by Hélène Pinet in the catalogue of the exhibition *Le corps en morceaux* [exh. cat., Musée d'Orsay and Schirn Kunsthalle] (Paris, 1990), 171–175.

21 Cornelia Carr, ed., *Harriet Hosmer: Letters and Memories* (New York, 1912), 92 (for Browning's aversion to the *formatore*); Dolly Sherwood, *Harriet Hosmer: American Sculptor, 1830–1908* (Columbia, Mo., 1991), 92. What Carr claimed to be the "original" plaster cast was given to the Schlesinger Library by Isabella Carr Thompson Leighton with the Hosmer collection. See Carr 1912, 345, n. 10. But if a piece mold was employed, then more than one plaster may have been taken from it.

22 Entry by Butler in Butler, Lindsay, et al. 2000, 390–391.

23 "Main sortant de la tombe," Paris 1986, 391.

24 Entry by Butler in Butler, Lindsay, et al. 2000, 406–407. Similarly, the plaster cast given to Malvina Hoffman in The Metropolitan Museum of Art, New York, was presumably a reward to her for helping put the Hôtel Biron in order (408, n. 2). Not everyone admired this work: see the discussion in Paris 1990, 174–175.

25 Entry by Butler in Butler, Lindsay, et al. 2000, 331, n. 16.

26 Butler, Lindsay, et al. 2000, 331–333.

27 For Hébrard in general, see Lebon 2003, 64–65, 182–188, and for Vesuvian patina, 184–185.

28 Lebon 2003, 186, n. 4, quoting Hébrard's words in Clément Vautel, "Un Fondeur Artiste," *La Vie Illustrée* (July 8, 1904).

29 For Falguière, see above all Léonce Bénédite, *Alexandre Falguière* (Paris, 1902); and Anne Pingeot, "Le Fonds Falguière au Musée du Louvre," *Bulletin de la Société de l'Histoire de l'Art Français* (1978): 263–290.

30 Entry by Lindsay in Butler, Lindsay, et al. 2000, 111–116, n. 16.

31 The original setting is described by Henriette Caillaux, *Aimé-Jules Dalou* (Paris, 1935), 99–100.

32 Lindsay in Butler, Lindsay, et al. 2000, 114, n. 16, where it is also explained that there may have been an intention to deflect attention from the blame attached to the duke's father for his imprudent precipitation of the Franco-Prussian War.

33 Lindsay in Butler, Lindsay, et al. 2000, 112, n. 18.

34 John Postle Heseltine is typical of the collectors around 1900 who valued sketchy and fragmentary pieces from the Renaissance and later, including works by modern artists.

35 Both transactions with Norton Simon and Paul Mellon are described in Anne Pingeot, *Degas, Sculptures* (Paris, 1991). Further reflections on the question of Degas' intentions will be found in the forthcoming systematic catalogue of the waxes in the National Gallery of Art by Daphne Barbour, Suzanne Glover Lindsay, and Shelley Sturman.

36 Most relevant is the relief of Scipio in the Louvre (then in the Rattier collection), which was disputed between Leonardo and Verrocchio in the late nineteenth century but is now generally considered to be a modern imitation. A full discussion of its status is supplied by G. Passavant, *Verrocchio* (London, 1969), 199–200. See also the relief of Alexander the Great by Verrocchio or a follower in the National Gallery of Art and the metalpoint drawing by Leonardo in the British Museum, which are conveniently illustrated and ably discussed in Andrew Butterfield, *The Sculptures of Andrea del Verrocchio* (New Haven, 1997), 156–157.

37 Georges Dupré (1869–1909) worked as a chaser before he entered the École des Beaux-Arts and won the Prix de Rome in 1896. *Meditation* and *Greetings to the Sun*, both created in the following year, are his most famous medals. The chief source for our knowledge of his work is the account by François Mazerolle, "Georges Dupré," *Gazette Numismatique Française* (1902): 225–233.

38 See Emmanuel Héran et al., *Alexandre Charpentier (1856–1909): Naturalisme et art nouveau* [exh. cat., Musée d'Orsay] (Paris, 2008), for more on this relief and related work by the sculptor.

POSSESSION

Georges Alfred Bottini (French, 1874–1907), *Sagot's Lithography Gallery,* 1898, color lithograph, image 28.9 × 18.6, sheet 38 × 28, National Gallery of Art, Washington, Rosenwald Collection 1953.6.8 (Parshall fig. 10)

Félix Hilaire Buhot (French, 1847–1898), *The Devil as Printer,* 1878, etching with drypoint (state ii/ii), plate 12 × 15.8, sheet 14.6 × 19, National Gallery of Art, Washington, Ailsa Mellon Bruce Fund 2008.1.1

Eugen Napoleon Neureuther (German, 1806–1882), *Self-Portrait in the Etching Studio,* 1839, etching, plate 26.2 × 20.4, sheet 34.1 × 25.8, National Gallery of Art, Washington, Ailsa Mellon Bruce Fund 2005.20.2

Adolphe Martial Potémont (French, 1828–1883), *Seat of the Society of Etchers, 79 rue de Richelieu,* 1864, etching, plate 28.5 × 38.9, sheet 30 × 40.1, Baltimore Museum of Art, The George A. Lucas Collection, purchased with funds from the State of Maryland, Laurence and Stella Bendann Fund, and contributions from individuals, foundations, and corporations throughout the Baltimore community 1996.48.2436 (Parshall fig. 12)

Félicien Rops (Belgian, 1833–1898), *Gaspard de la nuit: Fantasies in the Manner of Rembrandt and Callot* (frontispiece to Aloysius Bertrand, *Gaspard de la nuit*), 1868, etching and aquatint on Chinese paper, plate 19.8 × 12.9, sheet 25 × 19.8, National Gallery of Art, Washington, Rosenwald Collection 1946.11.189 (Parshall fig. 13)

NATURE AND THE CITY

Adolphe Appian (French, 1818–1898), *Nocturne (Fisherman in a Boat),* 1887, etching with monotype wiping on Chinese paper (state i/iii), plate 31.2 × 46.3, sheet 32.7 × 48, National Gallery of Art, Washington, Gift of Jacob Kainen 2002.98.371

Adolphe Appian (French, 1818–1898), *At Valromey,* 1868, etching with drypoint (state ii/ii), plate 13.8 × 23.8, sheet 14.2 × 24.2, National Gallery of Art, Washington, Gift of Gaillard F. Ravenel and Frances P. Smyth-Ravenel 2000.7.1 (Parshall fig. 5)

Félix Bracquemond (French, 1833–1914), *The Moles,* 1854, etching (state v/vii), plate 27 × 19.8, sheet 37.6 × 28.2, National Gallery of Art, Washington, Ailsa Mellon Bruce Fund 1975.33.1

Félix Bracquemond (French, 1833–1914), *The Raven,* 1854, etching on chine collé (state v/vi), plate 23.3 × 18.4, sheet 31.9 × 23.4, Baltimore Museum of Art, Bequest of Dr. Grace McCallum 1948.143.3

Félix Bracquemond (French, 1833–1914), *Top of a Barn Door (Le Haut d'un battant de porte),* 1852, etching (state iii/x), plate 30.5 × 40, sheet 31.7 × 41.5, National Gallery of Art, Washington, Rosenwald Collection 1944.8.5 (Parshall fig. 4)

Rodolphe Bresdin, in the style of (possibly J. Benazech), *Fantasy Farm House,* 1853, pen and black ink and gray wash with touches of red-brown crayon, and surface scraping on Bristol board, 60 × 45.8, National Gallery of Art, Washington, Woodner Collection 1991.182.22

Félix Hilaire Buhot (French, 1847–1898), *The Spirits of Dead Cities,* 1885, etching, roulette, drypoint, lift ground, aquatint, scraping, and burnishing (state v/vi), plate 29.2 × 39.1, sheet 36.9 × 54.7, National Gallery of Art, Washington, Rosenwald Collection 1943.3.1262 (Parshall fig. 6)

François Nicolas Chifflart (French, 1825–1901), *Cholera in Paris,* 1865, etching with drypoint, plate 23.9 × 31.9, sheet 31 × 44.5, National Gallery of Art, Washington, Ailsa Mellon Bruce Fund 2002.136.8 (Parshall fig. 17)

Charles François Daubigny (French, 1817–1878), *Ruins of the Château de Crémieux,* 1850, etching and roulette on chine collé (state ii/ii), plate 12.2 × 19.8, sheet 28 × 41.6, National Gallery of Art, Washington, Ailsa Mellon Bruce Fund 1975.34.67

James Ensor (Belgian, 1860–1949), *The Cathedral,* 1886, etching on Japanese paper (state iii/iv), 1st plate 24.3 × 19, sheet 39.8 × 28.5, National Gallery of Art, Washington, Rosenwald Collection 1948.11.63 (Parshall fig. 9)

Victor Hugo (French, 1802–1885), *Landscape,* 1868, etching, plate 22 × 14.6, sheet 36 × 25.2, National Gallery of Art, Washington, Rosenwald Collection 1980.45.854

Max Klinger (German, 1857–1920), *The Allee (Die Chaussee),* from *Vier Landschaften* (Opus VII), 1883, etching and aquatint (state iii/iv, third or fourth printing of five), plate 52.7 × 37.2, Private Collection

Max Klinger (German, 1857–1920), *Bear and Fairy,* from *Intermezzi* (Opus IV), 1881, etching and aquatint on chine collé (state ii/ii), plate 41.4 × 29, sheet 62.3 × 45, National Gallery of Art, Washington, Gift of the Epstein Family 2001.132.56 (Hertel fig. 4)

Max Klinger (German, 1857–1920), *Moonlit Night,* from *Intermezzi* (Opus IV), 1881, etching and aquatint on chine collé (state iii/iii), plate 41.5 × 29.5, sheet 62.4 × 44.8, National Gallery of Art, Washington, Gift of the Epstein Family Collection 2001.132.60 (Parshall fig. 15)

Max Klinger (German, 1857–1920), *Siesta I,* from *Radierte Skizzen* (Opus I), 1879, etching and aquatint on chine collé (state iii/iii, fourth printing of four), plate 21 × 30.1, sheet 39.6 × 54.7, National Gallery of Art, Washington, Gift of the Epstein Family Collection 2001.132.40 (Parshall fig. 14)

Charles Émile Jacque (French, 1813–1894), *Mousetrap,* 1860, etching on chine collé (state ii/ii), plate 12.7 × 16.2, sheet 18.4 × 26.5, Private Collection

Ludovic Napoléon Lepic (French, 1839–1889), *Shore of the Escaut: Turbulent Sky,* 1870/1876, etching with monotype wiping, plate 34.4 × 61.5, sheet 74 × 89.3, National Gallery of Art, Washington, Gift of Ruth Cole Kainen 2006.162.12 (Los Angeles and Chicago only)

Adolph Menzel (German, 1815–1905), *Bear Pit in the Berlin Zoo,* 1851, lithograph on chine collé (state i/iii), image 24.8 × 19.7, sheet 43.8 × 36, National Gallery of Art, Washington, Rosenwald Collection 1943.3.6143 (Hertel fig. 5)

Charles Meryon (French, 1821–1868), *The Clock Tower, Paris,* 1852, etching with engraving on blue-green paper (state iii/x), plate 25.5 × 18.2, sheet 29 × 21.9, National Gallery of Art, Washington, Gift of R. Horace Gallatin 1949.1.32 (Parshall fig. 19)

Charles Meryon (French, 1821–1868), *Collège Henri IV (or Lycée Napoléon),* 1864, etching (state v/xii), plate 29.8 × 48.5, sheet 35.5 × 54, National Gallery of Art, Washington, Rosenwald Collection 1943.3.6146

Charles Meryon (French, 1821–1868), *Collège Henri IV (or Lycée Napoléon),* 1864, etching (state xi/xii), plate 29.8 × 48.5, sheet 35.5 × 53.8, National Gallery of Art, Washington, Rosenwald Collection 1943.3.3122

Charles Meryon (French, 1821–1868), *Gallery of Notre Dame,* 1853, etching with engraving on blue-green paper (state iii/vi), plate 28.3 × 17.5, sheet 38.5 × 26.5, National Gallery of Art, Washington, Gift of R. Horace Gallatin 1949.1.36

Charles Meryon (French, 1821–1868), *Ministry of the Marine, Paris,* 1865, etching (state vii/vii), plate 16.8 × 14.8, sheet 24 × 20, National Gallery of Art, Washington, Gift of Mrs. Harold Ober 1968.9.2 (Parshall fig. 16)

Charles Meryon (French, 1821–1868), *The Morgue, Paris,* 1854, etching with drypoint (state iii/vii), plate 23.2 × 20.5, sheet 36.1 × 27, National Gallery of Art, Washington, Rosenwald Collection 1943.3.6172

Charles Meryon (French, 1821–1868), *The Vampire (Le Stryge),* 1853, etching on blue-green paper (state v/x), plate 17 × 12.8, sheet 26.8 × 19.4, National Gallery of Art, Washington, Gift of R.Horace Gallatin 1949.1.27

Emmanuel Phélippes-Beaulieux (French, 1829–1874), *Heath,* 1860, etching and roulette, plate 25.5 × 29.8, sheet 49 × 63.6, National Gallery of Art, Washington, Rosenwald Collection 1964.8.1369

Emmanuel Phélippes-Beaulieux (French, 1829–1874), *Tourist,* November 22, 1858, etching and roulette, plate 6.6 × 7, sheet 14.6 × 11.2, National Gallery of Art, Washington, Rosenwald Collection 1964.8.1371

Félicien Rops (Belgian, 1833–1898), *Satan Sowing Tares over Paris* (frontispiece to *Sataniques*), 1882/1883, softground etching, plate 27.9 × 20.7, sheet 37.2 × 26.5, National Gallery of Art, Washington, Rosenwald Collection 1951.10.401

James McNeill Whistler (American, 1834–1903), *Nocturne*, 1878, lithotint with scraping on a prepared half-tint ground on blue chine collé (state ii/ii), image 17.1 × 25.7, sheet 36.2 × 54.6, National Gallery of Art, Washington, Rosenwald Collection 1943.3.8664 (Parshall fig. 7)

REVERIE

Albert Besnard (French, 1849–1934), *The Cup of Tea*, 1883, etching with monotype inking (state ii/vi), plate 17.6 × 25.1, sheet 19.1 × 26.4, National Gallery of Art, Washington, Ailsa Mellon Bruce Fund 2005.151.1 (Clayson fig. 11)

Albert Besnard (French, 1849–1934), *Intimacy*, 1889, etching, plate 18.1 × 23.8, sheet 22.2 × 29.2, National Gallery of Art, Washington, Rosenwald Collection 1943.3.1470 (Clayson fig. 16)

Albert Besnard (French, 1849–1934), *In the Embers*, 1887, etching and roulette with drypoint (state iii/iii), plate 42.8 × 31.5, sheet 46.6 × 34, National Gallery of Art, Washington, Rosenwald Collection 1943.3.1476 (Clayson fig. 12)

Albert Besnard (French, 1849–1934), *Morphine Addicts*, 1887, etching, plate 23.8 × 37.1, sheet 32.6 × 43.6, National Gallery of Art, Washington, Rosenwald Collection 1943.3.1480 (Parshall fig. 1)

Albert Besnard (French, 1849–1934), *Woman with a Vase*, 1894, etching and aquatint (state iii/iii), plate 19.8 × 13.9, sheet 29.2 × 21.7, National Gallery of Art, Washington, Gift of Mr. and Mrs. Daniel Bell, in Honor of the 50th Anniversary of the National Gallery of Art 1992.59.21 (Clayson fig. 4)

Eugène Carrière (French, 1849–1906), *Sleep*, 1897, lithograph, sheet trimmed to image, 34 × 43, National Gallery of Art, Washington, Rosenwald Collection 1943.3.2733

Mary Cassatt (American, 1844–1926), *Before the Fireplace* (no. 1), c. 1882, soft-ground etching and aquatint (state iii/iii), plate 16 × 20.6, sheet 21.6 × 30.3 (ex-collection Edgar Degas), National Gallery of Art, Washington, Rosenwald Collection 1949.5.466

Jean-Baptiste-Camille Corot (French, 1796–1875), *The Dreamer (Le Songeur)*, 1854, cliché-verre, sheet trimmed within image, 14.3 × 19.6, National Gallery of Art, Washington, Print Purchase Fund (Rosenwald Collection) 1967.18.7

Edgar Degas (French, 1834–1917), *Woman Reading*, c. 1885, monotype, plate 38 × 27.7, sheet 44.3 × 32.5, National Gallery of Art, Washington, Rosenwald Collection 1950.16.292 (Clayson fig. 10) (Chicago only)

Fernand Khnopff (Belgian, 1858–1921), *Memory of Flanders: A Canal*, c. 1904, conté crayon over graphite, 25 × 41.5, Hearn Family Trust (Parshall fig. 21) (Washington and Chicago only)

Käthe Kollwitz (German, 1867–1945), *Self-Portrait at the Table*, c. 1893, etching and aquatint with drypoint (state iv/vi), plate 18 × 12.8, sheet 31.4 × 22.4, National Gallery of Art, Washington, Rosenwald Collection 1943.3.5260

Edvard Munch (Norwegian, 1863–1944), *Girl at the Window*, 1894, drypoint and roulette (state v/vi), plate 21.8 × 15.8, sheet 48.2 × 34.5, National Gallery of Art, Washington, Rosenwald Collection 1943.3.9022

Edvard Munch (Norwegian, 1863–1944), *Moonlight*, 1895, drypoint, open bite, and burnishing (state iii/iv), plate 35.5 × 26.2, sheet 47.2 × 34.5, National Gallery of Art, Washington, Rosenwald Collection 1943.3.9021

OBSESSION

Anonymous (French?), *Ex Libris C. Patel*, c. 1890, etching, aquatint, and roulette, plate 12 × 9, sheet folded in half, 32.8 × 50.2, National Gallery of Art, Washington, Ailsa Mellon Bruce Fund 2000.127.14.1

Edgar Degas (French, 1834–1917), *Woman by a Fireplace*, 1880/1890, monotype, plate 27.5 × 37.7, sheet 32.7 × 49, National Gallery of Art, Washington, Collection of Mr. and Mrs. Paul Mellon 1985.64.168 (Clayson fig. 18) (Los Angeles and Washington only)

James Ensor (Belgian, 1860–1949), *Lust,* 1888, etching (state ii/ii), plate 9.8 × 13.8, sheet 15.8 × 25, National Gallery of Art, Washington, Rosenwald Collection 1964.8.2753

Max Klinger (German, 1857–1920), *In Flagranti,* from *Dramen* (Opus IX), 1883, etching (state vi/vi, eighth printing of ten), plate 45.5 × 32.1, Princeton University Art Museum, Gift of Carl E. Schorske in honor of Professor Hajo Holborn 2004 _ 261.1 (Hertel fig. 14)

Max Klinger (German, 1857–1920), *A Glove* (Opus VI), 1880, ten etchings in proof impressions on chine collé, National Gallery of Art, Washington, Anonymous Gift 1995.82.1–10
1. *Place,* etching and aquatint (state i/ii, first printing of five), plate 25.7 × 34.7, sheet 34.5 × 52.8, 1995.82.1
2. *Action,* etching (state i/ii, first printing of six), plate 30 × 21, sheet 53.8 × 34.8, 1995.82.2
3. *Yearnings,* etching and aquatint (state i/iv, first printing of six), plate 31.6 × 13.8, sheet 33.7 × 15.8, 1995.82.3
4. *Rescue,* etching (state i/ii, first printing of seven), plate 23.6 × 18.1, sheet 52.8 × 34.8, 1995.82.4
5. *Triumph,* etching (state i/ii, first printing of five), plate 14.4 × 26.8, sheet 34.8 × 53.2, 1995.82.5
6. *Homage,* etching (state i/ii, first printing of five), plate 15.9 × 32.7, sheet 34.7 × 53.1, 1995.82.6
7. *Anxieties,* etching (state i/ii, first printing of five), plate 14.3 × 26.8, sheet 34.5 × 52.6, 1995.82.7
8. *Repose,* etching (state i/ii, first printing of five), plate 14.3 × 26.7, sheet 34.7 × 53.5, 1995.82.8
9. *Abduction,* etching and aquatint (state i/ii, first printing of five), plate 12 × 26.9, sheet 34.8 × 52.9, 1995.82.9
10. *Cupid,* etching (state i/ii, first printing of five), plate 14.2 × 26.3, sheet 34.7 × 53.2, 1995.82.10

Edvard Munch (Norwegian, 1863–1944), *The Vampire II,* 1895, lithograph (state i/x), sheet 38.4 × 57.8, Epstein Family Foundation (Los Angeles and Washington only)

Odilon Redon (French, 1840–1916), *This Is the Devil, Bearing the Seven Deadly Sins Beneath His Two Wings,* from *Tentation de Saint-Antoine,* 1888, lithograph on chine collé, image 25.1 × 20, sheet 44.2 × 30.9, National Gallery of Art, Washington, Ailsa Mellon Bruce Fund 2006.150.2 (Parshall fig. 2)

Odilon Redon (French, 1840–1916), *Temptation of Saint Anthony* (frontispiece to *A Gustave Flaubert*), 1889, lithograph on chine collé, image 28 × 20.3, sheet 50.5 × 36, National Gallery of Art, Washington, Rosenwald Collection 1943.3.7378

Franz von Stuck (German, 1863–1928), *Sensuality (Sinnlichkeit),* c. 1891, etching, plate 21.7 × 17.8, sheet 49.5 × 38.2, Baltimore Museum of Art, Gift of Blanche Adler 1929.17.21.8

Henri de Toulouse-Lautrec (French, 1864–1901), *Wounded Eros,* 1894, lithograph on Chinese paper (second edition), image 29 × 22, sheet 35.5 × 25.5, National Gallery of Art, Washington, Rosenwald Collection 1952.8.361 (Parshall fig. 20)

Anders Zorn (Swedish, 1860–1920), *An Irish Girl,* 1894, etching, plate 27.3 × 19.8, sheet 39.3 × 31, National Gallery of Art, Washington, Rosenwald Collection 1943.3.8840 (Clayson fig. 13)

ABJECTION

Albert Besnard (French, 1849–1934), *Apotheosis,* c. 1886, etching (state i/ii), plate 31.6 × 24.7, sheet 51 × 32.5, National Gallery of Art, Washington, Gift of Mr. and Mrs. Daniel Bell 1997.91.1

Albert Besnard (French, 1849–1934), *The Suicide,* c. 1886, etching and aquatint (state iii/iii), plate 32 × 24.8, sheet 51 × 32.7, National Gallery of Art, Washington, Gift of Mr. and Mrs. Daniel Bell, in Honor of the 50th Anniversary of the National Gallery of Art 1991.28.4

Max Klinger (German, 1857–1920), from *Dramen* (Opus IX), 1883, Princeton University Art Museum, Gift of Carl E. Schorske in honor of Professor Hajo Holborn 2004_261.3–5
1. *A Mother I,* etching and aquatint (state iii/iv, fifth printing of seven), plate 45.3 × 31.8 (Hertel fig. 11)
2. *A Mother II,* etching and aquatint (state v/v, seventh printing of nine), plate 45.4 × 31.8 (Hertel fig. 12)
3. *A Mother III,* etching (state iii/iv, fifth printing of seven), plate 45.4 × 35.9 (Hertel fig. 13)

Käthe Kollwitz (German, 1867–1945), *At the Church Wall,* 1893, etching with drypoint (state ivb/vii), plate 25.2 × 13, sheet 39 × 26, National Gallery of Art, Washington, Rosenwald Collection 1947.12.60 (Hertel fig. 9)

Käthe Kollwitz (German, 1867–1945), *Need (Not),* from *Ein Weberaufstand* (no. 1), 1893–1897, lithograph (state ii/iii), image 15.4 × 15.3, sheet 19 × 18.4, National Gallery of Art, Washington, Rosenwald Collection 1943.3.5311 (Hertel fig. 3)

Käthe Kollwitz (German, 1867–1945), *Woman with a Dead Child,* 1903, etching and softground etching with drypoint, proof impression worked up with graphite, charcoal, and gold wash (state iv/x), sheet trimmed to and within plate mark, 41.7 × 47.2, National Gallery of Art, Washington, Gift of Philip and Lynn Straus, in Honor of the 50th Anniversary of the National Gallery of Art 1988.67.1 (Hertel fig. 17)

Edouard Manet (French, 1832–1883), *Absinthe Drinker,* 1862, etching and aquatint (state iv/v), plate 28.7 × 15.9, sheet 32.8 × 20.5, National Gallery of Art, Washington

Edvard Munch (Norwegian, 1863–1944), *The Sick Child,* 1894, drypoint, roulette, and burnishing (state vi/vii), plate 38.5 × 29.2, sheet 48.5 × 38.2, National Gallery of Art, Washington, Rosenwald Collection 1944.14.61

Henri de Toulouse-Lautrec (French, 1864–1901), *The Madman (Le Fou),* 1895, lithograph (first edition), image 24.3 × 14.5, sheet 38.1 × 28.2, National Gallery of Art, Washington, Rosenwald Collection 1952.8.391 (Parshall fig. 20)

Henri de Toulouse-Lautrec (French, 1864–1901), *Le Tocsin,* 1895, color lithograph (first edition), image 57 × 45.3, sheet 65.4 × 49.9, National Gallery of Art, Washington, Rosenwald Collection 1952.8.455

Adolphe Léon Willette (French, 1857–1926), *Hanging Clown,* 1894, lithograph on Japanese paper, image 28 × 19, sheet 46.5 × 29.2, National Gallery of Art, Washington, Gift of the Virginia and Ira Jackson Collection 2004.162.41

VIOLENCE

Albert Besnard (French, 1849–1934), *The Murder,* from *L'Affaire Clémenceau,* 1885, etching and aquatint on green paper (state ii/ix), plate 16.9 × 11.3, sheet 27.5 × 21.7, National Gallery of Art, Washington, Gift of Mr. and Mrs. Daniel Bell, in Honor of the 50th Anniversary of the National Gallery of Art 1992.59.12

Albert Besnard (French, 1849–1934), *The Rape,* from *La Femme,* c. 1886, etching, proof impression touched with graphite (state i/ii), plate 32 × 24.9, sheet 45.8 × 31.6, National Gallery of Art, Washington, Gift of Mr. and Mrs. Daniel Bell, in Honor of the 50th Anniversary of the National Gallery of Art 1992.59.14

James Ensor (Belgian, 1860–1949), *Exterminating Angel,* 1889, etching, plate 11.8 × 15.7, sheet 29.5 × 40.2, National Gallery of Art, Washington, Rosenwald Collection 1964.8.715

Eugène Grasset (French, 1841–1917), *The Acid Thrower (La Vitrioleuse),* 1894, photo-relief with watercolor stenciling, sheet 39.9 × 27.6, Virginia and Ira Jackson Collection

Käthe Kollwitz (German, 1867–1945), *Scene from "Germinal,"* 1893, pen and black ink with gray washes heightened with white, 46.5 × 60.5, Anonymous Loan

Käthe Kollwitz (German, 1867–1945), *Scene from "Germinal,"* 1893, etching with drypoint (state iiib/iv), plate 22.5 × 53, sheet 39.5 × 63.5, National Gallery of Art, Washington, Rosenwald Collection 1943.3.5258 (Hertel fig. 16)

Odilon Redon (French, 1840–1916), *Cain and Abel,* 1886, etching, plate 18.5 × 12, sheet 33 × 25.2, National Gallery of Art, Washington, Gift of Ruth Cole Kainen 2006.57.27

Henri Rousseau (French, 1844–1910), *The War,* c. 1895, lithograph on orange paper, image 21.5 × 32.5, sheet 25.7 × 38.5, National Gallery of Art, Washington, Rosenwald Collection 1964.8.1502

DEATH

Albert Besnard (French, 1849–1934), *The End of It All,* 1883, etching (state iii/v), plate 24.1 × 20.8, sheet 32.5 × 25.5, National Gallery of Art, Washington, Gift of Mr. and Mrs. Daniel Bell, in Honor of the 50th Anniversary of the National Gallery of Art 1991.28.2

Rodolphe Bresdin (French, 1822–1885), *The Comedy of Death,* 1854, lithograph (state i/vi), image 21.7 × 15.1, sheet 47.8 × 31.3, National Gallery of Art, Washington, Ailsa Mellon Bruce Fund 1983.92.1

Jean-Baptiste-Camille Corot (French, 1796–1875), *Young Girl and Death,* 1854, cliché-verre, sheet trimmed to image, 18.5 × 13.1, National Gallery of Art, Washington, Print Purchase Fund (Rosenwald Collection) 1967.18.8

Jules Ferdinand Jacquemart (French, 1837–1880), *The Executed Criminal Mamiya Hajime, Assassin of Europeans, before the Temple of Kamakura, Japan,* 1867–1868, etching with drypoint, plate 15.7 × 23.6, sheet 30.8 × 43, Baltimore Museum of Art, Garrett Collection 1946.112.2560

Edouard Manet (French, 1832–1883), *Civil War,* 1871, lithograph on chine collé (second printing), image 39.4 × 50.7, sheet 47.6 × 60.4, National Gallery of Art, Washington, Rosenwald Collection 1943.3.5758 (Parshall fig. 18) (Los Angeles and Washington only)

Edouard Manet (French, 1832–1883), *Dead Matador,* 1868, etching and aquatint (state v/vi), plate 15.4 × 22.2, sheet 19 × 24.6, National Gallery of Art, Washington, Rosenwald Collection 1943.3.5763

Odilon Redon (French, 1840–1916), *Saint George,* 1880s, reworked c. 1892, charcoal heightened with pastel, 53.7 × 37.5, National Gallery of Art, Washington, Gift of GTE and the New Century Fund 2000.14.1 (Washington only)

Alfred Rethel (German, 1816–1859), *Another Dance of Death II,* 1849, wood engraving, image 22.4 × 32.5, sheet 27.5 × 37, National Gallery of Art, Washington, Ailsa Mellon Bruce Fund 1971.28.7 (Washington and Chicago only)

Alfred Rethel (German, 1816–1859), *Another Dance of Death VI,* 1849, wood engraving, image 22.4 × 32, sheet 27.5 × 36.3, National Gallery of Art, Washington, Ailsa Mellon Bruce Fund 1971.28.5 (Washington and Chicago only)

Alfred Rethel (German, 1816–1859), *The Dance of Death of 1848,* 1849, six wood engravings on one sheet, 71.8 × 118.4, UCLA Grunwald Center for the Graphic Arts, Hammer Museum 1967.34.3 (Los Angeles only)

Alfred Rethel (German, 1816–1859), *Death as a Friend,* 1851, wood engraving, image 30.2 × 27.2, sheet 51 × 38.8, National Gallery of Art, Washington, Rosenwald Collection 1951.10.112

Karl Stauffer-Bern (Swiss, 1857–1891), *Male Nude,* 1886, etching on chine collé (state vi/vi?), plate 29.8 × 59.3, Richard A. Simms Collection

BOOKS

Gustave Doré (French, 1832–1883), wood engravings for Blanchard Jerrold, *London: A Pilgrimage* (London, 1872), National Gallery of Art, Washington, William B. O'Neal Fund 2007.98.1 (Parshall fig. 8)

Gustave Doré (French, 1832–1883), wood engravings (by Georges Rouget) for Pierre Dupont, *The Legend of the Wandering Jew* (Paris, 1856), National Gallery of Art, Washington, William B. O'Neal Fund 2002.33.1

Edouard Manet (French, 1832–1883), ten transfer lithographs (including four repetitions on Chinese paper) for Edgar Alan Poe, *The Raven (Le Corbeau)*, translated by Stéphane Mallarmé (Paris, 1875), Collection of Mrs. Paul Mellon, Upperville, Virginia

Various artists, etchings for Philippe Burty and Alphonse Lemerre, eds., *Sonnets et eaux-fortes* (Paris, 1869), National Gallery of Art, Washington, Gift of Richard A. Simms, in Honor of the 50th Anniversary of the National Gallery of Art 1991.26.1

SCULPTURE

Louis-Ernest Barrias (French, 1841–1905), *Nature Unveiling Herself before Science*, model 1895/1899, cast c. 1900, bronze with silvering and malachite, without base 57.2, National Gallery of Art, Washington, Gift of Frank Anderson Trapp 2004.166.1 (Penny fig. 1)

Joseph Pierre Braemt (Belgian, 1796–1864), *Charles de Brouckère, Mayor of Brussels* (obverse), *The Cholera Epidemic of 1849 and 1854* (reverse), 1854/1856, bronze medal, struck, 8.75, National Gallery of Art, Washington, Gift of Mark and Lynne Hammerschlag in Honor of Nicholas Penny

Alexandre-Louis-Marie Charpentier (French, 1856–1909), *Allegory of Painting* (obverse), *Intertwined Branches of Laurel and Evergreen* (reverse), 1897, silver medal, 5.3 × 4.1, National Gallery of Art, Washington, Gift of Mark and Lynne Hammerschlag 2004.156.4.a (Penny fig. 14)

Sir Alfred Gilbert (British, 1854–1934), *Comedy and Tragedy: "Sic Vita,"* model 1891–1892, cast probably 1902/1905, bronze, with attached marble base 34.6 × 15.6 × 13.7, National Gallery of Art, Washington, Pepita Milmore Memorial Fund 1984.67.1 (Penny fig. 2)

Johannes Götz (German, 1865–1934), *Boy Balancing on a Ball*, model 1888, cast probably 1905, bronze, 24.6 × 7.6 × 7.3, marble base 3.7 × 9.2 × 6, National Gallery of Art, Washington, Gift of Dr. Dieter Erich Meyer 1976.3.1

Harriet Goodhue Hosmer (American, 1830–1908), *Clasped Hands of Robert Browning and Elizabeth Barrett Browning*, model 1853, bronze, 8.3 × 21 × 10.8, National Gallery of Art, Washington, Gift in honor of Margaret and Raymond Horowitz 2005.41.1 (Penny fig. 4)

George Minne (Belgian, 1866–1941), *The Little Wounded One II*, 1898, bronze, 25, Hearn Family Trust

Auguste Rodin (French, 1840–1917), *Figure of a Woman (The Sphinx)*, model early 1880s, carved 1909, marble, 59 × 62.1 × 58.3, National Gallery of Art, Washington, Gift of Eugene and Agnes E. Meyer 1967.13.6 (Washington only)

Auguste Rodin (French, 1840–1917), *The Sirens*, model before 1887, cast probably 1900/1920, bronze, 43.2 × 45.8 × 31.8, National Gallery of Art, Washington, Gift of David Baron in memory of his wife, Mary F. Baron 1978.71.1

Louis-Oscar Roty (French, 1846–1911), *The Body of President Sadi Carnot Borne to the Panthéon* (obverse), *France Mourning the President of the Republic* (reverse), 1894, silvered bronze medal, 7.8 × 5.7, National Gallery of Art, Washington, Anonymous Gift 2004.148.3.a–b (Penny figs. 12, 13)

A
Appian, Adolphe, 14
Aristotle, 96
Augusta, Empress, 122
Auzoux, Charles, 145

B
Banque de France, 131, 147, 149
Barrias, Louis-Ernest, 129, 131, 137
Bartsch, Adam von, 27
Barye, Antoine-Louis, 134
Bassanville, Comtesse de, 19
Baudelaire, Charles, 6–7, 14, 23, 36, 39, 66, 76
Bénédite, Léonce, 138, 142
Béraldi, Henri, 19
Bernini, Gian Lorenzo, 146
Bertrand, Aloysius, 30
Besnard, Albert, 13–14, 36, 47, 51, 53, 56–57, 61–62, 65, 67, 69, 71
Blanc, Charles, 4, 6–7
Boehm, Edgar, 132, 134
Bonnat, Léon, 25
Bonus-Jeep, Beate, 116
Bottini, Georges, 19
Boucher, François, 25
Bracquemond, Félix, 14, 25
Brahms, Johannes, 109
Bremer Kunsthalle, 86
Bresdin, Rodolphe, 21
Browning, Elizabeth Barrett, 138
Browning, Robert, 138
De La Bruyère, Jean, 30
Buhot, Félix, 14, 36

C
Cabanel, Alexandre, 13
Cadart, Alfred, 4, 6, 7, 21, 23
Carnot, Sadi, 149
Carpeaux, Jean-Baptiste, 142
Carrier-Belleuse, Albert-Ernest, 142
Cassatt, Mary, 45, 51, 53, 57, 61, 67, 71, 73
Cassirer, Bruno, 86
Cassirer, Paul, 86
Cellini, Benvenuto, 132, 134–135
Charcot, Jean-Martin, 5
Charpentier, Alexandre-Louis-Marie, 149
Chifflart, François Nicolas, 14, 36
De Chirico, Giorgio, 110
Claussin, J.-J., 3–4
Cochläus, Johann, 33
Codman, Ogden, 134
Collas, Achille, 134
Collins, Wilkie, 30
Compagnie des Bronzes, Brussels, 134
Coppier, André-Charles, 56, 62, 71
Corot, Jean-Baptiste-Camille, 14
Corry, John, 19
Courtry, Charles, 25
Croswell, Sally Hicks, 138
Cruet, Paul, 138

D
Dalou, Aimé-Jules, 138, 145–146
Darwin, Charles, 5
Daumier, Honoré, 109
Deering, Charles, 67, 69
Degas, Edgar, 36, 47, 57, 61, 67, 73, 146–147
Delacroix, Eugène, 47
Desiderio da Settignano, 147
Donatello, 135
Doré, Gustave, 14
Drouot, 25
Dupré, George, 147
Durand-Ruel, Paul, 25, 53
Dürer, Albrecht, 19, 33

E
Eastlake, Charles Locke, 19, 21
École de Médecine, Paris, 129, 131
Ensor, James, 14, 76
L'estampe originale, 56
Evelyn, John, 25

F
Falguière, Jean-Alexandre-Joseph, 142–143, 145
Von Falke, Jacob, 15, 18–19, 21
Flaubert, Gustave, 14
Flaxman, John, 131
Freud, Sigmund, 5, 71, 116
Frick, Frank, 25
Friedländer, Max, 118

G
Gautier, Théophile, 4–5
Gemito, Vincenzo, 132, 134–135, 137
Giambologna, 134–135
Gilbert, Alfred, 132, 134–135, 137
Gilbert, W. S., 137
Von Goethe, Johann Wolfgang, 103
Van Gogh, Vincent, 86
De Goncourt, Edmond, 21
De Goncourt, Jules, 21
Gonon family, 134
Goupil, 21
De Goya, Francisco José, 88, 98
Gramont, Duc de, 145–146
Die graphischen Künste, 88
Graul, Richard, 88

H
Habermas, Jürgen, 116
Haden, Seymour, 14
Hamerton, Philip Gilbert, 7, 30, 33
Handke, Peter, 83–84
Hauptmann, Gerhart, 84, 113
Havard, Henry, 22
Hébrard, Adrien-Aurélien, 142–143, 145–146
Herterich, Ludwig, 113
Holbein, Hans, 88, 122
Hölderlin, Friedrich, 109–110
De Hooch, Pieter, 104
Hosmer, Harriet, 138
Huysmans, Joris-Karl, 19, 21

J
Jacquemart, Jules Ferdinand, 25
Jamnitzer, Wenzel, 135
Joan of Arc, 147

K
Khnopff, Fernand, 39
Kladderadatsch, 86
Klinger, Max, 14, 33, 36, 83–88, 90, 93, 96–98, 103–104, 109–110, 116, 118, 120, 122, 125
Kollwitz, Käthe, 14, 83–87, 90, 93, 97–98, 103–104, 109–110, 113, 118, 120, 122–123, 125
Kollwitz, Peter, 116
Kurzweil, Maximilian, 47

L
Lebrun, Charles, 146
Lehrs, Max, 87
Leonardo da Vinci, 147
Lepic, Ludovic Napoléon, 57
Lhermitte, Léon, 25
Liebermann, Max, 14, 83–88, 90, 93, 97, 104, 110, 113, 116, 118, 120, 122–123, 125
Lucas, George, 25

M
Mallarmé, Stéphane, 5, 76
Manet, Édouard, 36, 56, 76, 79
Marx, Karl, 5, 84
Marx, Roger, 3
Menzel, Adolph, 87, 96–97, 103
Merrill, Elizabeth, 138
Meryon, Charles, 5, 14, 25, 36
Meyer-Graefe, Julius, 97
Monet, Claude, 142
Munch, Edvard, 36

N
Nadar (Gaspard-Félix Tournachon), 25
Neureuther, Eugen, 88
Nisini, Giovanni, 135

P
Palazzolo, Albino, 146
Palmer, Mrs. Potter, 67
Pauli, Gustav, 86
Petit, Georges, 25, 142
Piranesi, Giambattista, 19
Poe, Edgar Allan, 5, 66, 76, 79
Potémont, Adolphe-Martial, 23

R
Raphael, 33
Redon, Odilon, 14, 21
Rembrandt van Rijn, 3–5, 7, 13
Rethel, Alfred, 84, 122
Revue Indépendante de Littérature et d'Art, 57
Rodin, Auguste, 65, 125, 138, 142, 146
Rops, Félicien, 14, 30
De Rothschild, Marguerite, 145–146
Roty, Louis-Oscar, 147, 149
Royal Society, 25
Runge, Philipp Otto, 88
Rysbrack, John Michael, 131

S
Schmid, Max, 109
Schopenhauer, Arthur, 84
Société des Aquafortistes, 4, 6
Société des Peintres-Graveurs Français, 53
Société Nationale des Beaux-Arts, 145
Society of Painter-Etchers, 23
Susini, Antonio, 134

T
Tissot, James, 14, 73, 76
De Toulouse-Lautrec, Henri, 36

V
Verrocchio, 147
Victoria, Queen, 145
Vinnen, Carl, 86

W
Wharton, Edith, 19, 21, 132, 134
Whistler, James McNeill, 14, 45, 47, 56, 69

Z
Zola, Émile, 5, 13, 84, 109, 113
Zorn, Anders, 51, 65, 67

All works from the National Gallery of Art courtesy of the Board of Trustees, National Gallery of Art, Washington.

Dean Beasom: Parshall figs. 11, 18 (digital technician Christina Moore), 21; Clayson figs. 1, 6, 7, 18

Ric Blanc: Hertel fig. 15, 17; Penny figs. 12, 13

Philip Charles: Penny figs. 5–7, 9

Lorene Emerson: Parshall figs. 1–10, 13–20; Clayson figs. 2–5, 10–16, 20; Hertel figs. 3–9, 16, 22; Penny, fig. 10

Lee Ewing: Clayson fig. 9; Penny figs. 1, 4

Julia Sybalski: Penny fig. 11

Clayson fig. 8, Photograph © 2009, Museum of Fine Arts, Boston

Clayson fig. 19, © 2008, Art Gallery of Ontario

Hertel figs. 2, 23, Bildarchiv Preussischer Kulturbesitz/Art Resource, NY; fig. 2, photograph Christophe Irrgang

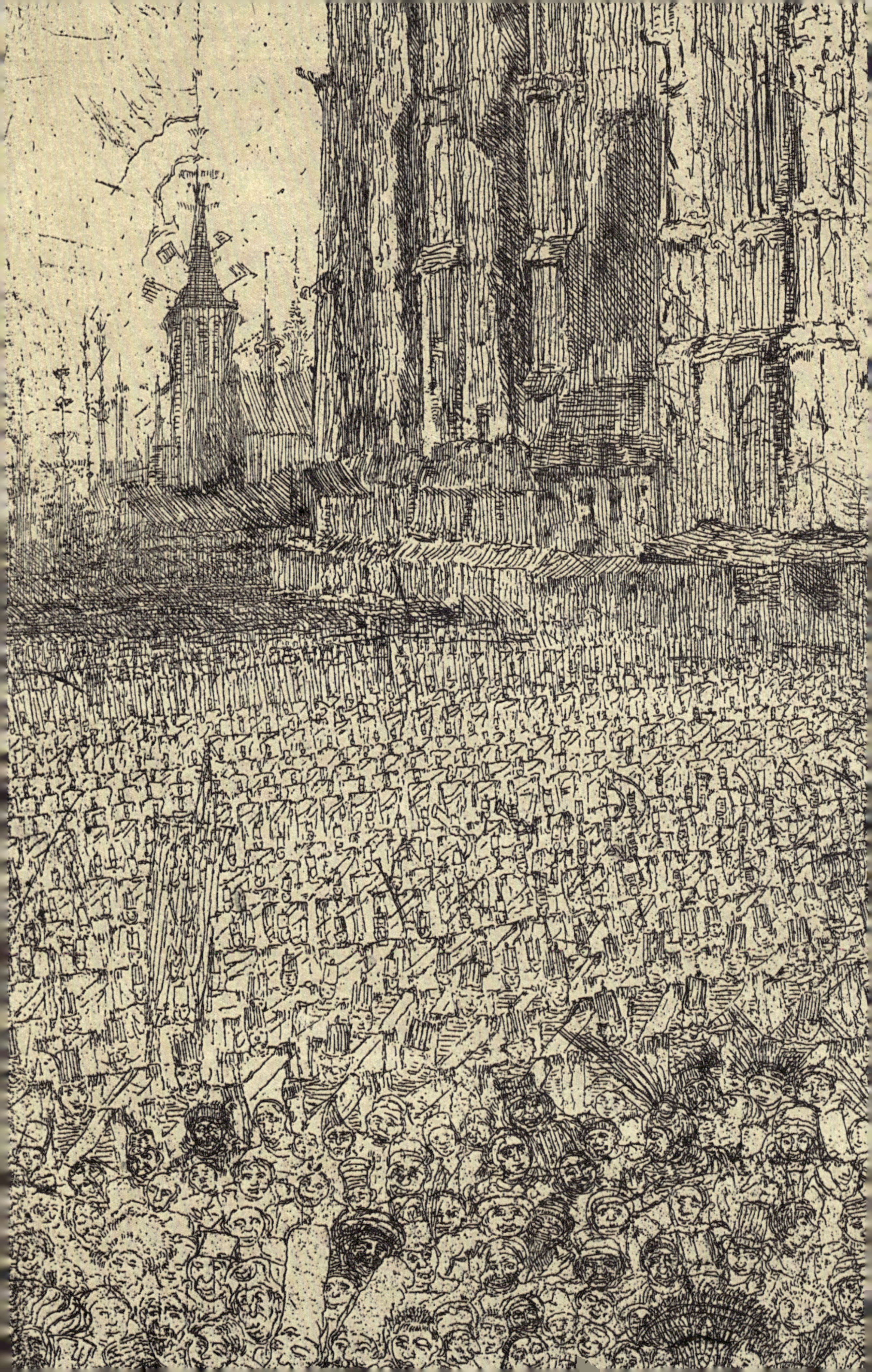